COACHING SOCCER SUCCESSFULLY

Roy Rees
Director of Coaching, Texans Soccer Club

Cor van der Meer
Community Colleges of Spokane

Human Kinetics

Library of Congress Cataloging-in-Publication Data

Rees, Roy.
    Coaching soccer successfully / Roy Rees, Cor van der Meer.
      p.   cm.
    Includes index.
    ISBN 0-87322-444-2
    1. Soccer--Coaching--United States.   I. Van der Meer, Cor.
  II. Title.
  GV943.8.R356   1996
  796.342'07'7--dc20   96-15148
                                          CIP

ISBN: 0-87322-444-2

Copyright © 1997 by Roy Rees and Cor van der Meer

Developmental Editor: Jan Colarusso Seeley; **Assistant Editor:** Lynn M. Hooper; **Editorial Assistant:** Coree Schutter; **Copyeditor:** Bob Replinger; **Proofreader:** Pam Johnson; **Indexer:** Theresa Schaefer; **Graphic Designer:** Keith Blomberg; **Graphic Artist:** Tara Welsch; **Photo Editor:** Boyd LaFoon; **Cover Designer:** Jack Davis; **Photographer (cover):** F-Stock/John Laptad; **Photographers (interior):** Nita L. Dyslin, Carol Fields, Rick Harrison, Rob Kelly, R. Montgomery, Cathy Perry, Michael Pidding, Heather Wolfe; **Field Diagram Illustrator:** Craig Ronto; **Printer:** United Graphics

Printed in the United States of America   10 9 8 7 6 5 4 3 2 1

Human Kinetics
Web site: http://www.humankinetics.com/

United States: Human Kinetics P.O. Box 5076, Champaign, IL 61825-5076
1-800-747-4457
e-mail: humank@hkusa.com

Canada: Human Kinetics, Box 24040, Windsor, ON N8Y 4Y9
1-800-465-7301 (in Canada only)
e-mail: humank@hkcanada.com

Europe: Human Kinetics, P.O. Box IW14, Leeds LS16 6TR, United Kingdom
(44) 1132 781708
e-mail: humank@hkeurope.com

Australia: Human Kinetics, 57A Price Avenue, Lower Mitcham, South Australia 5062
(08) 277 1555
e-mail: humank@hkaustralia.com

New Zealand: Human Kinetics, P.O. Box 105-231, Auckland 1
(09) 523 3462
e-mail: humank@hknewz.com

To my immediate family—particularly my wife, Ann, who typed and retyped the text as it took shape—and to my larger family, the Texans Soccer Club, many of whose players are featured in the illustrations.

—R.R.

To my most diligent teacher—the game; to the game's indulgent assistants—those who coached me; to the source of my rich memories and future challenges—my players; and to the best teammate I ever had—Sandra, my wife.

—C.v.d.M.

Contents

Foreword   vii
Acknowledgments   viii
Introduction   ix

PART I   **COACHING FOUNDATION**   **1**
Chapter 1   Developing a Soccer Coaching Philosophy   3
Chapter 2   Communicating Your Approach   13
Chapter 3   Motivating Players   25
Chapter 4   Building a Soccer Program   35

PART II   **COACHING PLANS**   **49**
Chapter 5   Planning for the Season   51
Chapter 6   Planning Practices   67

PART III   **COACHING DEFENSE**   **73**
Chapter 7   Basic Defensive Skills and Positions   75
Chapter 8   Teaching Defensive Skills   89
Chapter 9   Teaching Defensive Tactics   109

PART IV   **COACHING OFFENSE**   **129**
Chapter 10   Basic Offensive Skills and Positions   131
Chapter 11   Teaching Offensive Skills   145
Chapter 12   Teaching Offensive Tactics   163

PART V   **COACHING MATCHES**   **181**
Chapter 13   Preparing for Matches   183
Chapter 14   Handling Match Situations   189

PART VI   **COACHING EVALUATION**   **195**
Chapter 15   Evaluating Your Players   197
Chapter 16   Evaluating Your Program   209

Index   219
About the Authors   226
About ASEP   228

Foreword

As soccer coaches, we expect much from our players. And they, in turn, should expect and receive much from us. That's the magic of the coach-player relationship.

Veteran coaches Roy Rees and Cor van der Meer know that this relationship begins with the coach. A prepared coach can meet this responsibility; an unprepared one cannot. *Coaching Soccer Successfully* covers all aspects of what it takes to be prepared and effective in your role.

And who better to learn from? Roy and Cor have a wealth of education and experience to draw from—their own. They've coached youth to elite levels; men and women; school, club, and national teams. Their win-loss records are outstanding no matter who they've coached, and they are among the more highly respected teachers in our sport.

My own experiences as an author add to my appreciation of this effort. *Coaching Soc-cer Successfully* is both comprehensive and detailed. Part I on Coaching Foundation is reason alone to buy the book. But there's much more. Sections for teaching offensive and defensive skills and strategies are perhaps the highlight. From start to finish you'll find valuable practice and game coaching tips to improve how you work with your players.

Roy and Cor have done a great service to the soccer coaching profession by sharing their wealth of knowledge in *Coaching Soccer Successfully*. Take the opportunity to read and learn from them. And keep the book handy on your office shelf for quick reference—and a better season.

Jerry Yeagley
Head Soccer Coach
Indiana University

Acknowledgments

My final thanks must go to the players I coach and have coached. They have been my teachers. Their trust, integrity, competitiveness, sportsmanship, warmth, ability, and performance have been and continue to be the joy of my life. I would like to mention my appreciation of all those players—from six-year-olds, competitive club players, college players, and professional players to World Cup players—who have helped shape my coaching philosophy. At times I labored to find the right answers to problems, but now, with over 35 years of experience coaching players at all different levels and from many different countries and cultures, I find little that is "new." My deeply-felt thanks to those many thousands of players whom I have coached—I hope you enjoyed it as much as I did.

—Roy Rees

That morning, May 10, 1945, I was hungry—but then I had been hungry for a long time. We had been occupied for five years, and the last few of them had been particularly cruel. As I stood on a road in the woods, I heard the rumbling noise of heavy machinery. Soon a gigantic tank plodded its way around a bend. Above the tank's turret flew the star-spangled banner. I had been liberated. I was free.

After the initial joy came the sadness, as I realized that many young men and women had given their lives so that I could live in freedom. At that moment I silently vowed that if in some small way I could ever acknowledge the sacrifices made by those who fought in World War II, I would do it. Here is that acknowledgment.

I'm grateful to so many other people—my mother who instilled in me my competitive drive, my father who died young but not before teaching me that displaying poor sportsmanship while winning results in an empty victory, my teachers who taught me the value of education and curiosity, my coaches who took endless hours to teach us youths the fundamentals—they all contributed to this book.

Later in life other coaches generously gave their time to help me better understand our game. I will be grateful forever to people like Jimmy Gabriel, Bobby Howe, Tony Waiters, Clifford McCrath, Billy McNichols, Jan Smisek, Alan Hinton, and so many others. I have also learned much from the coaches who coached against me in our conference, in particular, from David Ryberg. I give special thanks also to Dr. Frank Smoll, who taught me that there is so much more to coaching than knowing how to play the sport. From a coaching perspective, the last 11 years have been exciting and rewarding, and I am thankful that my college and its athletic director, Dr. Maury Ray, created an atmosphere of trust, so conducive to a coach's growth.

All these people contributed to this book indirectly. The efforts of several others were more direct. I'm referring to the thoroughly professional people at Human Kinetics. In particular, I want to thank Karen Partlow, who started me dreaming about writing this book; Ted Miller, who made me realize that the dream could come true; Jessie Daw, whose encouragement pushed the dream along; and Lynn Hooper, who made sure that the dream had a perfect ending. Most of all, I shall be forever grateful to Jan Seeley for the guidance, prodding, cajoling, and constant encouragement that I needed to not give up on the dream.

—Cor van der Meer

Introduction

The idea for this book was first discussed some years ago in Anaheim, California with Karen Partlow of the American Sport Education Program. At first Karen's proposal was somewhat overwhelming. The scope of the book seemed too comprehensive. After some days, though, the awe and anxiety were replaced by feelings of excitement. Here, at last, was an opportunity to offer all those who love and coach our great sport a book that not only presents a fresh and contemporary approach to technical and tactical development of players and teams, but also dares to address all the other prerequisites necessary to coach soccer successfully.

After the few years it has taken to write this book, Karen's concept has become a reality. The goals that we set with the American Sport Education Program in the beginning have now been attained. All coaches—and in particular those who coach at the junior high and high school levels—will find helpful and practical advice within the pages of *Coaching Soccer Successfully*.

This book is based on the assumption that your players are of junior high and high school age and therefore have some playing experience. That's why we decided to spend little time here on basic technique development. Instead, we've made sure these pages are chock-full of innovative and practical information. For instance, we show you how to use match simulations—small-sided, conditioned games—to effectively develop and improve your team's technical and tactical understanding of soccer.

Part I begins by showing the need for a solid coaching foundation, which includes developing a strong, consistent philosophy of coaching; developing practical methods of effective communication; and developing an understanding of motivation. Approaches to building a successful soccer program are also thoroughly discussed.

In Part II, coaches can learn how to save time by following our suggestions for planning for the season and preparing for practices. Part III concentrates on how to coach basic defensive skills and tactics, while Part IV deals with offensive skills and tactics. Part V takes the coach to the field for some meticulous insights into effective coaching during matches, and Part VI shows how success is perpetuated by courageously evaluating your players, staff, and program.

All of the above details may give reasons enough to write this book. However, there was an even more important motivation: Soccer is our life. It has been good to us. We have much to be grateful for. We hope that we are giving something back by sharing our experiences with dedicated coaches, so that they can in turn have a positive influence on America's greatest asset—its youth.

Part I

Coaching Foundation

Chapter 1

Developing a Soccer Coaching Philosophy

Your success as a soccer coach is totally dependent on the strength of your philosophy. This philosophy is your plan, guide, and map to achievement. With it, you'll find coaching to be exciting, challenging, and rewarding. A soccer team needs a leader with a strong and realistic concept of direction. After all, no sport places more physical and psychological demands on athletes than soccer. Some call it a long, high-speed game of chess.

Soccer presents a particular challenge to new coaches. Unlike other sports, soccer has a well-developed club system in the United States. Through the efforts of U.S. Soccer (formerly the United States Soccer Federa-

tion) and its youth branch, the United States Youth Soccer Association, as well as the American Youth Soccer Association, Soccer Association for Youth, and others, millions of young athletes are playing soccer. The players on your team have probably been playing for several years. These players may have had access to well-structured player development programs. Chances are they will have a fair amount of soccer knowledge and experience. The question is, are you prepared to coach them? If you don't feel you are, don't despair. There is help available.

This book is one good source of help. It is written for all soccer coaches, but especially the high school coach.

You can also call your state youth soccer association. These associations offer literature, visual aids, and coaching clinics.

If you live near a college with a varsity soccer program, call the coach and ask for help. Most coaches are willing and able to help. It is to the advantage of coaches at higher levels to help you if they want you to prepare players for their future teams.

To be a successful soccer coach requires an eagerness to meet the challenges of coaching and a thorough understanding of this often misunderstood sport. Mastering the Xs and Os of the sport is just a small part of it. More important is that you have a plan for success.

Building a Coaching Foundation

Several crucial ingredients are needed to create a plan for success. To begin ask yourself these questions:

- What are my objectives as a coach?
- What objectives do I have for each athlete?
- What objectives do I have for the team?
- Why do I want to be a coach?
- Am I willing to give the time and effort to become the best coach I can be?
- Am I willing to put the needs of my athletes before my own?
- Which is of greater importance to me—the performance of the team or the outcome of the match?

Your answers to these questions will reflect your coaching philosophy. This philosophy is your guiding force for every coaching decision you make. You have developed your philosophy from your earlier soccer experiences, perhaps as an athlete; books you have read; methods you have learned from other coaches; clinics you have attended; videos and films you have seen; and your personality.

Personal Experiences

Certainly the experiences you had as an athlete and the methods used by those who coached you will carry over into your coaching methodology. For instance, if your soccer-playing days were loaded with fun, you probably make sure that your players also have a lot of fun. If, on the other hand, your former coaches were sticklers for skill development, you probably emphasize that part of training. Also, if your former coaches were obsessed by winning records, winning might be your foremost consideration. Regardless, your experiences will carry over into your methods of coaching.

On the other hand, you may be one of the many soccer coaches who has had little or no playing experience. That's not a problem. In fact, it may be an unexpected benefit.

Most veteran coaches in other sports have relied on only one educational resource—former coaches. If the former coaches had weaknesses, those shortcomings probably surfaced in the next generation of coaches. For many soccer coaches, however, there have been few, if any, role models—good, bad, or indifferent. And not so many years ago, other sources of soccer coaching information were hard to find.

Books

When I first started giving soccer clinics, coaches often asked me where they could get more knowledge. Somewhat flippantly I would tell them to visit their local library. One coach told me that he had, but found nothing there about coaching soccer. I visited the library. He was right; there was nothing there. I promptly wrote two books—*Guide for Soccer Coaches* and *Keeper of the Goal*. Since I wrote my first two books, many books have been published on our great sport. Some are better than others, but I've never picked up a book on soccer that did not give me some new ideas. Books are a great source for learning.

    CASE IN POINT

Reinier, my oldest son, was an excellent basketball player, a fine wide receiver, a strong pitcher, and for a while held the Oregon high school record in the 100-meter dash. Gerard, my younger son, excelled at football, weights, and automobile racing. I had no background in those sports, but I wanted to support and encourage my sons. That required knowledge of the sports, which I found in the many excellent books written on those subjects. In time I became an assistant to a sports broadcaster during live broadcasts of basketball and football games over radio station KVAN in Vancouver, Washington.

Clinics

Clinics are a must for every coach. I can hear you say that a clinic is only as good as the clinician. Not true. Even if the clinician leaves something to be desired, you can benefit by talking with and learning from other coaches who are attending.

We coaches too rarely seek information from, or share experiences with, our colleagues. I used to finish my clinics with a question-and-answer period. I don't do that anymore. It is usually a waste of time because, in most cases, the coaches would not ask questions. Instead, they would make a statement or not participate in the discussion. If you want to increase your knowledge, ask questions. Some good examples are the following:

- Our opponent next week plays five men back. How can we beat it?
- One of my best players turns very negative when things go wrong. Any suggestions?
- You have talked about a 3-5-2 system. Who supports the attack more, the outside or the inside midfielders?
- One of our parents has been behaving destructively during matches. How would you handle him?

Other coaches are our greatest source of knowledge. But we must make an effort to tap into this knowledge, be it by attending clinics and asking questions, or by reading books like this one. And don't just learn from one coach. No coach knows it all.

 OF APPLES AND ORANGES OR COACHES AND REFEREES

When I was the program coordinator for the local youth sports association, I instituted two new programs, a weekly coaches' meeting and a weekly referees' meeting. The purpose of these meetings was to provide an opportunity for coaches and referees to freely discuss their ideas or problems and learn through this communication. The first few meetings flopped. The problem wasn't attendance; it was what the coaches and referees chose to talk about. They focused their conversations on last Saturday's match, the highs and the lows. Neither group asked for help or advice.

So, I tried another approach. I had the referees give assignments to the coaches and the coaches give assignments to the referees. We gave up after the referees chose for the coaches such subjects as "How to buy the right-sized muzzle" and "How to learn the Laws of the Game while being double-parked." Likewise the coaches came up with assignments for the referees like "Who in town makes the best eyeglasses?" and "How to get from penalty area to penalty area without benefit of a taxi or an oxygen tank."

I was about to give up on the meetings when a thought struck me. At the next meeting I gave assignments to two coaches. One was "How do you beat an offside trap?" and the other was "Design a functional practice for forwards." I instructed the coaches to study the assignments and report at the next meeting. I designed similar assignments for the referees. Future meetings were very successful. Coaches felt comfortable discussing certain problems when they had time to prepare. There was much exchange over a wide variety of subjects benefiting all who attended.

A final note about clinics. A clinic does not have to be soccer specific to help you be a better coach. Go to clinics that deal with sports injuries, sport psychology, nutrition, drug abuse, time management, risk management, sports law, motivation, management skills. Clinics dealing with other sports are also great for picking up new approaches to our game. In short, try to attend any clinic that could help you better serve your players, staff, and school.

Videos

Films and videos are another great source for learning. I conduct advanced coaching clinics, which include much theory that often is difficult to remember. To help the coaches I use specific video footage from matches. When we cover different styles of play—Italian, German, South American, English, and so forth—I can show those styles to coaches, and they can more readily grasp their differences.

Principles like depth, balance, and support in the defensive third are much easier to convey when I can show teams executing them.

Because so much happens off the ball, I often watch match videos in slow motion. Try it, especially after a goal has been scored. Try to figure out who caused the goal.

One of my favorite video clips is Marco van Basten scoring a goal for the Netherlands in the 1988 Europe Cup match against Germany. We use this clip in clinics and ask the coaches to determine who caused the goal. At about the 85th minute the match is tied at 1-1. After a slow buildup in the back, typical of the Dutch, Ronald Koemans receives the ball. Koemans spots a wide-open Jan Wouters about 30 yards from the German goal. He passes to Wouters, who could have taken a shot from his position. Instead, Wouters scans the field and sees van Basten on a lateral run, two steps ahead of his marking defender. Wouters crisply plays the ball in the space in front of van Basten, who receives, pivots, and shoots, beating both the defender and goalkeeper Immel.

Most people like to credit Koeman's and Wouter's passing for the goal. After looking at the video slo-mo, you can see that when Koemans is in possession of the ball, teammate Ruud Gullit makes a brilliant run off the ball toward Koemans. With that run Gullit draws no less than three defenders out of position, leaving Wouters wide open. Thus credit Gullit with that one. Videos are fun and very educational if you try to see what's happening off the ball.

Staples of a Coaching Philosophy

Earlier in the chapter, I asked you to answer some questions to determine your coaching philosophy. Perhaps you haven't given the matter much thought. Maybe you never considered the value of a sound coaching philosophy. If not, it's time to do so.

Be Yourself

I have often dreamed of playing NBA basketball, but at five-foot-six, I know that Michael Jordan isn't lying awake worrying about me. Maybe I could be a quarterback. Think the NFL is looking for a 140-pound signal caller? Dan Marino, you're safe.

I have limitations, as do you and every athlete. The key is to understand those limitations through honest self-appraisal and then make the most of your potential.

All of us know coaches we greatly admire. We learn from them and sometimes use their ideas and methods. There is nothing wrong with that. But it's a mistake to pattern your

entire style after another coach. A copy can only be second best. In the end it is your personality that must prevail.

Among my friends and acquaintances I count such coaching greats as Tony Waiters, former Canadian national coach; Lothar Osiander, former U.S. Olympic team coach; Anson Dorrance, who so brilliantly coached the American women to the World Championship; Roy Rees, who was the U.S. boys' under-16 coach and is coauthor of this book; Bobby Howe, U.S. men's under-20 coach; and many others. All are successful, all reach their goals, but all use different methods to get to where they want to go. None copies the others, and no two have similar personalities. All have put distinct, personal stamps on the teams they have coached. They are strong because they are always themselves.

Sometimes coaches have difficulty defining their strengths. If that is true of you, ask family, members of your coaching staff, and others close to you what they feel your strengths are. Then work to enhance those strengths to become the best person and coach you can be.

Do a Reality Check

During a season of play, you and your team will go through many ups and downs—elation after a hard-fought win, heartbreak after a narrow defeat, fatigue after exhausting practices, joy of making the team, feeling of worthlessness when cut, helplessness after injuries, pride and satisfaction after a great effort, exhilaration of winning a championship, utter loneliness in the few minutes directly after losing a championship match.

Also, there will be jealousy and envy, embarrassment, temper flare-ups, blame, slumps, and more.

How do you handle these emotional peaks and valleys? What kind of example do you set for your players in dealing with setbacks? Your responses to such questions will reflect your motives for coaching.

Lead by Example

"Do as I say, not as I do" doesn't work in coaching. To be effective we must lead by example. If we want practices to start on time, we must be on time. If we want our players to respect each other, we must show respect to our players, our assistants, and our superiors. If we want our players to perform with a positive attitude, we can't coach negatively. Sometimes we probably aren't even aware of just how much our attitude and expectations affect the teams we coach.

 A MATCH LOST BY THE COACH

Two years ago, our only regular-season loss was to a very weak fifth-place team. I was terribly upset by the team's poor performance. But that night, as I replayed the match over and over in my mind, I concluded that the team did not lose the match, I did.

The morning of the match I had to make a court appearance as a witness. The case dragged on and on, so I got to the match shortly after it had started. My assistants had taken the team through the proper preparation, but when I showed up I was in a rotten, negative mood, which was no doubt reflected by my body language. The team picked up on my attitude and played a miserable match.

As the leader of our teams, we must set the tone. Think about your career, the high and low points. Then think about how you felt and acted at those times. See the pattern?

For a long time I have had a sign in my office for my players to read. It says, "You get what you expect to get." I have since added a note at the bottom, "That goes for the coach also."

We have a strong influence on our teams. So keep your example and lifestyle in line with your expectations for the players, and you will probably see the team behave as you hoped it would.

Keep Perspective

Early in my career I had some difficulty keeping things in perspective. I tackled tasks with single-minded enthusiasm. It often upset me when those around me would share my enthusiasm but not my single-mindedness. I've since learned that priorities may not always be mutual. We should not expect young athletes with busy social and academic lives to be single-minded.

As vice president of development for the Washington State Youth Soccer Association,

I manage the Olympic Development Program in our state. One of the player evaluation tournaments we conduct, the Big Sky Tournament, takes place on the first weekend in May. This is an extremely important tournament for players because many college coaches are on hand to watch.

Two years ago I received a phone call from an irate parent whose daughter was scheduled to play in the tournament on the girls' under-19 team. The parent's dilemma was that her daughter was required to leave for Boise, the tournament site, hours before her senior prom. The player's coach and the team's administrator had refused the parent's request to fly the girl into Boise Saturday morning, at the parent's expense, before the first match. They said that if the player did not travel with the team they would not allow her to play in any of the four scheduled matches.

After I hung up the phone a wave of anger hit me. Were our rules so important and so inflexible that we were going to keep a young person away from a once-in-a-lifetime event? All because of a soccer tournament? Especially when a little flexibility would allow the girl to compete?

I called the coach and the team's administrator and we talked about perspective. The player went to her prom, flew to Boise on Friday night, played in all four matches, and was selected to a regional camp. Shortly after the camp she received a scholarship from coach Dang Pibluvich to the University of Washington.

I am a stickler for rules. But flexibility is an asset that every coach should have. Too few of us take the perspective of our players. We want them to be totally dedicated to our program and the team. We want them to forgo all other activities, and when they don't we get angry. And then we wonder why they don't turn up for the next season.

Think for a moment of the commitments of your players. They face pressure to achieve academically. Some have part-time jobs. Others are members of church organizations. And others have family obligations. We must respect them, their priorities, and their schedules if we expect them to respect us.

Win on More Than the Scoreboard

The willingness to give your best and play to win is important. A lesser effort is dishonest and a discredit to the sport, the fans, and the team. Every team should want to succeed. Every coach should encourage the team to go for the win.

That doesn't mean that we must win every match. It does mean that we must try to win every match.

When we fail, but give it our all, then we didn't really fail because we tried to succeed. Maybe the other team was just better. In that case we have gained much more than we have lost from the experience. But when we lose a match for lack of trying, no matter who the opponent is, that is a shameful loss.

In 1988 we had a great season. In the quarterfinals of the playoffs we won 3-1. We won the semifinal by the same score. In the final we faced a team we had beaten twice during the season. I knew we had a problem. Our players thought that the match was going to be a piece of cake; our opponent was breathing fire.

After 90 minutes of listless play on our part, the score was 0-0. Five minutes into overtime we scored. The players viewing the outcome as inevitable relaxed and lost their focus. The opponent scored two quick goals and we went home as the runner-up. It took the team weeks to get over the disappointment. We knew that the other team didn't win the championship; we had lost it.

In 1991 we won our division and were seeded into the semifinals of our league championship. But as defending champions we had paid the price. That season each team played us hard and tough. The result was that we lost forward Joe Chadwell (12 goals in six matches) due to a broken tibia. In the last match of the regular season we lost another forward, Adeeb Al-Dhain, with broken ribs. That left us with Nicolas Reep as our only healthy forward.

We won the semifinal match 2-1. But we also lost Nicolas Reep with a badly rolled ankle. So we faced an extremely strong team in the final without any true forwards. What a match it turned out to be. Oh yes, we lost

1-0. But for 90 minutes the fans saw a tremendous demonstration of skill, sportsmanship, and desire. We didn't win on the scoreboard, but we did on the field. We held our heads high and we felt good about ourselves and each other.

Two losses. What was the difference? Performance, of course. The first match we lost to the opponent for lack of performance. The second match the opponent won in spite of our performance. After the first match there was shame and guilt; after the second match there was pride and confidence.

Playing to win is important and should be any team's goal. To coach successfully, however, we must be conscious of the team's performance rather than the result of the match. If we can truly and realistically evaluate the performance of our team, we can find ways of improving that performance. If we do that conscientiously, winning will take care of itself.

Other Measures of Success

Indirectly we can contribute to the welfare of soccer and the growth of our players by encouraging the players to become involved with local soccer organizations. Most of our players give back to the community by helping out as coaches, assistant coaches, or referees. Not only does the community benefit, but our players get a better understanding of the game, the challenges of coaching, and the difficulties encountered by officials.

After completing college some of our former players have accepted challenging coaching positions. In our immediate area five of our high school coaches are former Community Colleges of Spokane players. Several are distinguishing themselves as well-respected referees. When your former players continue with the sport, you'll know you have developed a successful program.

Coaching as a Mission

Dr. Rainer Martens in his book *Successful Coaching* says, "To coach, one needs the teaching skills of an educator, the training expertise of a physiologist, the administrative leadership of a business executive, and the counseling wisdom of a psychologist." Add to that the need to have a thorough knowledge of soccer, and what you once thought was an interesting pastime has suddenly become a demanding profession. But that's how it is.

None of us is born with all the qualities mentioned above. We have the opportunity to acquire them as we go along. We can grow constantly and get better with each season. That's what makes coaching challenging and exciting.

We are in a unique position to serve our players. We guide and travel with them through the entire emotional journey of a season. The practices. The matches. And everything else.

We all have dreams of being carried off the field on the shoulders of our players while holding that huge, golden trophy way up high. There is nothing wrong with such a vision as long as we are aware of the tremendous amount of effort, time, and dedication it will take from ourselves and our athletes, and as long as we are willing to pay the price for success through hard work, overcoming adversity, resolving conflict, and coping with stress and self-doubt.

Carrying the golden trophy is a great objective. Everybody likes winning. Every soccer coach wants to have a winning team, but you cannot build a house starting with the roof. There has to be a foundation; there has to be a framework. The foundation and framework are built during practices.

You must be willing to spend the time first to develop the athletes' physical condition and then to develop the players' technical abilities. Only after doing that can you worry about the team's tactical development. While doing all that, you should also realize that the development of any athlete is not complete without building the athlete's confidence and self-esteem. This is particularly important for the soccer player.

Soccer is not a coached sport. By that I mean the soccer coach does not have the luxuries that coaches in other sports have. For instance, in football the coach often calls every play; in baseball the manager flashes signals between every pitch; in basketball the coach has several time-outs in which to adjust strategy and is close enough to the play to direct it. But in soccer, once the opening whistle is blown, the players make all the decisions.

True, the coach may make some tactical adjustments, such as substitutions for players who are having a bad day. Or the coach might revise the game plan at halftime. That's about it. The secondary role of a soccer coach during a match is highlighted by the international rule that the coach may be seen but not heard during a match. This rule is also being adopted in the United States. Before long, the coach's ability to make substitutions will be restricted.

Thus, in a soccer match, the players are the decision makers. A player without confidence and high self-esteem is unable to make the necessary decisions or will hesitate before making decisions. Since soccer matches are played at lightning speed, such indecision is costly. To be successful as a coach and a team, it is essential that we work on the players' psychological strengths.

Only after developing the athletes mentally and physically can you realistically expect to have a team that can perform to the best of its ability.

We, more than any other adult figure, can lead them to be the best athletes, the best students, and the best citizens they can possibly be. With our guidance, our fairness, our impartial discipline, our honesty, our openness, and our work ethic, we can instill in our players the qualities needed to live happy and productive lives. That's coaching. That's our job. That's our mission. Let's get prepared.

Make Soccer Fun

Someone once asked me to define fun. I feel it means to present young people with realistic challenges and then allow them, without interference, to overcome the challenges. Success at anything is fun.

Close to my home is a large sports complex. On Saturdays it is packed from early morning till evening with young soccer teams. On occasion it is fun to go out and watch the very young ones play.

One morning a father came to pick up his son shortly after the match ended. The boy, still excited from playing, rushed to his dad yelling, "Hi, dad! We had fun." Dad came closer and said, "Hi, son. Did you win?" The

boy looked confused, turned to the coach, and asked, "Coach, did we win?" The coach said, "Well, if you don't count their eight goals, we won one-nothing." At that point the father lost interest.

The story is both amusing and sad. Amusing, because to the boy, having fun was of primary importance and the 8-1 score didn't detract from that fun. Sad, because to the father, the score was all important.

Some years ago, in Vancouver, Washington, I watched an under-12 match. It was pretty lopsided. Halfway through the second half the blue team was ahead 6-0. I learned from one of the parents that the green team had never won a match. I wondered how the coach of the green team felt about that. I positioned myself close to him so that I could hear his comments. Just then the green team executed a perfect wall pass. The coach became unglued. "Did you people see that?" he yelled. "A perfect wall pass. For weeks we have been working on that and they did it. They did it!"

Here was a coach whose team had not won a match in the entire team's history, whose team was losing 6-0, but who was elated when his team performed a skill they had practiced. I admired that coach.

Young players are not wrong for wanting just to have fun. Nor are fathers or mothers wrong for wanting their children to win. And the coach who went crazy over the successful wall pass may not be a great coach. What I am saying is that all three—wanting to have fun, playing to win, and striving to improve and develop skills—should be part of your soccer coaching perspective.

At this point it should be obvious that to be a soccer coach means more than just knowing the sport. In fact, the coach must be capable of setting clear objectives for himself or herself and for the athletes, while keeping in mind that there is more to a young athlete's life than soccer.

To help athletes reach their objectives, you must be willing to spend the time to get to know them and to let them know who you are and where you stand. If you want them to overcome weaknesses, you should not be afraid to expose personal shortcomings. In fact, the ability to laugh at yourself is an important asset.

Summary

The components needed to develop your coaching philosophy and thereby lay a foundation for your players and team to perform at peak are as follows:

- Evaluate your objectives and your current qualifications to coach.
- Be hungry for knowledge. Read, attend clinics, watch and analyze matches, talk with fellow coaches.
- Be yourself, check realities, lead by example, and keep things in perspective.
- Coach to succeed by focusing on performance rather than immediate result.
- Improving performance is a win-win challenge.
- Balance the need to succeed with liberal amounts of fun, laughter, and good humor.
- Respect the sport, players, fans, officials, opponents, and everything else associated with your team and program.
- Accept challenge and maintain an enthusiastic attitude.

Chapter 2

Communicating Your Approach

Success in any relationship depends on clear, effective communication. When a message is transmitted, both the sender and receiver should have a clear understanding of its content. The message should not be open to any interpretation other than the one intended by the sender. That may sound simple, but when relationships sour, it is usually the lack of effective communication that caused the breakdown.

Many communication styles can be effective. You may be an individual who speaks rapidly and excitably, or you may be very calm and laid-back. It doesn't matter as long as the content of your message is logical and interpreted the same by all.

Coaching by its very nature is communicating. The better you develop your communication skills, the more successful you will be when communicating with

- your players, on and off the field, about positive and negative subjects,
- your assistants and staff, about goals and progress,
- your superiors, about budgets and administrative policies,
- officials before, during, and after matches,
- parents, with questions about their son's or daughter's playing time,
- faculty, to gain their respect,

- the student body, to entice them to come to matches,
- the community, for support for your program, and
- the media, to write and talk about your program.

While this list is incomplete, it nevertheless gives a good idea of how much communication a coach needs to do.

Keys to Effective Communication

It is important that you choose the right words to transmit your messages. However, there are other keys to effective communication. We also receive messages. The understanding of those messages depends on our ability to listen and interpret the content. Attentive listening is one of the communication skills we must learn or improve.

People also transmit messages through gesture, body language, and voice pitch. In effective communication the nonverbal messages play a crucial role because they often indicate the true state of mind of the sender. Here again, the message needs to be interpreted skillfully.

Sending Messages

Even if you've sent a clear and consistent message, how do you know it was received as you intended? A simple way is to ask the receiver to repeat the message. Another way is to ask a few quick, pertinent questions about the message. I encourage you to use these methods with your players.

When we wrongly assume that athletes know how we feel about them, we need another form of reality check, so part of my postseason activities includes a conversation with each athlete to discuss the next season.

Receiving Messages

Receiving messages is as important to coaches as sending them. Yet this is a coach's most neglected skill.

Effective, active listening is hard work. It requires full attention, accurate interpretation, and constructive response. That takes time that coaches on a hectic schedule often don't believe they have. Sometimes we don't have time to listen because we are too busy correcting errors caused by earlier faulty communication. Let me give an example.

John Blake takes care of our travel arrangements. For one of our trips he had chartered a bus to pick us up at 10:00 on a Friday morning. A few days later I told John that I wanted to leave earlier. The next day he handed me a slip of paper and said that the woman at the bus company needed to know what time the bus and driver should report. I said, "8 A.M." I was busy and never looked at the slip of paper. Well, on it were the name and phone number of the woman at the bus company. Obviously, John expected me to call but I assumed that *he* would call. We departed at 10 A.M.

We can't afford not to listen.

Another reason you should learn to listen is that an active listener is someone your athletes want to talk to. Players will open up to you more. They will share with you their dreams, hopes, and anxieties. You will thus get to know them better. Remember, you can't coach an athlete you don't know.

At the end of each season our players evaluate the program and the coaching staff with only the athletic director in attendance.

Keys to Becoming a Better Listener

- Face your athlete squarely and lean toward him or her.
- Be relaxed.
- Assume an open posture.
- Maintain eye contact.
- Paraphrase messages with questions such as, "Are you saying that . . . ?"
- Listen with empathy; try to understand the sender.
- Don't judge the message until it is delivered fully.
- Don't judge the sender by appearance or reputation.
- Listen for main ideas in the sender's statements.
- Get rid of distractions.
- Actively practice your listening skills.

After that the athletic director meets with the head coach and goes over the results of the meeting with the athletes. One of the questions the director asks the athletes is, "How well did the coach communicate?"

After my first year at the school the answers to this question were somewhat mixed. All felt that I was an excellent communicator. However, some stated that in one-on-one conversations they felt uncomfortable because I seemed to be tense and rushed. Although I didn't enjoy admitting it, after reviewing the conversations I had with some of my athletes, I concluded that they were right. Since then I have worked hard on my one-on-one skills, especially in confrontations. I did that by becoming a better and more attentive listener.

It is not difficult to become a better listener. Body posture alone can tell the athlete that you are ready to listen.

Open-Door Policy

Have you ever been in a situation where you felt you had a problem or needed counsel and the only one who could help you was your boss? Do you remember that it took some courage to walk into your supervisor's office and present your situation? Do you also remember how badly it hurt when your boss said something like, "Can't it wait? I'm extremely busy right now"?

When I first started to coach (our athletes say that was around 1846), the job consumed all of my time. I saw interruptions as major distractions. Often I was abrupt and frequently asked the interrupter to come back some other time. Of course, they never did.

Now I know that a part of good communication is being available. So when I arrive at my office, I open my door and it stays open until I leave for the day. My staff and athletes know they can come in anytime. Often when a staff member or an athlete walks in, it's because he or she has a problem or needs advice. If it's a problem, I want to know about it because I have learned that a minor problem will become a major one if it's not solved quickly.

I can hear many of you ask, "With that open-door policy, how do you get anything done?" Actually, I get a lot done.

To begin with, solving minor problems takes less time than solving major ones. Also, from a former business associate, I learned a little trick. She told me that I should schedule in time for interruptions during my day. If the interruptions come I am ready; if not, I have the luxury of some extra moments to work on a task I would not have gotten to otherwise. The open door shows that I am available and that I care.

Nonverbal Communication

Coaches must be good communicators, and most of us are great with words. It's equally important to realize that we send numerous nonverbal messages. With our hands, body, and face we can express disgust, disbelief, surprise, confusion, anger, joy. We often express our emotions better through nonverbal messages than through the spoken word. If these nonverbal messages don't correspond with the verbal ones, miscommunication will occur.

In our classes we do a little exercise to highlight the problem of verbal-nonverbal incompatibility. You can try it right now. Sit in a chair, put your head between your knees, and say loudly, "I feel great." Doesn't sound very convincing, does it? Now, stand up tall, raise your arm way up, clench your fist, lift your head, smile, and say loudly, "I feel terrible."

I know those are extreme examples, but it's not much different from telling an athlete that you are very interested in what he or she has to say, but once the athlete starts to talk, you stare off in another direction. Suppose, after your left forward badly misses a shot at goal, you throw your hands in the air as if to say, "Dear Lord, why me?" Do you think it does any good to follow it up with a half-hearted, "Good try, Jimmy"? Not likely.

It truly amazes me how much can be accomplished without benefit of the spoken word.

 A VISIT TO BABYLON

Some years ago, while still living in Vancouver, Washington, I had the opportunity to coach the Terriers soccer team. The Terriers represented the Washington School for the Deaf. All my players would be deaf. How was I going to communicate? I couldn't even sign. I had my doubts about the situation. But after an awkward first session the players and I started communicating very effectively. We didn't use the spoken word. We didn't need to. Our facial expressions, gestures, body language, demonstrations, and pure enthusiasm were all we needed. We had a great time.

I communicated successfully with the Terriers through nonverbal messages. However, nonverbal messages are sometimes misleading and often misinterpreted; a coach must be aware of, and careful with, this form of communication. We also should match our nonverbal messages with our spoken words.

Communicating With Players

Although your communication principles should never change, the style you use to communicate should change to meet the needs of the situation. The style of communication you use to talk with your spouse differs from the way you talk to your boss. The style you use when hauled over for a traffic violation certainly differs from the style you use to communicate with your children. The style you use when discussing a problem with an athlete may be friendly, angry, comforting, or threatening. In a one-on-one conversation in the privacy of your office, you can be far more direct than if the athlete is with the entire team.

Never Humiliate

You must be careful not to say anything that will make the athlete look bad in the eyes of teammates. The athlete will accept a negative statement about his or her effort made in your office but will never forgive you for making that statement in front of his or her peers. Not only that, but the other athletes may sympathize with the scolded one, and you lose all around. If you have a problem with an athlete, handle it in private.

Even in private be careful of what you say and how you say it. Attack the problem, not the person. There is a big difference between saying, "Heather, you are stupid," and, "Heather, that was a stupid thing to do." The first statement attacks Heather personally. The second attacks something Heather has done. She will never agree with the first statement but may agree with the second.

Athletes need confidence; humiliation destroys confidence.

In discussions with my players I like using "I" statements instead of leading with the word "you." I feel it is less intimidating and protects a player's self-esteem. For instance, when a player hasn't been playing too well, instead of saying, "You are playing terribly. Why?" I prefer to say, "I feel that you are far more capable than what you have been showing me. Do you feel the same way?"

The first statement puts the player on the defensive, and the player shuts you out. The second statement doesn't accuse and puts the player at ease. It makes the player realize that you are there to help solve a problem. Usually the conversation that follows is revealing and fruitful.

Another method I like using, especially during a confrontational discussion, is to start out with an agreement. It can go somewhat like this:

"Before we get into this discussion let's agree on something. I feel that with work and dedication you can be an excellent player and a real asset to the team. Do you agree with that statement?"

After the player agrees, I continue, "OK, we agree. Then I must tell you that I have difficulty understanding how disruptive behavior at practice, like what happened today, contributes to our expectations. Can you help me understand it?"

Again, I believe that this method shows the player that I am ready to help solve a problem. A rewarding discussion usually follows.

In all confrontations stay focused on the problem. Don't attack the person. A player who makes a mistake, or even two or three, is guilty of bad judgment. It doesn't necessarily make the player a bad person.

Most people feel that after a confrontation there must be a winner and a loser. One person's will must prevail. That's not true. A good communicator will try to create a win-win situation. It can be done as follows:

- State the problem, preferably using "I" statements or an agreement.
- Allow the other person to state his or her views and thoughts.
- Listen to what the player says or doesn't say.

- Restate the player's feelings and thoughts, making sure that both of you understand exactly how the player feels and thinks.
- Find the common grounds in your feelings and thoughts.
- Find alternate solutions to any remaining problems.
- Make a new agreement.

Communicating at Practices

Most coaches I have met and dealt with like the command style of coaching, or what I call coaching down to their athletes. They probably feel that the players are the students and they are the teacher. I don't agree with that style of communicating, especially during practices.

I prefer the "level" style of communicating with athletes, interacting almost as if we were peers. In many ways we are. We are partners working together to solve problems and maximize our performance.

Communicating During a Match

In most of the world a soccer coach may be seen but not heard during a match. That traditional restriction is being opposed by some coaches in the United States. I favor

the ban on touchline instruction during matches. Players' total concentration should be on their performance and the opponent—not on their coach. That doesn't mean that you can't offer an occasional comment. But don't bombard your players with instructions while they are on the field.

Instead, be an active observer during your matches. Bring your trusty clipboard and make notes about the things that go right and wrong. These notes are great cues for preparing your next practice and will help you make tactical adjustments during the match or at halftime.

As you observe from the touchline, control your body language. If you look irritated, upset, or uninterested, your players are likely to play sluggishly. Conversely, if your gestures are positive, encouraging, and enthusiastic, your team will show more zip.

 PLAYERS READ YOUR BODY LANGUAGE

For two years I coached Adam Johnson, a fine defender. After one match one of my assistants, Rick Harrison, told me that he had noticed that after every play—a good clearance, a super tackle, or a mistake—Adam would immediately look to the touchline, searching me out to read how I felt about the play. I started watching; Rick was right. Adam constantly looked over at me.

I met with Adam a few times, mainly to assure him of my confidence in him. I also became very aware of my body language and rewarded Adam with a thumbs-up, a smile, or a shake-it-off gesture. I was rewarded in return with Adam's slow easy grin. Soon he looked over at me less and less. I kind of missed it. Adam went on to Huntingdon College in Alabama on a fine scholarship. I told his new coach, Todd Schilperoort, this story. Today Adam plays for and is part owner of the Yakima Reds, a United States Interregional Soccer League (USISL) team.

Communicating Off the Field

You have a great opportunity to influence your athletes through your communication with them off the field. After a season of practices and play you may know your players better than their classroom teachers do. Some athletes will confide in you more than they will their parents.

Your off-field communication with players might consist of an occasional phone call during the off-season. It might be a postseason meeting in your office. It might be something as simple as a "hello" in a hallway.

Look for other ways to express your interest in your players. For instance, I keep track of all my former and present athletes' birthdays. My wife, Sandra, has designed some special birthday and Christmas cards related to soccer. Once a month I check my computer for birthdays and make sure that a card arrives on each athlete's birthday. Everyone gets a card at Christmastime.

Sometimes your off-field communication with players can have a tremendous payoff.

I really believe that you measure your success as a coach with the number of personal, long-lasting relationships you build with your athletes. You build those relationships off the field, by caring and showing that you care.

I treasure the phone calls, visits, and letters I get from former athletes. They wouldn't take the time if they didn't care.

 THE BARTMAN STORY

Rick Mullins (nicknamed The Bartman) played for our school for two years. He is a fine athlete; outside midfield was his spot. He impressed me as an intelligent individual, but his academic achievement was not great. His grade point average hovered around 2.0.

First, Rick and I had some long conversations. After that, one of my assistants started working with him. He helped Rick select classes, we counseled him, and slowly we saw his GPA improve to a 3.0. The Bartman went on to Central Washington University. Recently, Rick wrote me, "Coach, you won't believe this but my GPA at Central is 3.7. Thanks, thanks, thanks." As I took my handkerchief out of my pocket I wondered if anything compared with the thrill of being a coach.

Communication Mistakes That Hurt

Sometimes we get so busy that even when we see a problem developing, we don't step in to prevent it. Or, maybe, we feel that somehow the problem will resolve itself. Afterward we wish we had another chance to help those who got hurt. Too often we don't get another chance, but if we learned from such mistakes, we haven't totally lost.

One particular case I remember vividly—not proudly, just vividly.

 HASTE AND WASTE

The end of our 1994 season was hectic. With two rounds of matches to go there were four teams with a chance at first place in the division. Our last two matches were back-to-back and out of town. On Friday we were in Bellevue, Washington (300 miles one-way), and on Saturday we played in Tacoma (320 miles) against Pierce College. A loss against Pierce would have meant a play-off match on Sunday. Luckily we won. However, that put us in a quarterfinal match on Monday in Portland, Oregon (600 miles).

Dr. Maury Ray, our athletic director, gave us permission to fly to Portland, but I could take no more than 15 players, two coaches, and a trainer. We usually travel with 18 players. We quickly selected the 15 who would go. It had been my intent to meet, before the team meeting, with the three players we had not selected. Time got away from us and I didn't get it done. During the meeting I realized the error and I asked the three players to stay after the meeting so that I could explain my reasoning.

One of the three was a forward named Tony Frieske. Tony had suffered from an ankle injury most of the season, but he had come on as a substitute in the Pierce match and was instrumental in winning the match. He was riding high. Of course, during our hasty team meeting he crashed down. He did not stay after the team meeting. That evening he did not return my several phone calls. We left the next morning.

I have met with Tony since and he accepts the reason for my decision. I believe that I have undone some of the damage, but I can never make up for the pain I caused him that day. What I can do is never let it happen again.

Communicating With Others

As a coach you work with two teams—the one that plays soccer on the field and the team that consists of assistant coaches, trainers, managers, program administrators, information directors, and so forth. Both teams must be focused on the same goals and philosophy. They can do that if they have played a role in establishing the goals and philosophy.

Good play by the team on the field requires explicit communication. Suffice it to say that open communication by and with the support team is essential to overall success.

Communicating With Assistants and Staff

You must communicate with your immediate staff—assistants, trainers, and managers—on a daily basis. Two-way discussions with the assistants may involve talking about progress to date, effectiveness of the daily plan, adjustments to the daily plan, the next practice, the next match, player progress, and player concerns.

Listen carefully to what the assistants are saying. From their statements you can determine if everyone is still pulling in the same direction. They may also have suggestions for improvement. Most of all, players frequently find it easier to talk to an assistant coach than to the head coach. This indirect communication between the team and the head coach is extremely valuable in detecting problems in an early stage.

 THE ONE WHO ALMOST GOT AWAY

We have three goalkeepers on our roster. Ryan Porter, one of the goalkeepers, saw a fair amount of action during his freshman year. During his sophomore year he had to compete for playing time with two excellent freshman goalkeepers. Ryan must have realized that he would see limited playing time, if any at all. From Jim Martinson, my assistant coach, I found out that Ryan was thinking of quitting. I didn't want him to quit, because Ryan had other assets that greatly helped our team. He is a very positive person with a superb sense of humor. He was a constant inspiration to the team and helped us keep things in perspective. I needed Ryan.

During a meeting I tried to explain my feelings to Ryan. I told him that he would not play much, but that his contributions to the team culture, or team spirit, were as valuable as a stellar performance in goal. Ryan understood. He stayed. At the end of the season he visited me and thanked me for talking him out of quitting. He said to me, "I had the funnest time of my life."

Your players' welfare should be of constant concern to you. So, there should be open and daily communication with the trainers. I require a daily report about the progress of our injured athletes and discuss with the trainer the effectiveness of the rehabilitation plan.

I also invite comments from our trainers about our physical conditioning program and solicit their suggestions on injury prevention.

Your program, practices, and other events will run smoothly as long as your managers know exactly what you expect of them. Precise communication on a daily basis will help them stay effective and motivated. It also pays to listen to them. They also may have suggestions to improve certain routines.

The everyday activities of the team and the people directly involved will be efficient if everyone knows the goals for the day. Good communication accomplishes that, but you must create the time and the atmosphere in which your people feel comfortable to exchange thoughts, feelings, and reports.

Be aware of a potential problem in communication with assistants and staff. As a head coach, you are a supervisor. But you will very quickly lose the respect of those you supervise if you disobey or bad-mouth your superiors. If you don't respect your supervisors, why should your staff or players respect you?

Communicating With Officials

Over the years I have seen the quality of referees improve dramatically. But for every 10 referees recruited, 8 quit during their first year. Those who quit cite the verbal abuse they took during matches as a major reason for their decision.

Coaches, players, and fans seem to feel that a referee must be perfect during his or her first match and then improve. But even the best referees make mistakes, just like coaches and players. When the North American Soccer League (NASL) was still active, the referee was considered efficient if 85 percent of the calls were correct and if the ball was in play for more than 55 minutes. Thus, a 15 percent error rate was acceptable. Now keep in mind that the majority of a referee's calls (60 percent) are judgment calls. It's not likely, but all may go against your team. Add 60 percent of 85 (or 51 percent) to the 15 percent error allowed; you may object to 66 percent of the calls made by a well-qualified referee. That may be difficult to accept, but these are the facts.

    COURAGE IN BLACK

In 1982 the World Cup Tournament was in Spain. One of the matches was between Poland and Russia. The two countries then were feuding bitterly. There were 45,000 fans in the stadium. It was an explosive situation. To this

day I still feel tremendous respect for that man in a black uniform, who calmly walked onto the field and officiated an almost perfect match (with, I must add, the help of the players).

Of course, not every referee has the qualities of the Poland-Russia referee. Many referees, however, could reach that level if we let them. For players and coaches the match is the ultimate teacher. So it is for the referee. The more matches a referee can officiate, the better he or she will become. If the referee can do these matches without the added stress of abuse from players, fans, and coaches, his or her decisions will be better. Players and coaches make mistakes, and we learn from them. Let's extend the same courtesy to our referees. Control what you can—your players, your fans, and yourself. You can't control the referee's performance. Why waste the time?

It's fine to discuss certain calls with the referee, but do so in a quiet, dignified manner. Don't put the referee on the defensive. Who knows, after the explanation, you may learn something.

Communicating With Parents

I hear coaches complain about certain parents. In most cases, the problem is a lack of communication. The coach doesn't communicate with the parents, nor does he invite the parents to communicate with him. Usually these coaches interpret any parent inquiry as a disguised complaint, a nuisance, or an encroachment on their authority. This kind of attitude hurts your program and your team.

There are many reasons for being candid with parents. Just as the players have a right to know their exact status on the team, so does the parent. For instance, a parent left guessing why a son or daughter isn't getting more playing time will turn negative and become a problem. If, on the other hand, the parent knows exactly how you feel about the child and your plans for development, he or she may become very supportive.

With careful communication, parents can become an integral part of your program and your strongest supporters. Not only that, you can use them to build a sound social structure for and around your team and program.

    FROM FOE TO FRIEND

Jeff and Amy Montgomery, brother and sister, played for us. Jeff had been very successful with us and his father was very supportive of the team. After Jeff left, Amy joined us. At first she had difficulty because she was not in match condition. I could see the chagrin on Mr. Montgomery's face when Amy did not get to play in the first few league matches. I decided to talk with him. I told him why Amy wasn't playing, but I also assured him that Amy was a quality player and that when we had overcome the problem, she would be starting. I also shared with him the training program we had laid out for Amy. Mr. Montgomery was happy and supportive again. At the end of the season he wrote us a letter. I'd like to cite one part of it: "Thank you for coaching our proud children, preparing them for a future life of successes and small failures, and teaching them to make the best of both. Thank you."

Communicating With Faculty

When it comes to athletics, every campus has two factions: those who enjoy sports and truly believe that they are an important part of human development and those who feel that academics is the only function of a school. Of course, I totally agree with and appreciate the first group. But I respect those in the second group, because most are dedicated, caring, and knowledgeable educators. Regardless, you can earn the respect of all faculty through conscientious communication.

Certainly, keep all faculty informed of the team's progress and away dates; check academic progress of your athletes; don't play an athlete who is in trouble academically (even if it hurts); and don't ever defend or attempt to intervene for an athlete who is academically ineligible.

CLASSROOM ON WHEELS

Matt Kinder, our captain, was scheduled to take an exam on one of our travel days. With the instructor's cooperation we solved the problem. We left Friday at 7 A.M. Matt was in the passenger seat of the van I was driving. Promptly at 8 A.M. I reached under my seat for a sealed envelope that contained the test. I handed it to Matt. During the next hour and a half, while we were traveling, Matt did the test. Upon completion he handed it to me. I sealed it in an envelope and delivered it to the instructor on Monday morning.

Communicating With the Student Body

There is nothing as exciting as playing in front of a crowd of cheering fellow students. But to get them there is not always easy. Many students have a misconception or distrust of athletes and athletics. Those feelings can be overcome.

Your players need to be involved in student activities and, if possible, student government. Certainly, they should show an interest in the other school sports and attend contests whenever possible. Their behavior on campus and in classes must be exemplary.

In our school we have, among other great clubs, a fine choir, a well-known jazz orchestra, a forensic team of national stature. I try to attend as many of their activities as possible. I also encourage my players to go. A quick note of congratulations to the director and the students after a successful activity in or out of town keeps them informed of my interest.

The hardest misunderstanding to overcome is the belief that athletes get preferential treatment. That just isn't so. In fact, athletes have to live with many rules, like eligibility, that do not affect the rest of the student body. Once the student body is aware of that, a lot of the distrust seems to vanish.

We use various tools to educate the student body. Eligibility rules are clearly displayed on all college bulletin boards. The grade point averages of our athletes are accumulated quarterly. The averages are published and compared to the college average in school newspapers. We have never been lower than the total college average. We don't allow our athletes to wear team uniforms, warm-ups, jackets, sweaters, or other equipment to classes. We also encourage our athletes to be members of any one of the numerous campus committees.

So, with some effort you can get the students to come to your matches. Make sure the announcer encourages sportsmanlike conduct by the fans and thanks them for attending.

Communicating With the Community

I am very grateful to live in a community that is very sport and youth oriented. I maintain an active mailing list of community leaders, business people, and other supporters. Anytime the team, or anyone associated with the team, experiences a significant event, we inform the community. In turn when we need funds or equipment for a special occasion, people are always ready to help us.

All our tournaments and clinics are fully sponsored. When two years ago we entered a team in the Cascade League during the off-season, league fees, travel costs, and uniforms were collected within 10 days. Whenever we get support from the community, all our players contact the sponsors with letters of thanks. I have visited many businesses that have displayed these letters on bulletin boards.

We also contact coaches and physical education instructors in elementary, junior high, and high schools. If they attend one of our matches they get to visit with our players. If they bring their team we have some small gifts or mementos for the players.

Communicating With the Media

One of our biggest challenges is to convince the media that soccer is newsworthy. Many coaches get angry that the efforts of their teams, especially during a successful season, aren't reported properly. I share that frustration. But step back a moment and look at what is happening.

Most sportswriters and broadcasters simply don't know soccer (I can't count the number of times I have had to explain the difference between a free kick and a penalty). The media, like you and me, tend to talk about what they know. Most have limited time and space in which to report, especially TV sports broadcasters. Those are but a few of the reasons for the lack of coverage.

My main advice is not to become discouraged, but to keep supplying the media with information in a professional manner. Provide them with your match schedules, highlights on some of your athletes, and any special honors you, your staff, or players have received. Report match results (win or lose) accurately and promptly. Be sure to have some highlights to report if asked for them. If your school has a sports information director, supply pertinent information and work closely with him or her.

The media can be friendly, open-minded, and supportive. You can't demand support but you can earn it. Keep the media informed. Report news accurately and promptly and be sure to present highlights. Be available when called on. Whenever a special event or an interesting story develops, call the media and share the story.

Summary

The following suggestions will help you to become a more effective communicator.

- Send clear and consistent messages. Invite comments.
- Become a better listener. Listen actively and determine whether you are interpreting messages accurately.
- Be congruous in your verbal and nonverbal communications.
- Choose the appropriate style of communication with players on and off the field.
- Make sure that communication with your assistants and staff are two-way discussions.
- Communicate respectfully with officials and superiors.
- Keep parents, faculty, student body, community, and media informed.

Chapter 3

Motivating Players

Wouldn't it be great if we had some simple words or a magic button to motivate each of our players? A five-minute "pride of the team" speech at orientation; a "do it for the Gipper" prematch pep talk; a fire-and-brimstone halftime sermon; and perhaps an "If you win, the pizza's on me" approach. In some situations, these motivational methods might work. But they aren't the ultimate answer. And they often backfire.

Some coaches will question the methods of motivation I will talk about. They might still feel that fear is a great motivator, but I'd rather coach a team of happy, risk-taking, innovative, and motivated athletes than a herd of psychological cripples.

 A FAMOUS HALFTIME TALK

One of the finest gentlemen I know is C. Clifford McCrath, coach of soccer at Seattle Pacific University. SPU is a soccer powerhouse, and much of that success must be attributed to Cliff's tremendous motivational powers. At a dinner one night he told this story.

SPU was playing on the road and behind 2-0. At halftime Cliff gave the team one of his trademark speeches. When he was through the players were so fired up that they literally burst out of the dressing room. But there was a problem. The dressing room had two exits, one to the playing field and one to the swimming pool. Between the door and the pool was a deck about three feet wide. This was the first time in history that half a soccer team spent halftime in a swimming pool. It must have worked because according to Cliff they won 4-2.

What is Motivation?

Everyone fantasizes. Everybody has a dream. Some readily admit it. For others the dream may be deep seated. Some may even deny they have a dream. But it's there. Who hasn't entered the burning house and brought out the family dog? Who hasn't come to the rescue of the damsel in distress? What soccer player hasn't dreamed of being Romario or Michelle Akers and scoring the winning goal in a World Cup final. We dream, our players dream. A dream is a castle in the sky until you put a foundation under it. The foundation can be built when the dreamer believes the dream will come true and is willing to put forth the effort to validate the dream.

Some athletes pursue their dreams and fully expect to achieve them through hard work and dedication. They see each obstacle as a challenge and each setback as a call for a renewed effort to improve. They are self-motivated. Their motivation to succeed comes from within. This kind of athlete is easy to work with. All this player needs from the coach is an environment conducive to concentration, tools for development, and help with setting realistic goals.

Most athletes, however, lack either the belief in the dream or the willingness to spend the endless hours of hard work to achieve it. The coach needs additional tools to motivate these athletes to believe first that they can succeed and second that only hard work will lead to success. These athletes are extrinsically motivated; they need outside forces to help them achieve.

Years ago during an interview, a reporter asked what I felt was the most difficult part of coaching. I don't remember how I answered. But the question stuck with me. I know what my answer would be now: "To make athletes believe in themselves and each other."

Motivational Tools

There is no simple, standard approach to extrinsic motivation. What turns on one athlete may turn off another. Some of your players may have very low self-esteem, whereas others might have inflated egos. Even those who are cocky and display much bravado may be covering feelings of self-doubt. Athletes with true self-confidence are rare.

Athletes perform in a competitive environment where challenge, risk, and uncertainty are facts of life. Succeeding in sport competition takes courage, confidence, high self-esteem, and trust in self and teammates. Thus, motivation must start with the development of these personal qualities. To do that I use a number of tools that have helped me succeed:

- Relaxation
- Imagery
- Self-talk
- Goal setting
- Reinforcement

The most enjoyable part of coaching is motivating players. It is rewarding to see a timid, self-doubting, mediocre player turn into an assertive, confident, well-functioning athlete. And it's not difficult to promote such a positive change.

Relaxation

I have experimented with numerous relaxation techniques. All were beneficial, but with athletes progressive muscle relaxation (PMR) seems to work best. The athletes lie down or sit in a comfortable position, and a prerecorded cassette tape instructs them to tighten major muscle groups in a certain sequence, beginning with the hands, then arms, face, neck, shoulders, chest, abdomen, buttocks, thighs, and calves. When the muscles are relaxed, the athletes concentrate on the feeling of relaxation. The entire exercise takes about 20 minutes. By then they are in a pleasant state of relaxation.

Athletes benefit from being able to control their tension. When they are alert but relaxed, players can make better, quicker decisions during a match. An overanxious player will make incorrect decisions. Athletes are more motivated when they realize that they can control their anxiety. My team does PMR, as a group, before each match.

Imagery

I am a strong believer in the benefits of imagery. Athletes can improve their performance substantially through imagery sessions if the exercise is specific and the athletes are in a state of total relaxation. Once in a relaxed state, players can use imagery to rehearse a variety of aspects, like focusing on overcoming a weakness, embracing strengths, or mentally preparing for a match.

For instance, if players have a low opinion of their collective or individual abilities, they can't compete successfully. If they don't see themselves shining, they won't. To help players see themselves more favorably, I recommend they practice positive imagery techniques.

After getting into a relaxed state through PMR, players imagine themselves in action on the soccer field. Their mind's eyes should see the scenes vividly. They should hear the fans, the whistle of the referee, the shoe hitting the ball; they should smell the grass, the popcorn aroma coming from the concession stand; they should see the colors of the uniforms, the sky, the buildings in the background; they should feel the warmth of the sun, the tug of the wind. The scene must be vividly realistic. Still in their mind's eyes they enter the scene and play. They should do everything correctly. Anytime something negative slips in, players should return to positive actions immediately. Sessions of 5 to 15 minutes per day will cause dramatic changes in athletes. After a few weeks of imagery you will notice increased intrinsic motivation in your athletes. They are beginning to realize that the dream can come true.

Imaging Specific Performances

Once your athletes have developed the habit of imagery, they can start working on specific problems. They can work on the improvement of shooting, heading, passing, ball control, or any other soccer techniques. They can also image themselves playing relaxed and in a "flow state." The more specific, the better.

Imaging the Match

Because of our location we must travel no less than 300 miles to most of our away matches. When possible, I like to have the team arrive a day early because I feel it is important to have the time and opportunity to visit the opponent's field and the surroundings. Our visit lasts about half an hour. We walk the field, and if possible pass the ball around a bit. This walk-through makes our imagery about the next day's match more vivid and therefore more effective. On match day we are more comfortable and motivated, because we have already played—in our minds—on their field.

Self-Talk

I often tell my players, "Listen to what you're saying to yourself." This is a means of making players more aware of what they're thinking, positive or negative, about themselves.

Like you and me, athletes talk to themselves all the time. This self-talk influences their emotions, mental pictures, physical states, and behavior. How they are functioning is a product of what they think. Sad to say but many athletes think of themselves negatively. Their self-talk reflects that. Like an unchecked infection, these types of negative self-statements fester and spread throughout the individual. These put-downs serve no purpose other than to reinforce pessimistic attitudes, low self-concepts, and eventually, resignation.

Once players have become aware of the importance of positive self-talk, they can begin to regulate it. They can listen to themselves, catch the negative self-talk, challenge it, and change it into a positive conversation. It isn't easy, but it can be done, and once mastered the results are astounding.

To help players improve their self-talk, I like using an exercise designed by Tom Kubistant, author of *Mind Pump*. It's a simple exercise, and many have scoffed at it. To the skeptics I say, "Try it, what have you got to lose?"

During the first 12 days of practice we give the players 12 basic affirmations, one each day. They must memorize each affirmation and repeat it to themselves as many times as possible. At the end of the 12 days they must be able to recite all 12 and use the recital regularly, almost like a mantra.

1. Every day in every way I am better and better.
2. I like myself.
3. I am the captain of my ship; I am the master of my fate.
4. I trust my abilities.
5. I am relaxed.

6. I forgive my errors.
7. Sure I can.
8. I enjoy what I do.
9. I am on my side.
10. I always do the best job I can.
11. I am proud of my efforts.
12. I can do anything I choose to do.

Reprinted, by permission, from T. Kubistant, 1988, *Mind Pump* (Champaign, Illinois: Leisure Press), 105.

All my athletes master this basic set of affirmations. Later on we may use more specific affirmations. Self-talk also leads to improved intrinsic motivation. Not only do the athletes believe the dream can come true, they now know that they are worthy of success.

 ONE FORWARD'S AFFIRMATION

Jerry Havens, an outstanding forward, had trouble with his shooting. His shots were erratic. In a one-on-one conversation I asked Jerry what he thought of, or what he said to himself, directly before the shot. Very candidly he said that he feared missing the shot and communicated that fear to himself. We designed an affirmation for him: "I can make this shot." I asked Jerry to repeat that message to himself repeatedly, especially during practices before taking the shot. Over the next few weeks Jerry's shooting accuracy, speed, and power improved steadily. After leaving our school Jerry was recruited by Gonzaga University, where he holds the record for most goals scored in a season.

Goal Setting

One of the most effective tools to motivate athletes is goal setting. When used correctly this form of motivation allows an athlete to create a well-defined plan for improvement with measurable results at each step that lead to personal peak performance. If used incorrectly it can set up the athlete for failure.

It is a good idea to schedule a goal-setting session at the beginning of the season. Athletes involved in a team sport like soccer deal with two sets of goals—their personal goals and the team's goals. We should first help the players set their personal goals.

While setting long-term goals is beneficial, they won't do much to develop a player unless he or she establishes a set of realistic

intermediate goals and a set of daily goals. If the athlete reaches daily goals, he or she will improve. As the athlete improves, intermediate goals become more attainable. When intermediate goals are reached the athlete experiences the euphoria of success, and therein lies the great motivation of goal setting—measurable success at each step to long-term goals.

When I first start to help my athletes set goals for themselves and the team, I tell the following story:

A young child has just learned how to crawl. As an exercise to improve crawling and help the child become accustomed to stairways, his father shows him a large sucker. The father puts the sucker at the top of the stairs and tells the child that he may have the sucker if he crawls to the top. The child is enthusiastic and starts his climb. He climbs the first step with difficulty; the rug is rough and his knees hurt a little. But he is undaunted and attacks the second step. It is more difficult and his knees are turning red. Some of his determination vanishes. Nevertheless, the sucker beckons. He goes for step number three. He tries and tries but doesn't make it. His knees really hurt. Soon large tears roll down his face and he gives up. The father takes pity and rewards the child with the sucker for the good try.

Obviously, this kind of goal setting does more damage than good. The child has been set up to fail. He knows it. He also learned a very negative truth: you don't really have to succeed to be rewarded. After all, he got the sucker.

It would have been much better if daddy had put a small sucker on the first step and told his son that if he could climb the step today the sucker would be his. Tomorrow he could have put a sucker on the first and the second step and so on. Realistic, intermediate goals are essential for success.

When I talk about realistic goals, I'm talking about goals that are attainable and over which the player has control. Between the two of us we must decide if the intermediate goal is attainable in the player's present stage of development. If not, we should set a different, less demanding intermediate goal. In either case our next step is to determine what daily goals will have to be met to reach the intermediate goal. The goal must be attainable.

At the same time the goal must be realistic. Players, or coaches for that matter, have no control over outcomes. If a player sets a goal to be the leading scorer this season, yet last season did not score one goal, then the player is setting himself or herself up for failure. But if the player's goal is to improve by spending 20 minutes before or after each practice to work on shooting, he or she may not become the leading scorer but will certainly improve.

If it is the team's goal to beat Hayworth High, yet Hayworth High has a far better record, they will fail. But if it is the team's goal to prepare physically and mentally for the match, and if the team agrees to play at their individual bests, stay focused on the match, maintain a good attitude, communicate, and be hardy, they may surprise Hayworth.

For goals to be effective they must be performance oriented. Outcome goals seldom work. In the two examples above, the outcome goals are being the leading scorer and beating Hayworth High. The player and

team, respectively, do not have complete control over achieving these goals. The other two goals, to improve scoring by spending 20 extra minutes each practice and to be physically and mentally prepared for the match and agree to play at their individual bests, are performance goals. Players have complete control over these goals, and these performance goals will allow players to focus on important and controllable aspects of their matches.

After the players have set their individual goals for the season, you will find that there is much common ground. From this, develop the team goals and review them regularly.

Reinforcement

The most important principle of motivation is reinforcement. The idea is that rewarded behavior will increase in frequency, whereas neglected or punished behavior will decrease and eventually stop. While at first that sounds rather simple, here are the questions you'll need to answer to use reinforcement effectively with your players:

- What do you reward?
- What do you discipline?
- When do you reward or discipline?
- How do you reward or discipline?

Every play has its star. Every play has its supporting cast. Without excellent support the star can't shine, yet all the accolades go to the star when the play is successful.

It's easy for coaches, including me, to focus attention and praise on our star players and to be impatient and neglectful with those who are less skilled. To overcome this habit we have to remind ourselves that everyone on the team, not just the stars, must be motivated to play the match successfully.

Besides distributing rewards equitably, be consistent in what behavior you reward and when and how you reward it. This is easy to do if you base your rewards on effort, not performance or outcome. Even though your players may have vastly different skill levels, all of them can demonstrate a good work ethic. All can improve. Effort is easy to judge, and subsequently it becomes easy to be consistent in your praise.

At times you may want to praise a player for his or her effort in front of the team. This is especially true when most of the team seems to be giving less than 100 percent. Some players feel uncomfortable, however, when they are singled out. Instead, you might call the player out of the practice, or wait until after practice, and tell him or her you appreciate the hard work. I find these short one-on-ones invaluable. Try it. You're likely to find that the player works even harder after receiving your praise.

The Coach's Role in Motivation

Your goal should be to bring out the best in each player you work with. To do so, you must create an environment that satisfies athletes' basic needs. Some suggestions for doing that are the following:

- Get to know your players.
- Offer security.
- Show you care.
- Develop a positive team culture.
- Have fun.

Getting to Know Players

Get to know your players. Find out how well they take care of themselves. Are they being taken care of in their home life? If their means are inadequate for day-to-day survival, if they have to worry about their basic needs, they won't be able to reach their athletic potential. Maybe you can find them a part-time job or get them involved in a work-study program.

Offering Security

Provide your players with an understanding of their roles on the team, with assurance that their roles won't be diminished because of one bad performance. The easiest way to make players feel secure is to discuss with starters and nonstarters, individually, how you foresee them best contributing to the team. Make them feel that they can add to the team's success and that you consider each player important.

Showing You Care

Players need to know that you care for them. They will work and play hard for you if they know that you're concerned with them not only as athletes but also as human beings. If you show them that you care, they'll probably care more and they'll try to meet your standards.

 IT'S THE LITTLE THINGS THAT ARE IMPORTANT

James Jasso played for us for two years and was an exceptionally good attacking stopper. In one of our matches James looked out of it. I subbed for him and took him to the side to ask what was wrong. James said he felt uncomfortable because I had neglected to talk with him privately before the match.

The talk James was referring to was my habit of saying just a few words privately to each starting player before the match. They are simple words of encouragement. I just want them to know that they are not alone. I also touch them at that time. It might be my hand on their shoulder, a high five, a handshake, or a pat on the back. An old friend once told me that you can't dislike each other if you can touch each other. I believe it.

I assured James that my neglect was caused by the meeting with officials to go over certain league rules before the match. I had simply run out of time. James smiled, went back in, and did his usual superb job. He needed to know I cared.

Once your players have their basic survival needs met, feel secure, and know that you care for them, you can begin the task of improving their self-esteem, confidence, and feelings of self-worth.

Developing a Positive Team Culture

Nothing motivates a player as much as a positive comment from a teammate. From the moment training starts until the final match, our coaches freely praise outstanding effort. We encourage our players to do the same. When I hear one of our players make a positive comment to another player, I immediately take him aside and thank him for the contribution he has made to the team's

positive attitude. Soon all players begin to realize that we reward positive comments, and praise becomes the rule rather than the exception. At the same time we squelch all negative comments the moment they are made.

 THE "I'M OK, YOU'RE OK" GAME

Sometimes there may be some friction between players or some players' self esteem may be hurting a bit. When that occurs, I like playing a game I call, "I'm OK, You're OK." I admit the title isn't very original, but it works.

Before or after a practice, all players gather in our meeting room. Once the players are comfortable I ask them to say something positive about every one of the players. Usually a captain starts the game. She must describe a quality she likes about every player in the room. Thus, she may say: "Becky, I like your positive attitude," "Jen, I wish I could volley like you," and "Heather, I appreciate it when you encourage me after I make a mistake." She continues until she has made a positive comment about each player. When she is finished, the next player compliments everyone. The game continues until every player and the coaches have each had a turn.

The game forces the players to think positively about each other. Frequently, a player finds out that her teammate really appreciates her. Sometimes a player may discover that her teammates have noticed qualities in her that she was not even aware of herself.

Having Fun

If athletes did not have fun there would be no sports. In fact, the reason most athletes give for quitting is that it is no longer fun.

At one of my seminars I asked the coaches when soccer should stop being fun. One coach answered, "When they start playing select soccer." How sad. Of course, this same coach has a new team each year; his old players just don't want to come back.

Take a look at yourself. I've looked at myself. I'm a coach because I'm having a ball doing it. If it wasn't fun and exciting, I'd quit. How about you? If you are entitled to have fun, shouldn't your players have the same right? We have somewhat of a slogan before each match. Usually, my last words are, "Hey, trust yourselves, trust each other, and don't forget to have some fun out there."

Recall my definition of fun. I feel it means to present realistic challenges to young people and then allow them, without interference, to overcome the challenges. Success at anything is fun and very motivating.

Discipline

A soccer team is a small society, and like all societies it has laws, rules, and regulations. How those laws, rules, and regulations are

---

Letter of Agreement

My name is _____. During the upcoming season I will make the following contributions to the CCS soccer team:

- I will do my best academically.
- I will be on time for every practice.
- I will be on time for every match.
- I will give 100 percent in every practice and match.
- I will allow myself to be coached.
- I will respect my teammates.
- I will respect the authority of the match officials.
- I will do my best to achieve the goals of the team.
- I will maintain a positive attitude.

Signed _____ Date _____ Witness _____

Figure 3.1   A sample letter of agreement.

established is important. Some rules, like eligibility rules, are clear cut and the punishment is spelled out. Rules of that kind are beyond the control of the team and the coach. Other rules, particularly those concerned with behavior on and off the field, can be controlled by the coach and the team.

I believe that on- and off-field behavior is the responsibility of the entire team. Therefore the players should help devise the rules dealing with behavior. Shortly after practice starts, we have a team meeting and discuss the rules in depth. I explain why we need rules like on-the-road curfews, dress, and respectful behavior. The entire team agrees upon the rules and consequences of breaking them.

Then we draft a team-player contract and have the players read, date, and sign it. If later on a player's behavior is out of line, we can meet with him, bring out the contract, and inform him that he's violated the contract he made with the team. It's then up to him to explain his reasons. A typical contract should be short and simple.

Besides the contract, our players also sign a letter of agreement (see figure 3.1).

When a player breaks a rule or regulation, deal with the problem fairly, firmly, quickly, and calmly. Before anything else, make sure you have all the facts. Give the player an opportunity to explain. After the attempted explanation a player typically realizes that discipline is in order. Then the two of you can determine what form of discipline should be administered.

The disciplinary measures you apply should be constructive. Humiliation is destructive, and the player will never forgive you. I don't punish players with extra physical exercise, like running laps. After all, that kind of exercise is part of their conditioning program. Conditioning, especially in soccer, should be enjoyable.

Better methods of discipline include having players provide a certain number of hours of community service, attend a referee clinic, take part in a substance abuse class, and so forth.

Early in my career I would predetermine the punishment for each infraction. I soon learned that approach doesn't work.

 NOTHING IS SET IN STONE

On a road trip Scott Widener, probably one of the best defenders I have coached, broke curfew by 10 minutes. At that time I had a written rule that if a player broke curfew he could not play in the next match. On this trip our next match was in Longview, a town about 45 miles north of Portland, Oregon. Scott's grandparents lived in Portland and had traveled to Longview to see him play for the first time.

Before long, I realized the folly of my set-in-stone disciplinary policy. I suffered with the decision throughout the first half, but decided to admit my error to the team at halftime. I told the team that I was wrong to establish rules that were inflexible. I promised to review the situation with them when we were back home. I let Scott play the second half, and he played well. For the rest of the season Scott's behavior was excellent.

I had some concerns about how the team would view my inconsistent application of rules. At a subsequent meeting I found that my misgivings were unfounded. They applauded my flexibility and would have been disappointed if Scott hadn't played. They felt that sitting out the first half was punishment enough.

Discipline on the Field

I was taught that if you can break the other player's concentration you have a better chance of winning. Soccer requires total concentration; a player who loses focus may as well come out of the match. Confident players are less likely to be bothered by opponents' words or actions, or the calls of the referee, but even they can have an off day.

To me the most serious loss of concentration occurs when teammates attack each other. Sometimes a player may not be willing to accept responsibility for his or her errors and blames others. That player has lost focus. The player receiving the blame will also be less effective. Before long everybody is at each other's throat, unless you catch it in time. Be observant. The problem is that frequently you are too far away from the players to hear what is being said. Of course, the captain should play a role in this and make you aware of problems. Regardless, temper flare-ups, gestures of frustration, facial expressions, and other body language are good indications that you should make a substitution.

I feel it's also important that you establish some rules dealing with the issuance of yellow cards and certainly red cards. You must immediately deal with cautions, especially for dissent and unsportsmanlike conduct. The player receiving a caution has lost some control and should come out for a little while to cool down. If all your players, including your stars, know that on receipt of a caution they will be substituted, your team's number of yellow-card cautions will go down.

Being ejected from a match is serious business and in my opinion is uncalled for. The ejected player not only damages the reputation of the program, but also lets his team down badly. There is no excuse for that.

 THE COST OF A RED CARD

Kevin Scuderi played for our school as a wing forward. He was extremely quick and feisty, too feisty. In one match, after being tackled hard, he came up swinging. His punches missed, but the referee didn't and ejected him. After telling Kevin that his behavior was totally unacceptable, I sent him to the dressing room with instructions to meet me in my office directly after the match. After the match, before meeting with me, he bragged about his red card to his teammates. In my office he was in for a surprise—he had forgotten a team rule that states "Any player ejected from a match for violent misconduct or foul and abusive language may not play again until he has performed 10 hours of community service." I handed Kevin the address of a local youth center where he was to report the next day, a Sunday, at 7 A.M. for a day of cleaning windows. I never heard him brag again. By the way, we don't get red cards.

The assumption that the referee must control the match is incorrect. The referee applies the laws of the game. Coaches are responsible for the behavior of their players, the spectators, and certainly their own conduct.

Discipline Off the Field

As stated elsewhere, the success of your program depends a great deal on the goodwill of administrators, faculty, community, and the student body. Thus, on campus, the athlete is forever on display. If one causes a problem, all others and the program will be judged by the one student's error. We ask our athletes to behave exemplarily. We also ask them to police each other. In particular I ask the sophomores to help me catch problems early. The sophomores know that I will deal fairly with any problem and that I never reveal my sources. If giving the name of the offender makes the sophomore feel uncomfortable, I don't ask for it. As long as I know that a problem may exist I can solve it.

Off campus too, I need the help of the athletes. They will help if team pride exists. Again, the reporter does not have to be specific. He can merely ask that certain parts of our team policies, like drinking, be reviewed at the next meeting or practice.

All athletes should realize that on- and off-campus behavior reflects on the entire team and the program. Dr. Maury Ray, our athletic director, points out that when an athlete is arrested, the newspaper will not say "Jim Williams was arrested." It will say "Jim Williams, a soccer player at CCS, was arrested."

Consistent and fair discipline motivates because it gives players a clear set of boundaries that are the same for all players on the team. Again, it shows you care.

Sometimes silly things can motivate. I'm still trying to forget the aftermath of winning a conference championship. You see, halfway through the season, in a moment of madness, I told the team that if they won the championship, I would get my hair cut into a Mohawk. We won. Two days later my team came to visit me in my office and physically transported me to a nearby barber, who in 20 minutes managed to turn me into one of

the most ugly human beings on this planet. When I came home that night, my dogs barked at me. Three months later my wife moved back in. Well, I exaggerate a little. But I did look ugly.

Summary

Motivating athletes is a demanding but rewarding job. To make the task easier and to motivate your players more effectively, try using the following suggestions:

- Try to understand what motivation is and how to turn extrinsically motivated players into intrinsically motivated players.
- Schedule time to use the motivational tools of relaxation, imagery, self-talk, goal setting, and reinforcement.
- Understand your role in motivating your athletes. Get to know your players, offer them security, show them that you care, create a positive team culture, and allow them to enjoy themselves.
- Be consistent, flexible, and fair when applying discipline both on and off the field.

Chapter 4

Building a Soccer Program

I was hired as the first varsity soccer coach at the Community Colleges of Spokane in the spring of 1984. The Community Colleges of Spokane, a college district consisting of Spokane Community College, Spokane Falls Community College, and the Institute for Extended Learning, is a member of the Northwest Athletic Association of Community Colleges (NWAACC). The association has 28 member colleges. About 8 of those have been competing in soccer since the late 1960s, primarily in the soccer hotbed of the Seattle area. Today 14 members offer varsity soccer for men. In 1994 the NWAACC sanctioned varsity soccer for women for 8 of its members.

I accepted the job on the condition that I would be allowed three years to build the program. In 1987, three years later, we made it to the championship match. Since then we have won the championship once, were runners-up twice, captured third once, and have been divisional champions five times. Obviously, I'm extremely proud of the accomplishments of our college, teams, and athletes.

Since we are successful I'm often asked to share my secrets. I regret to say I have none. I can't draw a map for success, nor can I supply a proven plan or a magic formula. I believe we are successful because we have been willing to invest an inordinate amount of time to work, try, and plan the program. We have certainly worked hard to put an exciting product on the field by developing not only our players but also our ability as coaches, trainers, and managers. We have carefully cultivated support for our program from faculty, students, media, and community. We have identified our feeder system and established rules and policies that make the program run smoothly and effectively while creating an environment conducive to the development of team pride. There are no shortcuts.

Building a program depends much on the personality of the person doing the building. No single plan will work for everyone. I can only write about the things that worked for us. If some of that can work for you, use it. Don't forget that there are many successful soccer programs in our country. The coaches who made them work used methods of their own.

Developing a Style

When building a soccer program, one of the earliest and more difficult decisions you have to make is what style to adopt. The error we sometimes make is to decide style of play before becoming familiar with the factors that affect the style and not being flexible enough to make changes when needed. What works for one team may not work for others.

Assessing Personnel

Rinus Michels coached the Dutch national teams that made it to the finals of the World Cup in 1974 and 1978. He was credited with creating for them the total soccer concept, although he prefers to call it high-pressure soccer. In later years he tried to use that style when he coached Barcelona. Much to his frustration it didn't work. He analyzed the differences between the Dutch national team and Barcelona and observed that high-pressure soccer needs athletes in superb condition with a high work ethic. The Dutch satisfied that need; Barcelona didn't. He also felt that for the style to be successful there had to be an outstanding leader on the field. The great Johan Cruyff filled that role for the

Dutch. Barcelona didn't have such a leader. Being the brilliant coach that he is, Rinus Michels created a style of play for Barcelona that worked, and the club became a major power. It's ironic that Barcelona is now coached by Johan Cruyff.

Obviously, soccer is played in many different styles. The Brazilians refer to it as the beautiful game. Germans play with vigor, discipline, and speed. Italians exhibit tenacious defense with rapid counterattacks. The French are known for their midfield magic, especially during the days of Platini. As we saw, the Dutch invented the total soccer concept. The English like to bring the ball up quickly. It may seem that all these styles have very little in common, but all of them are dictated by conditions prevalent in their particular parts of the world.

The development of a style depends on a number of environmental factors. Climate is a strong influence. In the colder climates players like to run with the ball, while in hot climates energy preservation is important—players pass more, letting the ball do most of the work. Subsequently, field conditions are important. In wet climates, like in England, the field may be muddy and heavy, making play on the ground almost impossible. Dry, hard fields allow more play on the ground and a game with many more short passes.

The physical condition, technical level, and tactical understanding of the athletes come into play in style development. Certainly the personalities, temperament, and cultural background of not only the athlete but also the viewing public are also determining factors.

We all have favorite styles, and it is very difficult to compromise the desire to force a team to adapt to that style. But unless you know your players, the field conditions you have to work with, the time you have to spend with the team, your opponents, the level of officiating, your assistants, the support you will receive, and so forth, predetermining a style of play sets you up for disaster.

 CHILI-BURGERS AND CASSEROLES

A few years after coming to Spokane I was interviewed for the head coaching job at a high school. One of the athletic director's first questions was about the style of play I intended to use. I told him that I couldn't answer that. He

looked very disappointed, and I knew the interview was over. He didn't realize that I was just as disappointed. I didn't even bother to explain why I couldn't answer his question. I was disappointed because he asked such a question. As athletic director he should have known that no answer to his question was the best answer.

Some years later, after I had started coaching at the Community Colleges of Spokane, I met him again. He lamented that I would have had the job at his school if I had just answered his question. I told him one of my favorite stories.

I'm hungry and decide that I will fix myself a chili-burger. I will need a bun, hamburger, and chili, but when I open the refrigerator I find only potatoes, sauerkraut, and sausage. No way am I going to make a chili-burger. However, I can make a truly delicious casserole. So, I don't know what to cook until I know what ingredients I have available. He laughed and we shook hands. Two years later he gave me a superb compliment. The coaching job at the high school opened up again, and the athletic director hired my assistant.

Styles can range from the kick-and-run styles used by inexperienced players and teams to the styles of the world's great players and teams. The style you choose must depend on the assets you have. Once you choose a style, you should allow for adjustments.

Developing a System

The system of play you select will also depend on outside factors. You must not only adapt the system to the strengths and weaknesses of your team, but also consider the system used by the opponent and the strengths and weaknesses of their individual athletes. For instance, if the opponent plays with only two forwards, do you really need four players back? Might you strengthen your midfield by playing only three back in a 3-5-2 system? If the field is narrow could you use a 4-3-3 system? If the opponent has an attacking player who is exceptionally strong, you may decide to assign one of your players the singular task of marking that player. How do you then adjust your system to free the marking player from all other duties? If you play with one fewer forward you dimin-

ish your scoring chances. If you play with one fewer defender you are vulnerable to their attack. One fewer midfielder could mean giving up control of the midfield, which forces the team to play more long balls. If that is contrary to the team's normal style of play, can the team adjust?

Making changes in your system of play is difficult. You must always weigh the advantages of a change against the vulnerabilities it causes elsewhere. Regardless of how you change a system, you must be sure that the gains outweigh the losses and, more important, that you have players who understand the changes and can adapt to their new assignments.

Three years ago I decided that we had the personnel to play a 3-5-2 system. Even though we had talented players, we lost our first three league matches due to role confusion. The system needs two marking defenders, which increases the load on the sweeper and gives more defensive responsibilities to at least two of the midfielders. It didn't work. We reverted to a 4-3-3 system with a sweeper and a stopper and didn't lose another match that season. Most of the players had been playing 4-4-2 or 4-3-3 their entire playing careers, and three weeks of training didn't give them enough time to adapt to a new system.

When choosing your system of play for a particular match, the following exercise may be helpful. Start with a 3-3-3, as shown in figure 4.1.

That gives you good player distribution. Now ask yourself where the tenth field player would do the most good for the occasion.

In his book *Tactics and Teamwork*, Charles Hughes implies that we put too much emphasis on systems of play. He feels that when a team is in possession of the ball all players are attackers and when out of possession all are defenders. In a very general way that may be true, but I'm sure that every player on Mr. Hughes's teams had specific assignments. It is also true that changes in systems can play havoc with opponents.

The W/M system, so-called because when players lined up at the start of the match a W and an M could be drawn (see figure 4.2) with its two backs, three halfbacks, and five forwards, was stable and lasted for more than 20 years.

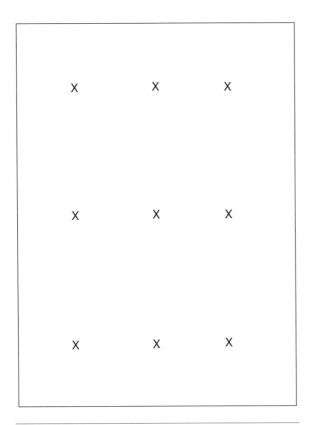

Figure 4.1   The 3-3-3 system.

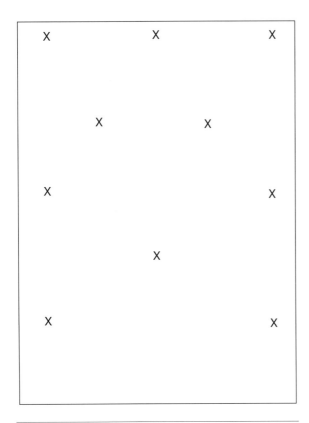

Figure 4.2   The W/M system.

In the early 1950s the Hungarian national team proved that the system had flaws. In 1958 the Brazilians changed their system and gave attacking duties to the halfbacks, thereby creating midfielders, and the W/M system was doomed. The W/M system defended with five players; the Brazilian system attacked with six. The W/M system attacked with five; the Brazilians defended with seven. Thus on attack and on defense Brazil played with numbers up. They scored frequently and were difficult to score on. People who saw the Brazilians play then said, "You know what they are going to do, but how are you going to stop them?" Anyway, the Dutch proved in 1974 that any system is vulnerable to high-pressure soccer. It is difficult to be creative when the opponent locks you into your half of the field and doesn't give you room or time to play.

Regardless of what style or system you adopt it should consider your viewing public. Our philosophy at CCS is that we owe our fans an exciting match. We take chances, we attack, we play to win, unlike many teams that are coached not to lose. Some use as many as six players back to keep the opponent from scoring while hoping that they may get that one breakaway that will give them a 1-0 victory. How dull.

Gaining Support for Your Program

After each of our seasons the colleges schedule a banquet for our teams. From four to five hundred people attend. Among the guests we usually find our chief executive officer, our three presidents, vice presidents, athletic director, program coordinators, faculty, classified staff, our trainers, and players, parents, and friends. It is festive and awesome. Without all those people we couldn't be very successful. We need them; we need their support.

It goes further than that. We also need the support of suppliers, sponsors, equipment managers, and groundskeepers. It hurts a program when a match worker is rude to one of the fans. Ticket takers, security personnel, and concession workers all need to have a positive attitude. Nothing gives people a better attitude than when they realize that they are appreciated. A few kind words, a thank-you card, a handshake, or a pat on the back goes a long way to say to a person, "Hey, I'm glad you're part of our program. It couldn't work this well without you."

Administrator and Faculty Support

You and I coach a team sport. Our teams can be successful only if our players support each other. In turn, our programs can be successful only if we generate the support of our schools.

Most of our administrators and faculty refer to our players as student-athletes. I like that description because it compliments my philosophy that our players are students first and athletes second. I firmly believe that my adherence to that sentiment is reflected in the academic progress of our players. The grade point average of our athletes is consistently higher than that of the total student body. When faculty realize that, they are more apt to accept our program. This gives me the opportunity to talk to them about the importance of a good athletic program.

Administrators vote on budgets, yours included. They decide which facility improvements get priority. Instructors give students permission to make up classes they can't attend due to training and travel schedules. You can receive backing from administrators and faculty by communicating frequently with them. Let them know that their support is important. Also make them aware that you are willing and available to cooperate by serving on committees and by promptly informing them of absenteeism.

Support and become involved with school projects. Take advantage of the many opportunities you have to discuss your program at informational meetings. However, while the soccer program is of extreme importance to you, all communications should indicate that the school comes first.

 PLANTING TREES FOR SUPPORT

A few years ago our horticulture department became involved in a beautification program. The project was to plant numerous small trees along the Spokane River, which flows by our campus. We were not asked to help, but I had heard that they needed volunteers. On the Thursday before the event I asked the team if they would be willing to help. The vote was unanimous. We made many friends on the next Saturday morning when the entire soccer team showed up to help.

Credit for much of the success of our soccer program must go to our athletic director, Dr. Maury Ray. Throughout the years he has strongly supported our program. In turn we have cooperated with him. Our teams are always well behaved both on and off the field. Our teams realize that they are part of one of the finest colleges in the nation. They also know that they represent a proud city.

I'm sure that Maury appreciates knowing that if a problem has occurred or is about to occur, I make him aware of it immediately. This allows him to create a comfortable atmosphere necessary for open communication. He also knows that I will not ask favors for an athlete who has goofed off. Like me, he is intolerant of students who do not apply themselves.

Maury expresses himself very well and often can relieve pressure with just a few words. When we were leaving for a play-off match, he came by my office and said that he hoped we would win but then added, "Regardless of the outcome I want you to know that you are doing a fabulous job." Such expressions of confidence go a long way in making the coach–athletic director relationship pleasant and effective.

All administrators are important to our program. Dr. Terry Brown, our chief executive officer, became interested in soccer when the son of one of his friends made the team. He came to watch a few matches. In the evening after work, Terry usually runs four miles. Since I often schedule players' or coaches' clinics in the evening, we have many opportunities to talk about the college and soccer during his cooldown. He asked numerous questions about the sport and my philosophy of coaching. He now attends our matches regularly. Even though he works somewhere between 12 and 14 hours per day, he never fails to send us a note with his compliments after a particularly good match. At the end of each season we also receive a letter from him. No matter what has happened or what the outcome of the season is, he always finds something very positive to say.

Support from administrators, faculty, and staff is essential to the success of a program. It isn't difficult to get. Most are not involved in soccer, but their children often are. Those children attend our camps, and if they have enjoyed themselves, learned something, and been treated with dignity and respect, they will carry the message home. Some parents have asked to borrow videos or books to better understand their children's sport. A few have even ventured into youth coaching and asked for our help. It takes good communication, cooperation, respect, an understanding of others' feelings and philosophies, and a readiness to help. Whenever you have difficulty with lack of support from an individual, you can usually trace it to an error on your part. When that happens it is time to seek out the individual and candidly discuss the problem.

Student Support

Nothing motivates your athletes more than being cheered on by a large group of fellow students. Getting that kind of support isn't always easy. Most students are pressed for time. Some have jobs. But you and the entire team working together can create student support.

The team must earn the respect of the student body. The athletes can accomplish that by exhibiting maturity, dignity, and class. They must respect their instructors, their classmates, each other, and most of all, their school. They must be willing to become involved with the activities of other student groups; they must integrate with the student body.

A coach has many opportunities to talk with student groups. When they do support your program, you should let them know that you and your team appreciate it. Many schools have in-house news bulletins. Often one of the compilers will want to interview you. That is a golden opportunity to let the student body know how you feel about them and their support at matches. Let them know just how important they are and don't forget to express your pride in the school. Be careful of what you say. Most people like a confident, positive coach; everybody hates a conceited braggart.

There is one more area of student support that is easy to tap. It never fails to surprise me how few soccer players will go watch a basketball game, how few baseball players attend a softball game, how few tennis players go to a volleyball game, and so forth. I don't see coaches cross-attending either.

 THANKS IRENE

One of the coaches I truly admire is Irene Matlock, our volleyball coach. She was hired about the same time that I was. She has built a program that has received national recognition. In 1994 Irene was voted national coach of the year.

Some years back, late in the season, our men's team played a must-win match at Shoreline Community College. It was a dreary day, rainy and cold. Our supporters were few. We were struggling. At the half the score was 1-1. A few minutes before the second half started our morale got a boost when Irene, her staff, and the entire volleyball team seated themselves behind our bench and began to cheer us on.

Unbeknownst to us, the volleyball team was playing in a cross-over tournament at Shoreline. Between their matches Irene decided to come give us a boost. Our soccer team was not going to let them down. We played an inspired second half and walked away with a 3-1 victory.

I don't know how many sports are played at your school. At our college we offer 15 sports involving more than four hundred students. Wouldn't it be nice if at every home match you could have a base group of four hundred cheering fans? Everybody loves a parade. Soon many other students would attend. That's why we make sure that our players attend the home matches of other teams.

Media Support

Your soccer program can really receive a boost if somehow you can get press coverage of your matches and your progress. It isn't easy. Soccer is the new kid on the block to most U.S. sportswriters and broadcasters. World Cup '94 helped some, but it is still difficult to get the coverage we feel we deserve.

Our program has seen its coverage increase year by year. Every one of our matches gets at least some space in the newspapers, and if broadcasters have time they mention us on the air. I believe that the accuracy and the quality of the information we supply have earned us their respect. Please understand we have never demanded respect; we have earned it.

A reporter who writes a story about soccer in general, or your program in particular, likes to color the story with easily available information. It behooves you to supply that information before the season starts. It may never be used, but the reporter is more apt to write a story if he or she doesn't have to spend time on the phone tracking you down and soliciting information. Shortly before the season prepare an informational packet that includes your roster, some highlights about players, a brief history of your program, some highlights of the preceding season, and your schedule. Be sure to include phone numbers.

Directly after a match, whether at home or on the road and regardless of the outcome, I call our local papers and broadcast stations. My report to the newspapers includes who we played, where we played, the final score and the score at halftime, the order of goals scored, who assisted, at what time (both ours and the opponent's), shots on goal (ours and the opponent's), saves made by both goal-keepers, our season record, our league record, and the opponent's records. I conclude with some highlights of the match. To the broadcast stations I report only the final score and our record, and I mention any of our players who had an outstanding match.

In the beginning reports may be ignored, but don't give up or become angry. Persist and always be courteous. Soon they will start to pick up on your reports, especially on slow news days. We get better coverage on Wednesday's matches than on Saturday's. On the weekend there is just too much competition.

Make sure that at the end of the season you submit a wrap-up and thank-you notes. The media can be of great help to your program. Respect them; they will reciprocate.

Community Support

During a normal year you will have many opportunities to meet people. Each of these opportunities gives you a chance to talk about your program. You have a family physician, a dentist, an accountant; invite them to matches as your guests. The guy who fixes your car, your barber, your grocer—invite anyone you meet. Accept opportunities to

talk at Kiwanis, Optimists, Lions, Eagles, and other order get-togethers and invite them. Invite to be your guests the people who supply your uniforms, balls, audiovisual equipment, and goal repair services.

Stage events that attract numerous people, like tournaments and camps, and then promote your program.

In the spring we run a five-a-side tournament. Over four hundred teams compete. During the two weekends of the tournament the players and our staff get to talk with many coaches, parents, and others who like soccer. Our summer soccer camps have become popular; again we talk to as many people as we can. If schedules are ready we distribute them. If not, we take names and add them to our mailing list for invitations and schedules to be mailed out later.

 SPECIAL MATCH

We dedicate one of our conference home matches to youth in general and five-a-side players and campers in particular. We usually pick a Saturday night match. All youth players wearing a team jersey or a tournament or camp T-shirt are admitted free. These nights have become very successful. Kids bring their parents. It is spectacular to see all the colors in our stands. Many come back to see subsequent matches.

All high school coaches receive our schedule with invitations for them and their teams. We also visit their practices when invited.

Local youth soccer associations are another source of community support. In turn, help them with coach and player clinics, lectures, workshops, and wherever else they may need you.

Your program will thrive if you actively seek the support and enthusiasm of the community.

Implementing the Plan

After you have developed your plan and laid the foundation for obtaining support for your program, you can start thinking of how to implement the plan.

Feeder System

The United States has been attempting to create a feeder system into the national teams for many years now. The program requires the existence of hundreds of local association or club recreational teams. Players from these teams could be selected to club select teams that compete within the boundaries of a local association. Players from the club select teams are selected to association select teams, often called premier league teams. From this level players are selected to a state's Olympic Development Program team. The ODP teams compete in the region, and from these teams four regional teams are chosen. Ideally, all our national players should come from the four regional teams. They don't, however, mainly because the national coaching staff have not provided consistent player development guidelines nor have they provided the necessary education for coaches. While most of our national players have developed outside the system, all were at one time part of the haphazard U.S. feeder system. Once all components are in place the feeder system will work.

You have a feeder system. If you are coaching a high school team and there is a junior varsity team, you must make the coaches of that team aware of the kind of player you need. If the JV team needs help, you and your staff should be available to provide the help.

Undoubtedly, there is a youth soccer organization in your community. Share your thoughts and goals with those coaches. They too are members of your staff, and with your help and suggestions they can feed quality players into your program.

If youth coaches and junior high coaches know what kind of player you want, and if you help them develop that kind of player, then players will enter your program with basic skills in place. You can start building on basic skills instead of spending endless hours coaching out bad habits.

Most of our players come from eastern Washington high schools. Our part of the state has an extraordinary number of excellent soccer players who have been developed by dedicated, astute coaches. I believe that my staff and I know every one of these coaches and know most of the players. We have met and worked with most of them in camps and clinics, go to as many of their matches as possible, and frequently host them at our matches and practices. Our players often visit the practices of youth teams, junior varsity teams, and varsity teams. During their visits they will help the coach with teaching a certain technique or tactic or will just talk to encourage players to work hard. Our players enjoy these visits. They know that young players see them as role models.

During our visits with coaches we have the opportunity not only to answer questions but also to let the coaches know about our program, philosophy, goals, preferred style of play, and the qualities we look for in players. These coaches are our partners. If they respect our program they will direct players to our college. Not all coaches agree with our philosophy and not all players come to CCS. But at least they all know who and what we are. They also know that we respect them for their abilities, and we show our appreciation by being available to them when they need us.

Establishing Rules

As I mentioned earlier, a soccer team is a small society. Like any organization it needs rules. If the coach sets all the rules, the players will feel acted upon. But if the players help establish the rules, particularly those dealing with demeanor and behavior, they are the actors. As the actors they will feel that the rules are theirs. If a player breaks a rule, it is a peer or team rule that was broken, not the rule of the authority figure.

I realize that many schools have set rules regarding practices like drinking or using drugs. Neither the coach nor the team can control those. They should endorse them. However, those rules are usually applied after an offense. I want the team to decide not to commit the offenses to begin with.

Neither do I want the team to determine specific disciplinary actions when a teammate commits an offense. Schools already recommend procedures for certain infractions. All other infractions should be punished after the offender has had a chance to explain his or her actions.

The coach can supply a list of subjects for the team to discuss, set policy on, and vote on. The list may include the following:

- Curfews
- Drugs
- Smoking
- Dress code
- Punctuality

You can add any reasonable item to this list. Sometimes the players will ask how other teams have voted on these subjects; there is nothing wrong with sharing that information. Returning players will usually set the tone for the meeting and the voting. Nevertheless the final vote should be on a secret ballot so that all players clearly have the opportunity to express themselves.

Once we tabulate the votes, we publish and share them. Again, I like to impress upon the players that these are their rules and that in the end it is their responsibility to enforce them.

Coaches often feel uncomfortable giving this kind of responsibility to young athletes, especially those of college age. I disagree. I feel that by showing my trust in them they will go to great lengths to maintain that trust. I've never been disappointed. It is also interesting to see that from team to team the rules never vary much.

Curfew

We play most of our matches at 1 P.M. On the recommendation of our nutritionist, we have advised the team to eat no later than four hours before kickoff. Therefore most players will want to get up before 8 A.M., and the team usually establishes an 11 P.M. curfew on nights before a match. When we are on the road the curfew is the same, but they add that lights must be off at midnight.

Drugs

Drugs are illegal, period! That includes steroids and the so-called socially accepted drugs like marijuana. I have never had a team that was not adamant about this rule.

Long before the team votes on a nondrinking rule, my staff and I spend some time with the team on the subject. After all, the stereotypical college-age player is a drinker. Again, I have found this not to be true with our athletes. I'm blessed with excellent help from people in our department. Cris Matthew, our nutritionist and health and wellness expert, and John Troppmann, our strength trainer, are very down-to-earth people. When they work with teams they never preach. In a few easy-to-understand explanations and demonstrations they can show our players how badly their performance is affected by poor nutrition and the use of alcohol. Invariably, after Cris and John's presentation the team votes to abstain from drinking.

Smoking

Smoking has also fallen into disfavor and the teams vote against it. For a while we had a problem with some players picking up the habit of chewing tobacco. When that occurred the team called its own meeting and voted against the use of chewing tobacco by any player. It stopped.

Dress Code

When the team starts to discuss the dress code, some of them don't see it as a very important subject. At this point the returning players always seem happy to explain that it is difficult to have pride in your team if the individual players don't take pride in themselves. That means that when the team represents the college or our city, players are expected to be well groomed and properly attired. For some reason a number of soccer players like to wear their hair long. That is probably because most of their soccer heroes have rather strange and lengthy coiffures. Our team doesn't rule out long hair as long as

the hair is clean and combed. In public places the team usually votes to wear sport shirts and clean jeans. The team does not permit players to wear outrageous T-shirts or any clothing with holes in it. Baseball caps are to be removed in public places. All players must wear their full warm-ups to matches.

Punctuality

I've only recently added punctuality to the list of subjects that I want the team to vote on. It isn't because it was a big problem; only occasionally was a player lax. I put it on the list because I want all players to understand that if they are not punctual it isn't just the coach who is upset. They are doing a disservice to the entire team, and therefore it should be a team rule.

As I have stated before, once a team has set the rules, I like to put the rules in contract form and have the players sign the contract. These are their rules and this is their contract with their team. Since it is their team, they will take care of it.

I have talked earlier about the evaluations of the program that the players do at the end of the season. One of the questions on the evaluation is "Did the coach use discipline fairly?" I was extremely thrilled when my athletic director informed me that one of the

players had answered, "Yes, he treats us like adults, so we behave like adults. Besides he allows us to set our own rules. I never broke any of them. I didn't want to be the only child on the team."

Yes, I do treat them like adults, because I have many other expectations of them. Not the least of these is exemplary behavior when we travel. The players understand that people who work in restaurants and motels have difficult, low-paying jobs. Those people don't need a group of smart-alecks to louse up their days. We are welcomed at the motels and restaurants we frequent. We know that after our visit our hosts think highly of us, the college, our city, and yes, soccer.

Team Pride

We often talk about athletes needing strong self-esteem. It should follow that teams need high team-esteem, or team pride. It is one of those intangible characteristics that spells the difference between success and failure. It is the quiet confidence that players have in each other, the coaching staff, the supporting crew, and the school. It is the characteristic that gives the team vitality and spirit.

It may sound somewhat corny when we say, "One for all and all for one," or, "The strength of the wolf is in the pack, and the strength of the pack is in the wolf." However, there is much truth in these statements. If the coach can create an atmosphere in which each player is willing to contribute to the efforts of the team because the player knows that each member of the team is ready to help him or her, then the coach is halfway home to creating excellent team pride. Players should be reminded of the proud history of the program. They should rejoice when goals are reached. They should be complimented when challenges are met. They should be allowed to grow to be the best they can be through positive instruction and encouragement.

The coach sets the tone for the development of team pride. Your love for the job, your pride in your school, your players, and your staff, and your preparedness will set an infectious example. Young people need standards and ideals to believe in. Your program can provide that.

Selecting the Starters

One of the more sensitive issues you deal with is deciding who will be among the starting 11 and who will play the role of substitute. You must keep in mind that most players equate playing time with self-worth. If you handle the decision improperly the players on the bench will feel like losers. You can't be successful if a number of your players feel that way. Eventually their discontent will hurt the entire team.

All players on the team should know why they are starting or not. At the same time all players should know that they are an important part of the team. The nonstarters should at least have an idea under what circumstances you will bring them into the match. It is true that players earn their starting positions, but I don't believe in setting up players against each other because one will win, but the other will lose. I shy away from any win-lose contest. I believe that by being candid, open, and honest I can create winwin situations.

 MIDFIELD DILEMMA

At the beginning of one season I started Wilbur Bishop, a freshman, at a center midfield position. After three matches I went back to sophomore Micah Prim even though Wilbur was the better player. Micah had one ability that was stronger than Wilbur's. Micah read the opponent's counterattack well and in most cases would win the ball back with good positioning and clean, decisive tackles before the opponent had a chance to get set. Since we were using a 3-4-3 system, we needed Micah's skill to keep some of the pressure off our back three. That strength regained him the starting position. I knew that Wilbur would be upset. Before making the switch I called in both players. I explained what I was going to do and why I was doing it. At the same time I promised Wilbur that we would work hard with him, and for that I solicited Micah's help because it was his last season with us. As the season went on Wilbur got more and more playing time. And when substituted Micah felt good about it, because his protégé came in for him.

One of the tools I use early in the practices is a form, which I call a sociogram, that asks for advice from the players. While the decision of who starts is ultimately mine, the sociogram gives the players a feeling of having a voice in the decision-making process. It asks questions like the following:

- Who do you feel is the best goalkeeper?
- Who do you feel is the best defender?
- Who do you feel is the best midfielder?
- Who do you feel is the best forward?
- If you had the opportunity to line up the team in a 4-3-3 system, who would you play on defense, at midfield, and as forwards?

Team Leader

I have said earlier that soccer can't be coached during matches. Instead, a successful soccer team has to have a strong leader on the field. Without such a person it is difficult to win consistently. Look at the world's successful teams and you always find that there was one player who led them. Look for the player whom the team respects, whose positiveness is infectious, who has a sense of humor, and who is responsible, is hardworking, stays focused, and has a vision. That player should be the captain of your team, the coach on the field. Since this role is extremely important, the coach should select the captain.

You Create Success

You can create a successful program as long as you take pride in your effort, are consistent in your decisions, and are capable of putting yourself in the other person's shoes. Take care of your athletes, concern yourself with performance rather than results, treat those involved with the program respectfully, be gracious in victory or defeat, keep your priorities in order, and keep in mind that your players will pick up the values and standards you set. These values can serve them the rest of their lives, not only as soccer players but also as human beings. Creating success starts with the coach.

Summary

To build a successful soccer program, you will need to give attention to the following subjects:

- Give careful thought to the development of style and system of play.
- Learn to assess your personnel and environment.
- Be willing to adjust your style and system of play.
- Gain support for your program from administrators, faculty, students, media, and community.
- Create a plan and implement it.
- Evaluate and nurture your feeder system.
- Carefully establish rules covering such subjects as curfews, drugs, smoking, dress code, and punctuality.
- Develop team pride.
- Select your starters and captain with care.
- Create your own success.

Part II

Coaching Plans

Chapter 5

Planning for the Season

In January, about a month after the season ends, we begin planning for the next season. We carefully prepare a budget. We inventory equipment such as uniforms, balls, and so forth, and place orders if necessary. We evaluate facilities and put desired changes out for bid.

This is also a good time to assess the efficiency of our medical screening, medical examinations, insurance settlements, and handling of injuries. We need to start planning our staff of coaches, managers, and trainers.

While the past season is still fresh in mind we may feel a need to alter our methods of player conditioning and find ways to make off-season conditioning more effective and rewarding. Finding ways to better bring home the message of balanced nutrition is another challenge that needs planning.

Using the results of the preceding season, we reevaluate the methods used to develop the team technically and tactically. If improvements can be made, we begin our planning. These evaluations should include our match tactics.

We plan the next season's schedule, propose travel arrangements, and find tournaments.

Last, but most important, we must evaluate and plan to improve our contribution to the development of our athletes' self-esteem, competitiveness, fairness, and ability to function successfully in society.

Your planning list should include the following items:

- Budgets
- Equipment and facilities
- Medical screening and insurance
- Medical care
- Staff planning
- Conditioning players
- Preseason planning
- Scouting opponents
- Travel
- After-graduation plans

Budgets

One of the items that needs an early decision is the budget. I like to refer to it as the "wish list." It consists of four main categories.

1. Services:
   This includes such items as printing and promotional materials, referees, and so forth.
2. Goods and equipment:
   This category is divided into three sections:
   - Supplies used up yearly, such as training and first-aid supplies, field paint, video and audio tapes, training uniforms, and practice and match socks
   - Supplies used up in two to four years, such as practice balls, nets, and corner flags
   - Supplies purchased on a rotation system, such as uniforms, warm-ups, and travel bags
3. Travel:
   This category includes transportation, meals, and motels.
4. Items we would like to have may include the following:
   - New VCR or camcorder
   - Ball-shooting machine
   - Additional goals
   - New cassette player
   - Shirts for the coaching and training staff
   - Extra rain gear

Items in the last category are not essential, but they help us function better and more efficiently.

Equipment and Facilities

We are a state institution, and all orders for goods and equipment amounting to more than $300 must go out for bid. This can present problems unless you are very specific in preparing your orders. For instance, if you list 24 white Umbro jerseys, suppliers will bid using the least expensive white jersey Umbro has available. That may not satisfy your need for a better quality uniform. So be specific. Include the model, the sizes you need, the height and the font of the numbers on the backs of the jerseys, the height of numbers and lettering on the fronts of the jerseys, and what kind of screen process you want. The more specific you are, the more likely you will get what you really want. This also makes it easier for your suppliers to prepare their bids because everyone is bidding on the same item.

I recommend that you buy equipment from well-established dealers and manufacturers. They will be there when you need to replace a broken or torn item. Also, buy the current style. Some manufacturers discontinue production of items after a certain time making it impossible to find a replacement.

Uniforms

I'm sure that you have heard the saying "dress for success." That doesn't apply only to business people; it also works for soccer teams. A well-made, clean, colorful uniform instills pride and confidence in players. Proud, confident players play better. Also, the uniform must be of good quality because it has to last three years.

We follow a rotation schedule. In year 1, we buy the away uniform, which, in the NWAACC, unlike the NCAA, is white. In year 2, we buy the dark home uniform, in our case blue. In year 3, we buy warm-ups and travel bags.

Footwear

Your team, like ours, probably plays on a variety of surfaces. In our part of the state it is usually dry, and surfaces are often hard, calling for a multicleated shoe. On the west coast, where we play most of our away matches, it rains often and players need a six-cleated shoe. On occasion we have to play on artificial turf that requires a turf shoe. Our budgets can't handle 60 pairs of shoes per team, so we don't supply shoes to our athletes. Cost is not the only reason. We'd never be able to satisfy all our players. If we were to supply shoes, I'm sure that no three players would agree on what kind to get. I don't recommend any one shoe; I just try to persuade our players to buy a well-fitted, comfortable shoe with good arch and other support.

Balls

While our conference recommends the use of a certain ball, the ball's manufacturer hasn't been all that active in our state. We're on our own.

Most balls are guaranteed for a year, although a better ball should last at least two years. Cost is important, but quality is essential. You can't expect players to improve technically if the ball they are using is of poor quality, improper weight or size, or under- or overinflated. I know that most balls are stamped "FIFA approved." All that means is that the materials used to manufacture the ball were approved by FIFA. Also, FIFA's spread of approved circumference and weight of a number 5 ball is rather large. There is a big difference between a 27-inch ball and a 28-inch one, between a 14-ounce ball and a 16-ounce one. A smaller, lighter ball is more difficult to control but it is livelier and will travel faster and farther. For high school play I would recommend a 28-inch, 14-ounce ball.

Don't compromise on the quality of your soccer balls and don't differentiate between practice balls and match balls. It is difficult for players who have been practicing with a certain kind of ball to play well with a totally different match ball.

Items we no longer use, such as uniforms, balls, and other equipment, we donate to the intramural program.

 THE BALL GAME

When I was coaching Team Vancouver, USA, we played in the Pacific Northwest Conference. Several of our opponents were NASL teams, among them the Seattle Sounders, Portland Timbers, and Vancouver Whitecaps. The NASL-

approved ball was of the largest size and weight allowed by FIFA. It was also inflated to the high limit. We decided to use an 18-panel Mikasa, which was quite small, light, and very lively. The Timbers complained about the ball when they came to our stadium. They blamed our upset victory entirely on the ball. Two weeks later we played them on their home field, Civic Stadium in Portland. After our warm-ups a Timber ball boy inadvertently had taken all their balls, including the match balls, to the locker room. When we kindly offered one of our balls to the referee, Portland's captain, Pat McMahon became unglued. He personally ran off the field and brought out the match balls. He looked over at me and said, "You're not gonna do that to me again." We didn't win that second match; we tied 1-1. Darn!

Training and Match Facilities

You can save much time by carefully planning your training and match facilities. I'm fortunate to have excellent facilities with a lot of space. Our match facility is a lighted stadium that seats approximately eight thousand. The playing field is 75 by 115 yards. It is lighted and we play most of our matches there. We also use it for 11-versus-11 practices.

Our training facility includes a grid area, a conditioning area, and two fields. One field is 75 by 115 yards; the other is small (55 by 100 yards). We use the small field for practice on the days before playing an away match against an opponent whose home field is small. All fields are clearly marked and have portable aluminum goals. We use 12 goals—2 in the stadium, 2 on each training field, and 6 in the training grid.

A quick word about goals: All goals are unsafe. They can tip easily. Even the wind can blow them over, especially the aluminum goals. Even though goals may be portable, you should anchor them once they have been moved. When stored, lock them up in such a way that they cannot be tipped over.

The training grid is an area of 40 by 60 yards (see figure 5.1). We have divided it into 10-yard squares, 4 squares one way and 6 the other, or 24 squares. The team works on one-versus-one or two-versus-one practices in a 10-yard square. When they move up to two-versus-two and two-versus-three, we increase the area to 10 by 20 yards. We accommodate three-versus-three in a 20-by-20-yard square, and so forth. Our five-versus-five sessions take up the entire 40-by-60 grid. The system saves a lot of time, because you are not forever setting up areas with cones. Also it keeps many practices off the playing field.

Another advantage of the grid system is that no one has to stand around. Once a technique or tactic has been demonstrated the team breaks into small groups and practices. Assistants and captains can oversee the practice, and I wander from group to group. There is no wasted time.

The grid has a goal on each 40-yard line and two goals on each 60-yard line, thus six goals. It is ideal for shooting practices and goalkeeper practices.

If you don't have the luxury of plenty of space, you can use areas on your playing field to accommodate your various practices (see figure 5.2). Penalty areas are ideal for working four-versus-two. The area between the halfway line and the penalty area line from the touchline to halfway across the field

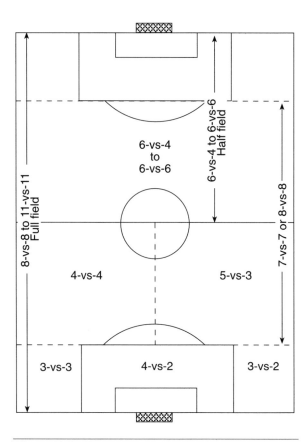

Figure 5.2   Practice areas.

is ideal for four-versus-four or five-versus-three practices. Moving the goals to the top of the penalty areas creates an ideal space for seven-versus-seven or even eight-versus-eight practices.

Medical Screening and Insurance

A player asks, "When will we start practicing?" Answer: "As soon as the weight of the paperwork equals the combined weight of the team."

That may be a bit of an exaggeration, but it seems that way at times. All of it has to be done while you are chomping at the bit, ready for action, ready to get onto the field, eager to get the ball rolling. Bite the bullet; the paperwork has to be done.

Our players report for orientation in mid-August, the day before we begin practices. Before they can practice, the following papers have to be filled out, signed by proper

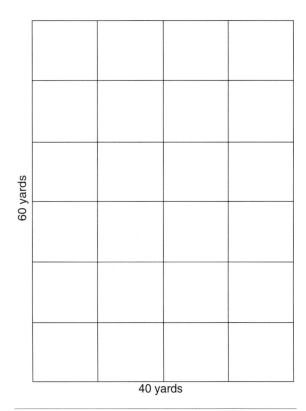

Figure 5.1   Training grid area (40 yards by 60 yards).

authorities, and submitted to the athletic secretary:

- Recruiting disclaimer
- Health history
- Medical examination results
- Athletic insurance information form
- Explanation of medical policies form
- Explanation of athletic policies form
- Informed consent form

Besides the forms, the players must also view a risk film, which points out the dangers of participation in a contact sport.

You may joke about all the paperwork; however, these are important steps designed to protect your athletes, your school, and you.

Medical Examinations

Of all papers filed, the results of the medical examination and the physician's approval to participate are probably the most important. Our conference doesn't accept these documents if the exams occurred before July 1. So, to accommodate our players, we bring in a physician in the evening of orientation day, and for a nominal fee he examines them.

Insurance

Information on insurance coverage is another important issue. Most athletic department insurance coverage is a secondary insurance that pays only after an athlete's personal insurance has been billed. Also this kind of insurance covers the athlete only during supervised practices or matches. If for any reason the student athletic insurance or parental insurance does not cover the charges, or denies a claim, the athlete and the parents are responsible for the bill.

Some schools allow students to buy student insurance at a relatively low fee. It provides 24-hour accident coverage. I encourage our athletes not covered by parental insurance to buy it.

It is essential that the school has on file a parental consent form that authorizes the school, the coaches, or qualified medical personnel to make decisions in case of medical emergency situations. The trainers and the coach should have copies of this document.

Providing Medical Care

It is a fact that no matter how careful you are or how conscientiously you train, injuries do occur. It's tough on you, on the team, but most of all on the injured player. Thank heaven for the unsung heroes, the trainers. These people are an extremely important part of your staff. Their ability can spell the difference between your player being out for the season or having the player back on the field in just a short while. Again, I'm fortunate to have at our college one of the finest teachers I have ever met. Her name is Phoebe Duke. She is in charge of our sports-training program. The trainers who come through her program are not only medically capable but also fully aware of the dilemmas a coach has when injuries occur. Phoebe, her trainers, and her student trainers are invaluable to our program.

Two trainers are present at all our practices and matches. Since we cannot depend on other colleges for qualified trainers, one of our trainers travels with us to all our away matches.

All of us should be aware that if injuries are treated quickly and properly, not only will the severity of the injury be reduced but the recovery time can be shortened significantly. While most injuries to soccer players deal with the knees and the ankles, on occasion you may be faced with fractures or injuries to the back, neck, or head. Having someone present who is thoroughly trained in handling these medical emergencies is of benefit not only to you but also to the injured player. The player benefits physically and, more important, psychologically.

 THE FASTEST RESPONSE EVER

Two years ago, late in one of our practices, Brandon Trowbridge, a midfielder, was clipped going up for a header and came down head first. He was unconscious, and both the trainer and I suspected a grave neck injury. The trainer, Tory Carle, immediately called 911 on his cellular phone. Before he had finished giving the address, two emergency medical technicians from our fire department came running onto our field and, with Tory's help, immediately started to work on Brandon. Several minutes later emergency vehicles appeared, and before long Brandon was transported to a hospital.

After the ambulance left I had an opportunity to chat with the two emergency technicians and wondered how they got to our practice field so fast. At Spokane Community College the tennis courts are next to the soccer facility. The two men had been playing tennis but had left their radios on. It really was the quickest response we had ever had. By the way, Brandon did not have a neck injury, but he did have a concussion. He rejoined us a few weeks later.

I don't want to make it seem that by having a trainer in attendance you are relieved of responsibility. You are not. Even if the trainer is certified, the final decision in any medical emergency is still the responsibility of the coach. Neither does it relieve you, or anyone on your coaching staff, from having to be well versed in first-aid procedures, cardiopulmonary resuscitation techniques, and at least some knowledge of bloodborne pathogens.

Our trainers keep a daily journal on all injuries. Once a player is in rehabilitation I require a daily report about the recovery. I need to know if the player is following the trainer's instructions conscientiously. The decision to declare a player fit again is mutually agreed upon by the trainers and me. I will not use a player whose injury may be aggravated, no matter how important the match.

Most schools have a physician to whom injured athletes are referred. It is normal procedure for the athletic trainer to make the player's first appointment with the team physician. The team physician may then refer the athlete to another doctor if necessary.

Our trainers handle nearly all our injuries. However, they are never overconfident. If they suspect anything out of the ordinary about a specific injury, they make a same-day appointment with the team physician. Our team physician happens to specialize in sports medicine. He may make some recommendations, but in most cases he confirms the trainer's diagnosis and approves the prescribed treatment.

If the team physician feels that the athlete has a problem outside the scope of his specialty, he may refer our player to another doctor. That has happened to us once with a player who had a heart arrhythmia.

There are two exceptions to our procedure of injury care. The first occurs when we feel that an injury is life threatening, in which case we seek immediate emergency medical help.

The other exception deals with the coach's responsibility. If you feel that an athlete needs to be seen by the team physician even though the training staff assures you such a visit is unnecessary, it is your right and responsibility to overrule the trainers. I have only done this twice; in both cases the trainers were right. I'm glad they were. I also know that as professionals they respect me for exercising my right and accepting my responsibility.

Again, people like your team physician are important members of your staff. Put them on your thank-you note list, make sure you keep them aware of the team's progress, and invite them to special team functions.

Staff Planning

The success of any program depends on the hard work and dedication of all the people who are directly involved with the program. Determine your immediate staff—assistant coaches and managers in particular—early

in the season so that you have ample time to prepare them and get them qualified.

Coaching Staff

Many of the high school soccer teams in our immediate area are coached by our former players or assistant coaches. Some are coaching at the college level. Since I encourage our assistants to find new challenges and further their careers, it means that we have a turnover of coaching personnel. Each time that occurs we must advertise the position. A committee makes the final selection, though it considers my recommendation.

A new assistant must be thoroughly trained, but more than that, must understand and subscribe to our philosophy. The college and our conference also require that the new assistant have certain qualifications. They include the following:

- USSF coaching license or expression of intent to pursue it
- Valid driver's license
- First-aid card
- CPR card
- Proof of having attended a class dealing with bloodborne pathogens
- Willingness to submit to a police background check
- Passing an exam regarding the understanding of conference policies, rules, and codes

All this takes time; thus, it is essential that your relationship with your assistants is of a nature that they will confide in you and give you early notice of their intent.

I'm blessed with quality assistants. All have extensive playing and coaching experience. They know the game and our players, and they support my philosophy of coaching. Their impact is valuable and part of every decision I make.

Managers

It takes a number of diligent people to get ready for a season. Fields and practice grids have to be groomed and lined, goals netted, balls cleaned and pumped up, other equipment repaired and checked for safety, training vests washed, uniforms issued, audiovisual equipment cleaned and checked, travel arrangements and motel reservations made. The list goes on.

No one person can do it all. We need nine managers to help us. The college employs some full-time and hires others for the season only. For instance, one of the college's program managers makes travel arrangements for all 15 of our athletic teams. His job is to reserve vans or a bus for a specified time and date, make motel reservations, and deliver to the head coach a check to cover meals and motels.

Another program manager is an administrative assistant. He checks the eligibility of our players and their academic progress, arranges for excused absences when players have to miss class time because of travel, oversees the design and printing of promotional items, does still photography, and supplies visual aids during matches.

The audiovisual production manager, the fields manager, and the equipment manager are present at all practices and home matches.

For matches at home we use a statistician and a spotter. We also use a greeter who meets the opposing team on their arrival and takes care of their needs. Our field manager is very carefully selected and trained because he supervises the other managers, except for the program managers (travel and administration).

We treat our managers with respect and dignity and make them feel part of the team. In turn I expect them to do their jobs promptly, correctly, and cheerfully. Budget restrictions don't allow us to take the managers to away matches, but they are part of every other team function. And, in the years that we made the play-offs, all managers traveled with us.

Of course, besides our managers, the college employs security personnel, concession workers, ticket takers, an announcer, and an activities director for special events before or after the match or during halftime.

Conditioning Soccer Players

Soccer has three major components. They are fitness, technique, and tactics. If a soccer player is not fit, his technique will suffer, especially late in the match. And, if a player's technique is not nearly perfect, working on tactics, no matter how simple, is a waste of time.

Physical fitness has many other advantages. If fit, the player's vision, awareness, instinctive reactions, adaptability, inventiveness, composure, skill, confidence, decision making, and hardiness all benefit. In addition, a fit player is much less likely to be injured, and when injured will recover more quickly. All athletes, particularly soccer players, must develop physical fitness before anything else.

Some players and coaches view fitness as a static condition. They believe that you can start a fitness program at the first practice and then peak at the first match a few weeks later. That's shortsighted. Fitness is an ongoing challenge in which the serious athlete constantly tries for improvement. Fitness is not a steady state; maintaining or improving it is a dynamic year-round process.

A balanced fitness program should be a part of every soccer player's lifestyle. I provide our fitness program the moment a player has indicated his or her intention of trying out for us. Many athletes are willing to train during the off-season. They understand the importance of fitness. Without pressure and competition, however, it is difficult for them to get match fit. When they report for the season the players are somewhat discouraged to realize that, even after their hard work, in-season conditioning is still an agonizing experience. Keeping that in mind, you might want to put more time in planning off-season conditioning.

To begin with, you should encourage the players to condition together, or in as large a group as possible. That will introduce the element of competition. In addition you should provide them with a workout program that is challenging but achievable, enjoyable but rewarding, intense but interesting, and gives means of measuring results.

The physical demands of our sport require that soccer players work on all five components of health-related fitness. While cardiovascular endurance and muscle endurance rate high on the list of soccer fitness components, you can't overlook the significance of flexibility, muscle strength, and ideal body composition. Since the players need such a variety of components, it is not difficult to lay out an interesting and challenging program.

Cardiovascular Endurance

Exercises for cardiovascular endurance may include running, power walking, aerobic dance, stepping, jumping rope, cross-country skiing, swimming, and cycling.

When designing cardiovascular endurance programs, most fitness experts like to refer to the "training pyramid." This pyramid is normally a four-to-six-month cycle with each stage building to the next (see figure 5.3). The first stage, called the *base* stage, consists of three to five workouts per week to build endurance. The workouts may vary from running to stair climbing to cycling. The main theme should be duration, not intensity. Players should exercise for 30 to 60 minutes per session.

The *build* phase has three workouts per week at higher intensity. This may include mile repeats or 800-yard runs. The theme is to go faster but not to cut back on the time of the session, which should be 30 minutes. Fartlek training, when a continuous tempo run is interrupted with short bouts of faster running, is another build workout of particular interest to soccer players.

Third is the *peak* stage. Players are now approaching their competitive season. Running workouts must be short but high intensity. It includes sprints of 10, 20, 40, 60, 80, and 100 yards. The normal work-to-rest ratio starts at 1:3. Thus if the first 100-yard run takes 15 seconds, there is a 45-second rest before the next 100-yard run begins. One month before the season starts the ratio is reduced to 1:2, and at two weeks before the season it is 1:1. A full set of sprints consists of 20 10-yard sprints, 18 of 20 yards, 16 of 40, 14 of 60, 12 of 80, and 10 of 100 yards.

The *maintenance* phase takes place during the season. The activities scheduled in daily practices help to maintain cardiovascular fitness, but I still recommend that you schedule at least one or two sessions per week of intense running workouts to truly maintain cardiovascular fitness throughout the season.

	Jan	Feb	Mar	April	May	June	July	Aug	Sep	Oct	Nov	Dec
Base—aerobic	▓	▓	▓	▓	▓							
Build—intervals						▓	▓					
Peak—sprints								▓	▓			
Maintenance										▓	▓	▓

Base phase—build aerobic base, longer bouts 30 to 60 minutes
Build phase—change to shorter bouts, higher intensity, intervals
Peak phase—short duration, high-intensity sprints (10 to 100 yards)
Maintenance—maintain by practicing sport and high-intensity sprints

Days per week for cardiovascular training

Base phase—three to five days per week
Build phase—three days per week
Peak phase—two to three days per week (prior to lifting or on nonlifting days)
Maintenance—three days per week, arranged around competitive schedule

Figure 5.3 Yearly cardiovascular periodization schedule.

When training time is lost, there is a definite decrease in aerobic conditioning. It's estimated that every week of lost training causes a 10 percent decrease in conditioning. Injured players should keep that in mind. They should maintain an aerobic exercise program that doesn't use the injured part of the body.

Muscle Strength and Endurance

It takes muscle strength to jump for a high header, to get off a hard shot, to stay on the ball when being charged. While you may not have given much thought to the need for developing muscle strength in soccer players, obviously this kind of exercise does benefit them, especially the goalkeepers. True, they shouldn't train for bulk, but tone and strength are essential. The players can develop muscle strength through such activities as working with free weights, weight machines, rubber bands or tubing, gymnastics, and calisthenics.

While muscle strength is significant, muscle endurance is of the utmost importance to the soccer player. Athletes can enhance this kind of endurance by working with lighter weights or resistance and increasing the repetitions of the exercises used to build muscle strength. Muscle endurance also benefits from any long-distance aerobic activity such as running, cycling, fast walking, or lap swimming.

I like using a training program that combines strength and endurance training by taking the program through three phases—the strength phase, the power phase (including plyometrics), and the maintenance phase (see figure 5.4).

The purpose of the *strength* phase is to develop a base or foundation on which to build. This is an introduction phase designed to prepare the muscles for more intense work that will follow in other phases. The rule is to have a high volume (sets by repetitions) and low intensity (weight). The initial program begins with light weight and three sets of 10 to 15 repetitions.

The *power* phase starts the change from high volume to lower volume and low intensity to higher intensity. The types of exercise change as well, incorporating more explosive lifts such as the power clean, hand clean,

	Jan	Feb	Mar	April	May	June	July	Aug	Sep	Oct	Nov	Dec
Preseason						▓	▓	▓				
In-season									▓	▓	▓	▓
Active rest	▓	▓										
Off-season			▓	▓	▓							
Strength phase		▓	▓	▓	▓							
Power phase						▓	▓	▓				
Plyometrics						▓	▓					
Maintenance									▓	▓	▓	▓

Strength phase—build strength, high volume/low intensity (three sets of 10 to 15 repetitions)
Power phase—change to low volume/high intensity, explosive lifts (five sets of 5 repetitions)
Plyometrics—reactive drills to promote explosiveness, box jumps, etc.
Maintenance—maintain strength during competitive season (two sets of 8 to 12 repetitions)

Days per week for strength training

Strength phase—3 days per week (Mon/Wed/Fri)
Power phase—4 days per week (Mon/Thur and Tue/Fri)
Plyometrics—2 days per week (prior to lifting or on nonlifting days)
Maintenance—2 days per week, arranged around competitive schedule

Figure 5.4   Yearly strength training periodization schedule.

snatch, and push press. The intent of this phase is to improve the transferability of strength training to the athletic movements players will be doing on the field.

Plyometric training during the power phase is of great value in the development of a soccer player's explosiveness. It usually includes reactive drills two days per week (prior to lifting or on nonlifting days).

Players perform the *maintenance* phase during the season. The purpose is to maintain the increased strength levels obtained during the preceding two phases. Strength training is designed to improve basic athletic components—strength, speed, and explosiveness. The time players need these the most is during their competitive season. Normally the in-season program calls for lifting twice a week, with one day being heavy and the second day light. Numerous studies have shown that one hard lifting session per week will adequately maintain strength levels.

Flexibility

A soccer player can improve flexibility by performing activities like yoga, static stretching, light swimming, or any other light activity that puts major muscle groups through a full range of motion.

A few cardinal rules apply when stretching for flexibility.

- Stretch the muscles on both sides of the body.
- Do not exceed the threshold for discomfort or pain.
- Do not bounce or jerk; gradually induce the stretch.
- Maintain each stretch for 20 to 40 seconds.
- Be aware if one side is more or less flexible than the other. It could be the result of structural difference, recovery from injury, or the possible development of an injury.

• Do not squeeze the knees. Be careful not to put too much pressure on the knee joint, especially when stretching the quadriceps.
• Stretch the muscles after a brief warm-up.
• Stretching after a workout helps to speed recovery for the next workout.

Body Composition

The capabilities of the human body are truly awesome. Think for a moment of all the intricacies the body must go through when a player receives a ball, controls it, turns, sees that space is available, attacks the space, avoids a tackle, views an open teammate, passes the ball, continues the run, receives the ball back, looks what the goalkeeper is giving, shoots, and scores. In those few seconds hundreds of muscle contractions have occurred, thousands of chemical reactions have taken place, energy has been expended, and calories have been burned. To do all that our bodies need three things—air, water, and food. For all of us, but particularly for the athlete, it is essential that the amount of water consumed be adequate and that the

food eaten be of high quality. After all, would you build an expensive race car and race it without enough coolant or with cheap fuel?

Very few soccer players drink enough water. Yet it is the nutrient that helps regulate the body's temperature, affects blood volume, aids in the body's chemical reactions, and carries off waste, among other functions. To depend on the body's thirst mechanism is wrong since it lags way behind the body's need for water. Obviously, soccer players should learn to force-hydrate themselves by drinking 8 to 10 glasses of water per day. They can easily check their hydration status. If they urinate in large volumes and if the urine is clear and colorless, they are probably drinking enough water.

We eat food for energy. The body's preferred source of energy is carbohydrates. Fat and protein can also be converted into energy, but the conversions are slow and inefficient. For good performance an athlete should eat a great variety of foods but give preference to pastas, whole-grain breads, potatoes, cereals, fruit, vegetables, and beans. All these are high in carbohydrates.

It is estimated that the current American diet obtains 40 percent of its calories from fat, 15 percent from protein, and 45 percent from carbohydrates. An athlete should attempt to consume a diet that gets 25 percent of its calories from fat, 15 percent from protein, and 60 percent from carbohydrates. A high-performance diet may even cut the fat to 20 percent.

It is difficult for coaches to control the diet of their athletes. All we can do is share the information with our players and their parents. I ask our players not to eat foods high in fat content on match day. It takes much energy to digest the fat. I also ask them not to eat anything during the four hours directly preceding the match. If they play with food in their stomach, energy loss occurs. The last thing I counsel them on is the consumption of sugar during the last hours before a match. Sugar creates a momentary energy burst, but it is of very short duration and is followed by an energy loss that requires a long recovery time (45 minutes).

Many young people are obsessed with their physical appearance. It's tragic that bulimia and anorexia nervosa (eating disorders) have reached epidemic proportions. These disorders are of a psychological nature and should be treated by experts. If you suspect that one of your players suffers from an eating disorder, get help. Usually the counselors at your school can handle these situations and if not, they have contacts who can.

Preseason Planning

During the month before the players report for the first practice, the coaching staff meets at least once a week. The purpose of those meetings is to prepare a plan for the upcoming season. The plan has to be somewhat general because at that time there are still several unknowns. We know the abilities of the returning players, and we have seen and met with the recruited players. Yet not until we have gone through several practices and seen all the players under the pressure of a match do we know if we can create the team culture necessary to play successfully with the new group. So whatever we plan, we need to be flexible.

Our conditioning and technique development program doesn't vary that much from year to year. Tactics, however, change each season and may change even during the season. Most changes are based on observations made during the preceding season. That includes the effectiveness of our tactics and the tactics used by our opponents.

While there are unknowns, much of the plan is consistent from year to year. Everyone on your staff should contribute to the plan. Once you establish the plan all should be thoroughly familiar with it.

These are the items that we incorporate into our master practice plan:

- Conditioning
- Technique development
- Principles of defense
- Principles of attack
- Compactness
- Defending and attacking on corner kicks
- Defending and attacking on direct and indirect free kicks close to the penalty area
- Defending and attacking on direct and indirect free kicks away from the penalty area

- Tactics for the throw-ins (possession or penetration)
- Tactics used for the kickoff (theirs and ours)
- Distribution from the goalkeeper (possession or penetration)
- Building up from the back
- Midfield tactics
- Setting the offside trap
- Beating the offside trap
- One-on-one tactics
- Combination plays
- Runs off the ball
- Crossing plays, both long and short
- Penalties

Once we complete this master plan, we schedule the subjects into a weekly and a daily plan (see the sample daily practice plan on page 70). Since the entire coaching staff contributes to the plan and helps with scheduling, all are well prepared for the start of practice. This makes our practices efficient and varied. Without a plan, or with the wrong one, you set up yourself and the team for failure. Success is not a chance happening; you plan for it.

Scheduling Matches

Like most college teams, we are restricted in the number of matches we may play during a season. Outside of the play-offs we are allowed two scrimmages and 24 matches. We may enter one tournament, which regardless of the number of tournament matches counts for one of our allowed matches. We may have as many as 19 conference matches, leaving us with 4 matches and two scrimmages to schedule on our own. We schedule these matches carefully so that the competition is challenging but not overwhelming.

We don't have time to play nonconference teams after the official start of our conference season. Furthermore, I don't want to set us up for unnecessary injuries. So we schedule all the extra matches during our preparation time. In the past we chose to play nearby four-year schools. With the numerous NCAA restrictions, however, that is becoming increasingly difficult. We still play Gonzaga University and Washington State University, not only because of tradition, but because we have a reasonable chance of beating them. I believe that preseason matches are best scheduled against competitive teams that your team has a chance to beat.

Soccer played at any level is exciting for the players. A match played against a vastly superior opponent, however, can demoralize a team. Playing against a very weak team provides no satisfaction, and your team will learn very little from such a contest.

Three years ago we traveled to Phoenix, Arizona, where we had the opportunity to play Yavapai College, the National Junior College champions, and Monroe College, the runner-up. We beat Monroe 2-0 and lost to Yavapai 4-3. That was probably one of our more exciting preseason weekends. It did much to boost our confidence.

We also select our tournaments very carefully. Again, we want to find good competition, but we also want to have a chance to win, if not the tournament, then certainly a number of matches. Our second concern is to find a tournament in which the style of play is like the style used by many of the teams in our conference. It prepares us better.

During my first three years at CCS we hosted a tournament so that we were in control of team selection. The main drawback is that in an at-home tournament, our players go home after matches. On a road trip they get to know each other better, and a lot of bonding occurs. So we prefer to travel to a tournament rather than to stage our own.

Regardless, it's beneficial to know at least some things about the opponent, like the system used, the identity of the strong players, tactics on set plays, where they defend, and so forth.

First work on your strengths and tactics; then adjust and work on the information contained in the scouting report. Figure 5.5 is one of our scouting report forms. Use it or adjust it to suit your needs.

Scouting the Opponent

There is no danger in learning all you can about your opponents. How you use the information, however, can be hazardous. Scouting reports can scare you to death or falsely reassure you. If you communicate these emotions to your team, you may be in for a rough time.

The other problem with a scouting report is that you may spend so much practice time on nullifying the opponent's strengths or capitalizing on their weaknesses that you don't have time to work on your strengths.

Traveling

The budgeting for travel, meals, and motels is an educated guess. At the time we set the budget we don't really know how the conference is going to align its members. Even when we know, the match schedule is not published until early May.

Regardless, our schedules in the past have called for seven trips for a total of about 4,200 miles plus two tournaments.

Traveling can be exciting, educational, and enjoyable, or it can be pure misery. It really depends on the behavior of the players.

Scouting Report

Team scouted_____Date_____Scout_____

Opponent_____Score T.S.____Opponent____

Weather_____Field Conditions_____Attendance_____

System: How many forwards?____How many at midfield?____How many back?____

Strengths of forward(s)_____

Weaknesses of forward(s)_____

Do they play over____, through____, or around____? Which side do they favor?_____

Roles and effectiveness of outside midfielders_____
_____

Roles and effectiveness of center midfielders_____
_____

Midfield strengths_____

Midfield weaknesses_____

Do they use a sweeper?___How deep does he play?_____Does he push up on their attack?_____

How far?_____When does he drop back?_____How far?_____Do his teammates trust him?_____

Tackling strengths?_____Distribution strengths?_____Temper?_____

What are his weaknesses?_____

Do they favor player-for-player in the back or do they defend zonally?_____

Strengths of the marking defenders_____

Weaknesses of the marking defenders_____

If zonal, are there weaknesses?_____

Effectiveness of the stopper_____
_____

Best way to beat their defense: over____through____around____Why?_____
_____

Keeper: Line____Sweeper_____Strengths_____

Weaknesses_____

Where does he like to distribute?_____

Name their key players:_____

Set Plays: Corners. Who takes them?___Near-post or far-post?___How do they attack the post and who is involved?_____

Free kicks. Who takes them?____Do they take them quickly?____Describe the play they used:_____
_____

When defending against a free kick is the wall set up quickly?_____Who sets up the wall?_____Do they allow defending players behind the wall?_____If the free kick is from far out, where do they defend?_____

Who clearly leads the team?_____

Additional comments:_____

Figure 5.5 Sample scouting report form.

Before a trip you should remind the team of their responsibility to their college, their city, and each other. I like to point out to them that I enjoy being a coach, but I am a very temperamental baby-sitter.

We usually travel in two 15-passenger vans. They are new vans; nevertheless, it is not the most desirable way of traveling. As I have stated earlier, we have to travel at least 300 miles one-way to our closest conference away match. Ideally, we should fly, or at least travel in a comfortable bus, but budget constraints put that out of the question. So we make the best of the situation. The vans may seem adequate for 18 players, a trainer, and two coaches, but when you add the luggage, balls, first-aid equipment, and water and ice containers, it becomes somewhat cramped. My major objection to traveling in two vehicles is that it tends to divide the team into two social groups. We try to make up for that by having our meals together, sightseeing as a group, and taking frequent rest stops.

Our team usually sleeps three to a room, on two beds and a roll-away. Each room has a room captain, and he is responsible for behavior in the room, which includes adherence to curfews, lights-out, and cleanup. We don't have problems when we travel. I don't believe that is because of the room captains; I believe our players behave well because from the day they first arrive we cultivate team pride.

After-Graduation Plans

The low cost of a community college education is attractive to many students and their parents. Also, at a community college the classes usually are smaller, and students have the opportunity to bring up their grade point averages in preparation for entering a four-year school.

There are two excellent universities in Spokane. Both offer varsity soccer for men and women. Many of our players apply to those schools. Some want to attend other universities, sometimes because of the soccer programs, but most often because the school is more desirable for their major. Since we are distant from the more densely populated areas, we try to help our students find the schools that would be best for them.

Youth and high school coaches can be of immense service to athletes trying to choose a college. You can help by finding out early which players want to go on after graduation. With the student prepare a profile that includes the player's background, statistics, cumulative GPA, major, goals, a practice schedule, and a match schedule. To this package add your observations. Be candid and honest; don't oversell or undersell the athlete. College coaches will appreciate your information, and if you are consistent, they will look at your players.

The package and a cover letter should be targeted to the universities in which your student truly has an interest. The cover letter, written by the student, should be addressed to the head coach using his or her name and title. The letter should give reasons why your student wants to attend that particular university. This is important. Please understand that most college coaches receive numerous letters each year. When those letters are addressed to "Soccer Coach" and don't include a name, the coach dumps them. Most of those letters are computer generated and mailed to almost every college in the United States. A number of college coaches won't even talk to a player unless that player has an application on file.

Summary

Planning for the season is hard work, but following these suggestions may make the task less overwhelming.

- Prepare your budgets carefully; include some contingency funds to cover the unexpected.
- Check your equipment and facilities thoroughly and, if replacements are needed, order early.
- Assess the efficiency of your administrative processes such as medical screening, examinations, insurance, and injury care.

- Determine who will be on your staff and how you will train them.
- Reevaluate and strengthen your conditioning plan, in particular your off-season program. Include nutritional information.
- Review and prepare, as much as possible, your plan for technical and tactical development of both players and team.
- Plan your training and match schedules, including possible tournaments, and make the travel arrangements.
- Analyze your program in its entirety to make sure that all who are involved have a chance to grow.

Chapter 6

Planning Practices

All the hard work in soccer is done at practice. In the practice we must work on the players' physical and mental condition, while developing them technically and tactically. It stands to reason that we should carefully plan all practices. Each practice should emphasize one or more specific components of soccer in an order that will allow gradual improvement.

I like working off a master plan that lists all the components that need attention. From the master plan I can then create my daily practice plans. The daily plans emphasize practice economy by combining as many components as possible. I like to do that through the use of small-sided, conditioned games.

Regardless, for practices to be effective they must be challenging, enjoyable, and provide all players with a certain amount of success. A practice without success is a

waste of time. We practice to remember success.

Practice Emphasis

Earlier I mentioned that I expect the players to report in good physical condition for the first practice. But I know that a player's concept of being fit is frequently not the same as mine. This means that we spend much time on physical conditioning during the early part of the practice season. This is a challenge for both the players and the coaching staff.

Our conference dictates that practice may not start until the third Friday in August and schedules the first conference match around September 15. That allows us less than four weeks to prepare. Any conditioning specialist will tell you that isn't enough time. Eight weeks is ideal; six weeks is workable. So the challenge is to get the players ready without causing injuries. At the same time you must find the time and energy to develop your players technically, and to do at least some work on individual tactics and team tactics.

The chart in figure 6.1 gives you a picture of how I schedule the three major components of soccer. When practice starts we spend the majority of time on conditioning and very little on tactics. As we go along the time spent on conditioning decreases and the time spent on individual tactics increases. By the end of the season we spend almost all our time on team tactics and very little on conditioning. From the beginning of practice until the end of the season, we work on technique improvement.

I don't believe in extremely long practices. However, again due to the shortness of our time to prepare, we start the practice season with two sessions per day. We do that for 10 to 14 days. The length depends on how well prepared the players are when they first report. Each session lasts about two and a half hours, which includes time to warm up, stretch, cool down, and an hourly water break.

Each session, especially during the first 14 days, includes hard physical conditioning. You must take care not to overtrain during that time. Every hard day of physical challenge should be followed by a day of lesser intensity. I have also found it better to schedule the purely physical work at the end of the practice. This way the players are less tired and have better concentration during the technique and tactics phases.

Master Plan

In our master plan I list all the components that we need to work on during our practices. Once we do this, it is not difficult to lay out the daily practice plans. See the sample master plan shown in figure 6.2.

Daily Practice Plans

At the beginning of the season you should prepare daily practice plans from your master practice schedule. Once the match season starts you should prepare practice plans based on review of the last match and the scouting report for the upcoming match. All practices, no matter what time in the season,

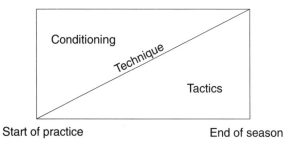

Figure 6.1 Scheduling the three major components of soccer throughout the season.

should include conditioning and technique development. Ideally the team should peak physically, mentally, technically, and tactically late in the season, when fatigue and play-off pressure start to take their toll.

Figure 6.3 shows a typical daily practice plan for a session during the preseason, presented in more detail than it appears on our plan. We spent the first 30 minutes on warming up the muscles and stretching them. We used the next 20 minutes to work on technique, choosing one of the components on our master plan. Here we chose passing. I like passing in triangles since it simulates game conditions by forcing the players to turn their hips toward the target. This doesn't happen when players pass in twos.

After the water break we worked on another item lifted from the master plan, support on defense. We used a number of grids and went for 30 minutes. We used another 30 minutes to practice support on offense, again using the grid layout.

We finished the work session with a strenuous conditioning exercise called horseshoe running. After that we warmed down with an easy around-the-field jog and a stretch down.

Getting Ready for Practice

Once classes have started, we schedule practices for afternoons only. Since the last classes usually finish at 2:00 or 2:30, practices start at 3:00 sharp. We expect players to be on time. Those who need taping must be ready at 3:00. The trainers will not tape once practice has started.

I don't allow dead ball shooting before a practice when players arrive early. I prefer that they play passing games of low intensity. Hard shooting can cause severe injuries if done before a proper warm-up.

Sample Soccer Master Plan

Team Development	Conditioning	Technique	Set Plays
Laws of the game	Physical	Ball control	Kickoffs
Player evaluations	Psychological	Passing	Goal kicks
Team evaluations		Tackling	Corner kicks
		Heading	Indirect free kicks
		Dribbling	Direct free kicks
		Shooting	Penalties
			Throw-ins

Defense	Offense	Midfield	Goalkeepers
One-versus-one	One-versus-one	Slow buildup	Shot stopping
Support	Support (angle, distance)	Quick attack	Punching, deflecting
Balance	Width and depth	Width and depth	Jumping
Depth	Combination plays	Redirection	Diving
Tactics for the sweeper	Crossing plays	Compactness	Cutting out crosses
Tactics for the stopper	Takeovers	Transition	Support of defense
Tactics for the marking defenders	Mobility		Distribution
Compactness	Creativity		
Transition	Compactness		
	Transition		

Figure 6.2 Sample soccer master plan.

During the first few minutes of a practice I like to bring the players up to date on whatever is newsworthy. That may include injury status of teammates, results from other competitions, standings, school news, and so forth. I also spend a minute or two on positive comments about the team's progress and set the challenges for the practice. Our before-practice talk is never longer than five minutes and is always positive. It sets the mood for the rest of the afternoon.

Practice Principles

Since practice is so important to soccer, I check every practice plan to see that it satisfies the principles I believe are needed for an efficient and effective practice. Practices must be economical and must combine the three major components of soccer—conditioning, technique, and tactics. Small-sided, conditioned games usually satisfy that principle.

It is essential that the practice be challenging but at the same time allow the team and each player to achieve at least some success in overcoming challenges.

Finally, the practice must be enjoyable.

Economical Practices

I have said earlier that soccer is not a coached game. Once the opening whistle in the match sounds, coaching stops. Except for injury or tactical substitutions and halftime instructions and adjustments, the coach can best serve his or her team by observing calmly and confidently. The quiet confidence will be transmitted to the team. If the coach gets

---

Sample Daily Practice Plan

15 min   Warm-up with ball and partner
From the goal line partner #1 sprints out about 30 yards. Partner #2 yells "turn" and serves the ball. Partner #1 receives and controls the ball, and dribbles it back. When partner #1 crosses the goal line, partner #2 runs out.

15 min   Stretch

20 min   Technique
Pass in threes while moving. Maintain shape of the triangle. Pass in both directions, using the inside and outside of the left and right foot. Pass for 10 minutes with the ball on the ground and do 10 minutes of chips.

10 min   Water break

30 min   Support on defense
One-versus-two. Use a 30-by-10-yard grid and one goal. One attacker starts attack at the top of the grid. Two defenders start at the goal line. Lead defender must communicate intent to commit to the ball. Lead defender must close down the attacker quickly without overrunning. Watch lead defender's body position and patience. Supporting defender must watch angle and distance of support. Supporting defender must communicate.

Two-versus-two. Use two attackers; otherwise, same as above. Supporting defender's role is to support the defender challenging for the ball but in such a position that if the ball is passed to attacker #2, the supporting defender can close down #2.

30 min   Support on offense
Two-versus-one. Same grid as above. Two attackers with the ball start at the top of the grid. One defender starts at the goal line. Coach the attacking players. Player with the ball should not put the defender between the ball and partner and should force the defender to commit before passing. The supporting player must provide a passing angle at a reasonable distance. Encourage wall passing and takeovers.

20 min   Horseshoes
Each player has a partner. Partner #1 sprints at full speed from the near goal to the intersection of the halfway line and the right touchline, then around the far goal to the intersection of the halfway line and the left touchline, and back to the near goal. When #1 enters the six-yard box, #2 runs while #1 rests. When #2 returns, #1 goes again until each player has completed five horseshoes. Do three sets.

15 min   Warm-down and stretch.

Figure 6.3   Sample daily practice plan.

---

nervous or uptight, so will the players. Their performance will suffer. The observations made in the match will set the schedule for the next practice.

Since it is impossible to coach effectively during a soccer match, the practices must duplicate match conditions. The best way you can do that is by designing small-sided, conditioned games that highlight a technique or tactic that needs attention. The method is often referred to as the whole-part-whole method. That is, observe the whole, see the problem, isolate the problem, and design a realistic game that allows the players to work on the problem. Once the players master the problem in the small-sided game, take it back into the match, the whole.

Small-Sided Games

Small-sided, conditioned games are the best coaching tool. The coach determines the number of players that will be involved based on the component he or she wants to improve. To work on defensive support, for example, the coach may begin with playing one attacker against two defenders and instruct the second defender in achieving the proper distance and angle of support. At the same time the coach may be giving information to the first defender.

The coach may also choose to put conditions on the game. For instance, if the team is practicing combination plays in a three-versus-three game, the coach may specify

ously in this type of game you can work on wall passing, through passing, back passing, and takeovers. The lone defender can be coached on positioning and marking space.

In a two-versus-two game you can coach overlaps, space seeking, and isolating one of the defenders to create a two-versus-one situation. The defenders can work on support on defense.

In three-versus-two you can instruct the offense to create width and depth while applying all the technique and tactics of the earlier games. The defenders work on support, space marking, and role switching.

The three-versus-three game calls for mobility and innovation by the attackers and the same plus good communication by the defenders. By the way, everything that happens in an 11-a-side match happens in a three-versus-three game. However, in a small-sided game players touch the ball more often, and the situations you want to work on occur more often. This kind of game is much easier to coach.

Four-versus-three, four-versus-four, five-versus-four, and five-versus-five games allow the players to work not only on the technique and tactics of the other small-sided games but also on position-related specifics, width, depth, player distribution, compactness, and transition.

Games that have numbers higher than five-versus-five lose the economy presented by a small-sided game.

Successful Practices

Nothing motivates as much as mastering a realistic challenge. All your practices should present realistic challenges to the team and the individual players. All practices should conclude with a reasonable amount of success. A practice that has no success is a wasted practice. That can become frustrating. At times you may present a challenge that somehow doesn't seem to work. Don't give up on the challenge. Evaluate it. Did the players understand what you wanted? Did you demonstrate it clearly? Was there ambiguity in the instruction? Did it conflict with earlier challenges?

Usually when an exercise, challenge, or small-sided game falls apart, you are per-

that every goal will count, but a goal scored after the execution of a wall pass will count for 3, or a goal resulting directly from a through pass will count for 2, or a goal resulting from a successful takeover will count for 2. In a heading practice, goals scored directly off headers will count for 5. Don't make the mistake of not counting goals scored by means other than the condition. You don't want to take away options.

Small-sided, conditioned games are match related. They allow your players to practice a technique or tactic under matchlike pressure. A small-sided, conditioned game must include opposition, a counterattack, and a goal.

Small-sided games can involve as few as 2 players or as many as 10. In one-versus-one games you can coach players in individual technique and tactics, both offensively and defensively. In a two-versus-one game you can coach the attackers to beat the lone defender by dribbling or by passing. Obvi-

forming in too small an area, there are too many people involved, or the basic technique is inadequate to overcome the challenge. Increase the space, use fewer players, or ease up on pressure to give more time to work on technique faults. Not having success at a certain endeavor is a coaching problem, not a player problem.

Enjoyable Practices

If you give players a choice of what to do at practice, they would all vote for a two-hour scrimmage. That's understandable; they love the game. That is their primary reason for being there. It stands to reason that if practices were fun and enjoyable, they would work hard for several hours.

Well, practices can be challenging and fun, or they can be pure drudgery. When you present players with realistic challenges and allow them to have a good time overcoming them, you will have a hard-working, enthusiastic team that gets things done. If your practices are dull and without much purpose the team will be discontented and tired.

Your preparation, good use of time, positive attitude, and ability to praise and compliment even minor successes will create an enjoyable atmosphere. In such an atmosphere it is much easier to work on the serious parts of the practice. Players in a positive mood are receptive to instruction and challenge. People, and athletes in particular, will have a high rate of success if they enjoy what they are doing. Having success is easy; just plan for it.

To make the practices enjoyable and fun for the players, your staff and you should keep the following in mind.

- Plan and be prepared for every practice. Make a time schedule for all elements of the practice and stick to it.
- Vary your practices. Don't work a subject to death; you can always go back to it.
- Make practices economical by keeping everybody involved. Work in grids so that several games can be played at the same time.
- Make sure that each challenge you present provides some success, not only for the team, but also for the players.
- Explain the purpose of each practice to your athletes. Encourage your players to communicate their feelings of success or confusion about the practice.
- Keep things positive and light-hearted. It will put players in a receptive spirit when it is time to do the serious coaching.
- Make sure you are enjoying yourself. Be rested, enthusiastic, caring, and compassionate. If you are having fun, players will too.
- Keep things in perspective. Soccer is a game, not a war.

It is my job to help players reach their potential and coach the team to success. I know that in soccer the only opportunity to do that is in practice. Thus I can best serve the team by thoroughly planning the practices and conscientiously executing the plan.

Summary

Probably the most important part of your job is planning your practices. The following suggestions will help to make practices successful.

- Emphasize what you want to achieve in the practice.
- Develop a detailed master plan.
- Extract your daily practice plans from the master plan.
- Keep your practices varied and challenging.
- Don't give long explanations that try to anticipate every possible problem. Get started and coach or use short explanations when problems occur.
- Combine conditioning, technique, and tactics in your exercises so that your practices use time economically.
- Use small-sided, conditioned games. They are the best tool you have.
- Make sure that each practice attains some level of success.
- Make sure that practices are enjoyable.

Part III

Coaching Defense

Chapter 7

Basic Defensive Skills and Positions

Defensive duties and responsibilities are assigned not only to the goalkeeper, sweeper, marking backs, and stopper, but also to wide midfielders, attacking midfielders (playmakers), and forwards. Therefore all players need to have defensive skills. Of course, players in certain positions need specific attributes to be effective. All players, however, must have the basic skills to defend plus additional defensive skills and attributes required by their positions.

We discuss teaching basic defensive skills in later chapters. For now let's take a look at the skills and attributes needed for specific positions from the goalkeeper to the forwards.

Goalkeeper

As the last line of defense and as the only player on the team allowed to use hands and arms to control, propel, or stop the ball, the goalkeeper deserves special attention. It is virtually impossible to have a successful team with a below-average goalkeeper. The goalkeeper is a special case in the team yet is a vital team member. The goalkeeper is expected to rescue the team with saves when defensive lapses have occurred and at the same time be an integral part of the defense by organizing the players in front of the goal.

THE LAST LINE OF DEFENSE

In the late 1960s I was the coach of the Liverpool University soccer team in England. In the 1968-69 season we were blessed with the most talented recruiting class in the university's athletic history, but in our preseason training camp the goalkeeper was injured and did not play again for over a year. We managed to advance to the national final but only by the narrowest of margins, often with scores of 4-3 or 5-4. Our lack of a dependable goalkeeper finally caught up with us in the Universities Athletic Union final where we lost by 4 goals to 3, after overtime.

Goalkeeper Skills and Attributes

In my experience I have found that all top-class goalkeepers have the following attributes:

- They are fearless.
- They relish body contact.
- They have quick reflexes or reactions.
- They are agile.
- They are above average in height.
- They have a dominant personality.
- They have good hand-eye coordination.

If any one of these seven critical attributes is missing, then it is unlikely that the goalkeeper will excel. I have known hundreds of promising goalkeepers who looked the part but were deficient in one or more of these attributes. Often I saw big, agile goalkeepers with quick reflexes who were outstanding in drill shnl-stopping situations but shied away from body contact. They failed to make the big save when physically challenged by opponents.

It is also essential that the goalkeeper be a good communicator since he or she is in the unique position of being able to see the other 21 players on the field most of the time. The goalkeeper must convey vital information to the nearest defenders so that they can organize themselves effectively and prevent shots on goal.

Goalkeepers should have well-developed skills in the following areas:

- Positioning—low shots, high shots, and recovery movement
- Stopping low shots
- Stopping high shots

- Punching the ball
- Dealing with crosses
- Distributing the ball—underarm roll, push pass, and overarm throw

Positioning

In saving shots on goal, the goalkeeper's distance from the goal line and the angle from the near post are of critical importance. A goalkeeper only a few inches out of position may concede a goal. My experience is that it takes a long time for goalkeepers to perfect their positioning. Many of the world's top goalkeepers are the oldest players on their team and are often in their late 30s or early 40s.

Too often we find goalkeepers in the youth leagues and in high school programs who concentrate most of their practice time on fitness or agility. Instead, their coaches should focus on getting them to perfect their positioning. We need to get an old head on young shoulders in a hurry.

Positioning for low shots. The basic set position in stopping low shots is illustrated in figure 7.1. Notice that the goalkeeper's feet are slightly apart with knees bent and pointing slightly forward. Hands face forward with fingers downward and thumbs on the outside. This is a classic set position from which the goalkeeper can thrust sideways to make a save. The goalkeeper must establish this basic set position, with feet motionless at the desired distance from the goal line and at the correct angle from the near post, a split second before the opponent shoots. The goalkeeper's weight should never be on the heels—otherwise he or she may fall backward when the shot is taken.

The goalkeeper's position (distance and angle) is largely dependent on (a) what is happening on the ball and (b) the options available to the opposing player on the ball. If an opponent is about to take a long-range shot from 25 or 30 yards, the goalkeeper's first priority is not to be so far off the goal line that the ball goes over him or her and drops into the goal. Rather, the goalkeeper should take a position at a point from the goal line where he or she might still be able to recover and tip a high shot over the crossbar.

Positioning for high shots. Again, in preparation for saving a long shot, the goalkeeper should adopt a modified basic set

Figure 7.1 The basic set position.

position a split second before the shot is taken. The goalkeeper should bend the knees only slightly, have a slight forward lean at the waist, and hold the hands higher in preparation for saving a probable high shot.

The goalkeeper should understand his or her personal optimum distance from the goal line if the opponent on the ball has the opportunity of "chipping" it. The goalkeeper should recognize that it is very difficult to chip a fast-rolling ball unless it is coming directly at the chipper. It is much easier to chip a stationary or slow-rolling ball. The goalkeeper must take a position at a distance from the goal line where it is still possible to recover and save shots that would have gone into the goal just under the crossbar.

Recovery movement. The recovery movement is a special technique that involves getting into position to save a high shot that is going over the goalkeeper but would drop into the goal. Too often we find goalkeepers moving directly backward with their backs to the goal, which makes it difficult to get height in their vertical jump. Instead, the goalkeeper's recovery movement should be a sideways one.

In saving a shot that is going high over the left shoulder, the goalkeeper should take a quarter turn to the left, take the left foot back and lift the right knee to cross legs by planting the right foot to the left of the left foot, thus enabling the goalkeeper to thrust upward off the right foot. The goalkeeper should keep an eye on the ball and swing the right arm upward and backward to propel the ball over the crossbar (figure 7.2). The foot movements are seen in figure 7.3.

To save a shot going high over the right shoulder, the goalkeeper should use a recovery movement that is a mirror image of the preceding description. The goalkeeper takes a quarter turn to the right by taking the right foot backward, planting it sideways across the field. The goalkeeper lifts the left knee and crosses the legs to plant the left foot beyond the right foot and straightens it vigorously to get upward thrust. The goalkeeper will always be looking at the ball. The goalkeeper swings the left arm upward and backward to hit the ball over the crossbar.

Figure 7.2 Tipping the ball over the crossbar.

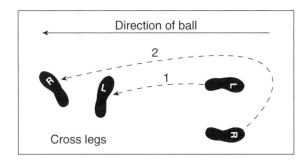

Figure 7.3   Foot placement in the recovery movement.

These recovery movements require much practice, and it is extremely important that the goalkeeper always be aware of position—distance and angle—from the goal line and near post.

Stopping Low Shots

I repeat that it is important that the goalkeeper be in the basic set position a split second before the shot is taken. This allows the goalkeeper to push off either foot to the right or to the left and extend the body in a side-on position. The goalkeeper should always push off sideways—maybe even slightly forward. Never allow the goalkeeper to dive with the chest to the ground. In the side-on position the goalkeeper should raise the upper arm high enough so that he or she can see through the "window" made by both arms.

Probably the greatest single fault in saving low shots is for the goalkeeper to have weight on the heels in the basic set position and fall down backwards, taking his or her face away from the ball when the opponent shoots. This action means that the goalkeeper is blocking the least amount of space, and it nearly always results in a goal being scored.

Stopping High Shots

Again, it is extremely important that the goalkeeper be in the basic set position a split second before the shot is taken. From the semicrouched position the goalkeeper pushes vigorously from the feet, thrusting through ankle, knee, and hip joints. At the same time the goalkeeper swings both hands upward to add upward momentum to the lift. If the shot is high to the right the goalkeeper leans to the right and pushes powerfully through both feet, although most of the power will come through the left foot. The goalkeeper straightens ankle, knee, and hip joints to generate lift, and at the same time throws up both hands so that the thumbs and forefingers form a W shape. The goalkeeper should try to get both hands behind the ball. The eyes should be on the ball from the moment it leaves the opponent's foot (figure 7.4).

Punching the Ball

It is often a risky business for the goalkeeper to try to catch the ball in a crowded goal area. It might be wise to punch the ball, particularly if the goalkeeper cannot get a clear run to the ball because of a congestion of players. Whenever possible, the goalkeeper should punch the ball high, far, and wide. Never should the goalkeeper punch it downward in front of the goal. To obtain height and distance in the punch, and to avoid mis-hitting the ball, the goalkeeper should try to get both fists to the ball. The goalkeeper should make the fists by folding the fingers and pressing both sets of upper finger joints together. The thumbs should point toward the ball and be placed on top of the forefingers (figure 7.5).

Figure 7.4   Saving a high shot.

The goalkeeper should try to get to the ball at a point in its flight higher than an opponent could possibly get his or her head to it.

Dealing With Crosses

Probably the greatest difficulty for most goalkeepers is dealing with crosses. Very often we find goalkeepers are adept at dealing with crosses from one side of the field but have huge problems in catching or punching the ball on crosses from the other side.

Very often, the root cause of the problem is starting in a position where it is difficult to move to the near- or far-post areas (figure 7.6).

Notice that the goalkeeper in figure 7.6 is positioned with both feet parallel to the side line with chest and feet facing downfield. It is difficult to make a quick, determined movement to the ball from such a position. Instead, the goalkeeper should take a position to deal with crosses by turning to face the opponent likely to cross the ball.

This allows the goalkeeper to make a rapid and decisive movement to the ball if it is

Figure 7.5 Making a fist.

Figure 7.6 The wrong starting position for crosses.

played into the near-post area. If the ball is crossed to the far-post area from the right wing goal, then the goalkeeper should follow the flight of the ball with the eyes and at the same time take the right foot back and the left foot across the body in a cross-step action. The goalkeeper might have to repeat this cross-step movement more than once.

If the ball is catchable the goalkeeper should attempt to catch it, but if there is any doubt the goalkeeper should help it on its flight path by swinging a straight left arm with outstretched fingers to lift and accelerate the ball (figure 7.7). If the goalkeeper cannot get to the ball or if there is heavy traffic of players at the far-post area, he or she should take a new position as in figure 7.8.

Distributing the Ball

With possession of the ball the goalkeeper can mount an immediate counterattack. The goalkeeper can distribute the ball with either

the feet or the hands. In most instances the goalkeeper will throw the ball. There are several different forms of throws:

- Underarm roll pass
- Push pass
- Overarm throw

Underarm roll pass.   If the goalkeeper has the opportunity of playing (passing) the ball to an unmarked teammate within a 10-to-30-yard range, often the best means of distribution is by using the underarm roll.

In executing the underarm roll the goalkeeper should concentrate on both accuracy and speed of the pass. The goalkeeper should deliver the ball to the exact spot a teammate indicates, through body movement, where he or she would like to receive the ball. The goalkeeper should also roll the ball at the appropriate speed whereby the teammate has the optimum opportunity to control it before being closed down by an opponent. The underarm roll pass is seldom played straight down the length of the field; usually, it is made to a wide player.

Push pass.   If the goalkeeper has the opportunity of throwing the ball to an unmarked teammate within a 20-to-40-yard range, then often the best means of distribution is by using the push pass (throw).

From holding the ball in the hands the goalkeeper takes it up to the throwing shoulder and straightens the elbow vigorously to propel the ball with the palm and fingers of the throwing hand. The other hand is used to balance the ball. The fingers of the throwing hand can also impart a slight spin on the ball by turning slightly clockwise immediately before the release. This allows the goalkeeper to "bend" the ball off the first bounce into the stride path of the receiving player.

Overarm throw.   This is by far the most common throw made by goalkeepers. From holding the ball in both hands the goalkeeper takes it backward in the palm and fingers of the throwing hand until the throwing arm is straight. The goalkeeper then swings the arm vigorously upward and forward, releasing the ball off the tips of the fingers. The advantage of the overarm throw is that it can be used to pass the ball over the heads of opposing players.

With practice the goalkeeper can also impart spin on the ball by "cutting" it off the

Figure 7.7   Helping the ball on its flight path.

Figure 7.8 Realigning the basic set position.

fingers; the little finger is pulled toward the ground a split second before release.

 OVER MY HEAD

Peter Schmeichel, Manchester United's Danish-born goalkeeper, has a prodigious overarm throw. He is capable of throwing the ball some 60 to 80 yards and brings gasps from the crowd whenever he uses this means of distribution. Very often, Manchester United has been able to begin its attack on the opponent's goal as a result of one of Schmeichel's long throws, often resulting in exhilarating end-to-end play. At the same time opponents have recognized the potency of Schmeichel's arm if they press up too much, and we often find Manchester United's opponents reluctant to advance in numbers up the field.

Sweeper

Most defensive units like to assume a triangular shape when faced with two opposing forwards. Two marking backs and one uncommitted player form the triangle (figure 7.9). In cases when the opponent uses three forwards, the defensive unit will assume the shape of a diamond with three marking backs and one uncommitted player.

The uncommitted player, or sweeper, is just that—uncommitted, with no assigned marking duties. The sweeper is the last defender, since he or she plays mostly behind the marking backs. From this position, the sweeper is the ideal person to direct the marking backs and other players helping on defense. For this reason alone, the sweeper should be an above-average player.

Besides directing the defense, the sweeper is also responsible for providing cover to the player challenging for the ball and, if the situation warrants, to double-team an opponent with a marking defender. The sweeper guards against unmarked players coming through, through passes behind the marking backs, and combination plays like a wall pass (one-two) that might beat the marking backs.

The sweeper's job is difficult. The position requires a player with a variety of skills and attributes.

Figure 7.9   The white sweeper (#10) moves to support one of the marking backs (#16), where she anticipates the ball will be played.

Sweeper Skills and Attributes

Most of the outstanding sweepers will have the following attributes:

- They are good "readers" of the game with the uncanny ability to anticipate the opponent's next move.
- They are intelligent with excellent analytical skills.
- They are well organized both on and off the field.
- They have leadership qualities and often take the role of team captain.
- They are good communicators.
- They have good ball skills.
- They can kick the ball well with either foot.
- They are good headers of the ball.
- They have good speed.

The sweeper is a key player in any defense and should take charge of most of the organization and reorganization of the team's defensive unit. The sweeper should constantly communicate with the marking backs and stopper(s) so that the defensive organization remains finely tuned throughout the match. The purpose of verbal connection with the marking backs is to ensure that whenever the opponents are likely to regain possession of the ball that the marking backs will be in good marking positions. This communication should take place just before the team loses ball possession. The sweeper should prepare for the worst.

The sweeper should be a level-headed player. A sweeper who loses his or her temper easily, or who retaliates, can be a liability since he or she often works close to or in the penalty area. A sweeper's misbehavior could result in costly free kicks or penalties.

Whenever an opposing team plays with three forwards the sweeper should instruct one of the stoppers to become the third marking back. If the opposing team plays with two forwards only two marking backs will be required, allowing the stopper to fill the space in front of the marking backs but behind the other midfielders.

Marking Backs

The job of marking just one player during a match may seem easy. Being a marking back, however, is probably one of the more difficult jobs. Knowing when and where to mark takes a good amount of intelligence and tactical awareness. Reading an action before it happens is another skill. The marking back should also know when and how to contain an opponent, stop the opponent from turning, and if turned, how to tackle the ball away.

 HOW PELE TAUGHT HOWE

Bobby Howe, presently the director of coaching for the Washington State Youth Soccer Association, tells a story of how he was assigned the duty of marking Pele in a match in England. He had been instructed that when the ball was played to Pele not to try to intercept. Instead, Howe was asked to contain him and stop him from turning with the ball. The instruction was based on the fact that Pele most always moved to the ball and through good body positioning would screen the marking back off the ball.

Bobby was surprised that when the first two balls were played to Pele, he did not move to the ball but instead waited for it. Bobby got bold and when the third ball was played to Pele, Bobby stepped in to intercept. Of course that was the moment Pele had been waiting for. He too stepped in, screened Bobby off the ball, turned with it, and delivered a nice shot at goal.

Marking Back Skills and Attributes

The best marking backs will have the following attributes:

- They are fast.
- They are aggressive and extremely competitive.
- They are strong and usually are tall.
- They relish body contact.
- They can concentrate on a task for a long time.
- They can kick the ball well with either foot.
- They are good headers of the ball.

By far the most important skill for any marking back is positioning relative to the immediate opponent and the ball. Most of the top marking backs, such as those in the Italian Serie A League, have their positioning worked out so that they can get to their immediate opponent just before that player receives the ball, yet be close enough to other opposing players that they can offer a degree of cover to the nearest defender (figure 7.10). Marking backs should also be willing to take

Figure 7.10 The white marking back (#9) is in good position to intercept a pass to the dark forward (#18).

direction and submit to the leadership of their sweeper and sometimes the goalkeeper.

Marking backs should understand that their problems virtually end if they can prevent their immediate opponent from receiving the ball, but their problems have just begun if they allow that to happen.

Stoppers

The role of the stopper(s) is to fill the space in front of the defense and cut off the supply of passes to the opposing forwards. The stopper should also act as a "sweeper" behind the midfield by offering defensive cover.

Stopper Skills and Attributes

Most of the better stoppers have the following attributes:

- They are very disciplined.
- They are fiercely competitive.
- They are extremely mobile with good speed and endurance.

- They are quick into the tackle.
- They are comfortable when the ball is in front of them. They play better when facing the opposing goal rather than with their backs to it.
- They are good passers of the ball.
- They are extremely good headers of the ball, meeting most punts or goal kicks of the opposing goalkeeper.

The stopper can often be thought of as the sweeper's foot soldier. The stopper should respond to the sweeper's instructions and fill the space in front of the marking backs, thus cutting off the supply of passes to the opposing forwards.

Whenever the ball reaches an opposing forward player, the stopper should "defend from the front" and sandwich the opposing player between himself or herself and the marking back (figure 7.11).

The stopper should also meet any opposing midfield player who attempts to dribble the ball into the area defended by the marking backs and the sweeper. The stopper should realize that if he or she is beaten by

Figure 7.11   The white stopper's (#10) position cuts off the passing lane to the dark forward (#18).

this dribbler then a major crisis will develop for the sweeper and marking backs.

Probably the skill that distinguishes the world's best stoppers, such as DeSailly from AC Milan or Dunga from Brazil, is their ability to track down opposing players who attempt to move into the space behind them. Such stoppers are extremely sensitive to any opposing player who attempts to move into the space behind them, while lesser players seldom notice opponents drifting into such vital spaces.

Stoppers are sometimes described as defensive midfielders, although defensive midfielders' responsibilities are not always restricted to the regular responsibilities of a stopper. The overwhelming function of a stopper is to *stop* both passes and opposing players, particularly opposing dribblers.

Wide Midfielders

Many coaches will place their weakest players in the wide midfield positions. This can often be a mistake and hurt the team both on attack and on defense. We will talk about their role on attack later. For now you should realize that these players are sometimes isolated from any immediate defensive cover, and the opponents can mount some telling offensive moves down the flanks. If the outside midfielder has been beaten the marking back and sweeper are in serious trouble. The marking back and sweeper now may have to contend with superior numbers on the flank and possible overlaps.

Wide Midfielder Skills and Attributes

In reality the wide midfield player must fulfill the requirements of three different positions at different times in the same match—wing back, wide midfield, and winger. First they should concentrate on the defensive aspect of all these positions. The best wide midfielders have the following attributes:

- They mark goalside and inside when the opponents have possession.
- They have great speed and endurance.

- They take up good covering positions when the opponents have possession on the opposite side of the field.
- They are good long passers of the ball.
- They can close down opponents without overcommitting.
- They know when to challenge and when to delay.

Wide midfield players defend a long narrow space on the side of the field some 70 to 80 yards long and 10 to 20 yards wide. They should concern themselves primarily with getting into good defensive position—goalside and inside—immediately *before* their team loses the ball. They will normally be required to cover a large area of the field so they must maintain their speed and endurance at a high level.

Attacking Midfielders (Playmakers)

I am reluctant to use the term "attacking midfielder" as this often presupposes that such a player does not defend. On the contrary, it is the duty of every player on the team to work hard to regain ball possession. Too often, I find so-called attacking midfield players and forwards standing around when the ball is lost and expecting others on the team to win the ball back.

Attacking Midfielder (Playmaker) Skills and Attributes

Some of the world's greatest soccer stars have been attacking midfielders (playmakers) such as Platini, Charlton, Dalglish, Cruyff, Baggio, Zico, and so on. Many of them had the following attributes:

- They shared in their team's defensive organization and could force the opposing team to play down channels and into their team's defensive strength.
- They were extremely fit, psychologically tough, and could tackle and take tackles without protestation or remonstration.

Probably the greatest single defensive skill that an attacking midfielder (playmaker) will show is the ability to calculate whether the forwards should press and harass to regain ball possession or whether they should drop back and regroup with the other members of their team. It is as if the playmaker has the uncanny knack of predicting what will happen to the ball a second or two before the event. The player can read from the posture of the opponent on the ball, from the positions of the supporting opposing players, and from the positions of teammates whether to give immediate chase by challenging hard for the ball or whether to retreat into a compact defensive unit farther back down the field. The attacking midfielder (playmaker) will convey the decision to teammates and they will respond accordingly.

Forwards

The coaches of most of the world's top teams would regard the forwards as the first line of defense. There is a great deal of merit in this as it is much easier to defend against a team that is forced to play down one channel of the field. If the forward(s) can harass the opposing defense and prevent it from passing the ball back and forth across the field, then it is easier for all the players behind the forwards to work out the channel where the ball will likely be advanced (figure 7.12).

All the players behind the forwards—midfielder(s), stopper(s), marking back(s), sweeper, and goalkeeper—can adjust their positions depending on how the forwards force the play.

Forward Skills and Attributes

Top-class forwards will have the following attributes:

- They are prepared to help their team on defense.
- They know how to challenge and when to commit.
- They know how to position themselves to take away the opponent's options.
- They know how to mark space.
- They know how to delay.
- They anticipate well and have good reaction speed.
- They have the ability to disguise their defensive intentions.

Figure 7.12   White is attacking. The dark forwards move into position to cut off the passing lanes to white #10 and white #9.

Forwards are expected to score most of their team's goals, but in the modern game forwards are also expected to play their part in defending. The defensive work of a team's midfield and defense is made infinitely easier if the team's forwards can harass the opposing players in possession of the ball and force them to play it down a well-defended area of the field. Forwards act as police officers who direct the traffic down certain roadways and prevent it from going down other roadways.

Summary

How well your team plays defensively will largely determine its success. Teams at the top of the league standings are usually the ones with the best defenses. This chapter highlights the following points to help you better understand the defensive skills and techniques needed by all players. It includes an explanation of specific skills and attributes for the various positions.

- All players have defensive duties and responsibilities.
- Players must have a keen understanding of the specific defensive duties and responsibilities of their positions.
- The goalkeeper is the single most important player in determining your tactical plan.
- Train goalkeepers to determine the correct position for all eventualities, stop shots, deal with crosses, distribute effectively, and cooperate with the defense.
- The sweeper must take charge of the team's defensive unit.
- Positioning is of utmost importance to the marking backs.
- The stopper's main job is to cut off the supply of balls to opposing forwards.
- The stopper should also be considered as a sweeper behind the midfield.
- The wide midfielders' primary concern is to get into a good defensive position immediately before ball possession is lost by the team.
- The attacking midfielder(s) must be able to judge when to stay up or when to drop back, depending on the action of their forwards.
- Forwards often are the first line of defense. They must be willing to help their team on defense.

Chapter 8

Teaching
Defensive Skills

Your players should always anticipate the loss of ball possession and guard against a possible counterattack, but at the moment the team actually loses the ball all players should think and act defensively. Thus, if the team loses the ball in its attacking third of the field, the forwards are the first line of defense. All players, from goalkeeper to sweeper to forwards, must learn to understand and perform defensive roles and responsibilities. They need to fully understand when role changes occur (transition) and what responsibilities they should assume.

The players must understand the importance of positioning, the significance of defensive shape, the purpose of distances and angles when marking or covering (supporting), the techniques of tackling, and when to leave their defensive positions to support or participate in the attack.

While all players should be aware of their defensive responsibilities, key defensive players, like the goalkeeper, sweeper, stopper(s), marking defenders, and any other player(s) with specific defensive duties, should be given the opportunity to solve defensive problems through matchlike practices you design.

To help you with those practices, and before going into teaching defensive skills, I will discuss small-sided, conditioned games and coaching in the game. Both tools have significant value and are highly effective when teaching defensive skills or, for that matter, any skill.

Small-Sided, Conditioned Games

In this kind of game you reduce the number of players from the usual 11 per team. You also introduce an additional condition that emphasizes the technique or skill you want to work on that forces the players into repeated responses to the condition. For instance, when practicing passing, the condition is "No more than three seconds on the ball for the player in possession." It will reduce the amount of dribbling and speed up ball movement from one player to another.

If we ask some of the greatest soccer players in the world, who might have been raised in Europe, Latin America, or Africa, how they learned to play the game successfully, they answer that they learned through repeated small-sided situations. Not only that, as young players they often would impose on these small-sided pickup games their own conditions, such as "Maximum of two touches on the ball for each player in each possession."

As coaches, we should learn from these answers and not spend too much time on "drills," which are far more appropriate for static games of the stop-start type. Soccer coaches should consider themselves *play architects* who design simple, fun-filled, small-sided, conditioned games that help young players learn through repeated, spontaneous, and continuous activity.

Coaching in the Game

The method of coaching I adopt during small-sided, conditioned games is "coaching in the game." With this method you instruct or advise the players regarding their defensive positioning immediately before or as the play develops. You should refrain from stopping the play and analyzing it after the event or from giving a sermon on what the players should have done. Rather, you must help them recognize cues in the "picture" as it develops so that they can make the appropriate decision to readjust or refine their defensive positioning.

I often find coaches focusing on the activity on the ball during practices. This is a mistake. The player on the ball needs to give undivided attention to the immediate task at hand; the player can't receive, assimilate, and react to coaching instruction when already fully engaged, both mentally and physically, in a confrontational situation. The timing of the instruction is wrong and will lead to stress.

Instead, you should focus your attention on players some distance from the ball. In this way, you will be able to analyze the defensive organization and deliver your instructions so that players have time to receive, assimilate, and react to them before the ball arrives. Your instructions should give players an opportunity to make the appropriate decisions. Make them aware that their defensive positioning depends on what is happening on the ball and the movement of other players.

You should be careful not to overcoach. At times it is necessary for young players to make mistakes so that they can learn from them.

When using the coaching-in-the-game method, you will occasionally need to freeze the play. On a given command—a shout of "stop" or a blow on the whistle—the players freeze in their positions. You can then point out to all the players some general coaching point you wish to make before resuming play. Use this coaching method sparingly. Overuse can lead to boredom and frustration among the players.

The coaching-in-the-game method puts a high premium on the coach's ability to analyze situations, make decisions, and deliver instructions in a split second. Not all coaches may presently have the skill to coach effectively through this method. However, they can develop the skill through practice. Strive to improve by observing other coaches, attending clinics, reading books, viewing videos, and so forth. In other words, while at present coaching in the game may be difficult, you can learn it.

DIFFERENT SKILLS

When coaching at the University of Liverpool in England, I had a visiting professor of botany from the University of Wisconsin as my next-door neighbor. We struck up a strong friendship, and each Sunday afternoon we would take a long walk together along the local country lanes. He would delight in pointing out to me the various species of wildflowers, shrubs, and trees, and accompanied each identification with a wealth of detailed information. Still, I saw only weeds, wildflowers, shrubs, and trees.

I later found out that the professor's son played soccer in Wisconsin so I decided to invite the professor to a Liverpool FC's midweek game. During the excitement of the game I would talk aloud and comment on aspects of the game: "Why doesn't the Liverpool defense play farther forward?" "Someone needs to close down their #10," "Liverpool must get the ball forward more quickly," and so forth. I sometimes caught him glancing at me with a puzzled look. He didn't understand or recognize what I was looking at. He simply followed the ball or looked at the activities of the famous KOP, which is the enclosure at one end of Liverpool's Anfield stadium where some 20,000 fanatical supporters cheer on their beloved Liverpool team.

Obviously the professor wouldn't have made a good coach in the game. But then I certainly would have flunked a botany exam. Both of us could have learned to become better in the other's specialty.

Basic Defensive Positioning

All players must understand that when the ball is lost, the opposing player now in possession has only three options—shoot, dribble, or pass. If your team loses the ball in your attacking third (their defensive third), a shot at your goal is highly unlikely. That leaves but two options—dribble or pass. Defenders are taught not to take risks in their defensive third of the field, so an attempt at dribbling through with the possibility of being stripped of the ball is also improbable. The only option left is to pass the ball. Here is one area where defensive positioning can play a vital role in winning the ball back. Cut off passing lanes. If the player with the ball has three passing options and your players take away two of them, the next touch on the ball becomes predictable. Your players may be able to intercept the ball

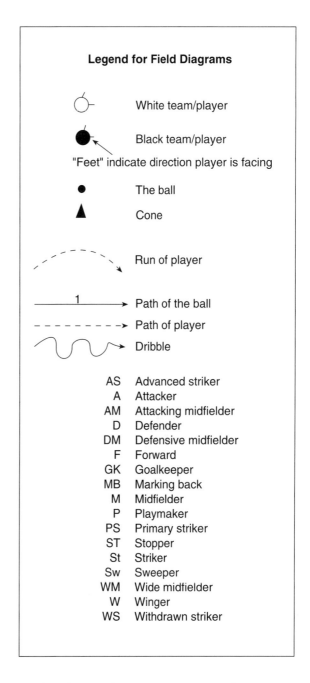

easily. If not, they can put immediate pressure on the targeted player.

In my opinion, defensive positioning is the most significant defensive skill you can teach. Defending players should know where to place themselves relative to opponents, teammates, and the ball at any given time. Sadly, positioning is not often thoroughly understood, and therefore its teaching is neglected.

In most instances, the position of a defending player should be goalside and inside the immediate opponent. Goalside is a position between the immediate opponent and the defending player's goal. Inside is a position between an imaginary line drawn from goal to goal and a line drawn from the immediate opponent toward the defending player's goal. Most young players understand what you mean by being goalside of their opponent but many have difficulty in understanding what you mean by being on the inside line. In my experience I found that most young players marked too tightly, too soon. I would often notice marking situations as shown in figure 8.1.

The white marking backs are marking much too tightly and are in no position to cut off passes through the middle of the defense. Moreover, they are not marking on the inside line. In figure 8.2 both marking backs have stepped into the *inside* position, thereby cutting off the passing lane through the middle of the defense. The wide midfielders have also readjusted their marking positions.

Another key factor in defending is the distance between the defending player and the immediate opponent relative to what is happening on the ball. The defender should take up a position based on these factors: How far away is the ball? Who has the ball?

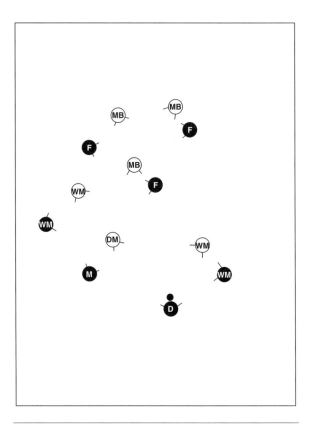

Figure 8.2 Goalside and inside.

Which way is the player in possession facing? In general, the farther away the ball, the greater the distance between the defending player and the opponent; the nearer the ball, the closer the distance between the defending player and the opponent.

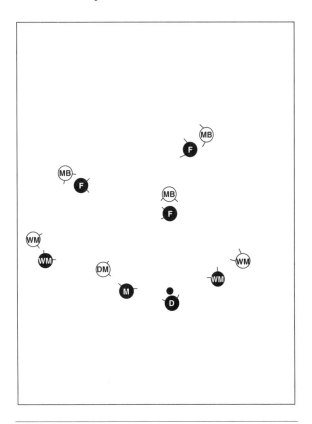

Figure 8.1 Goalside, but outside.

Rules of Defensive Positioning

As a general rule, defending players should concentrate on being

- goalside,
- inside, and
- at a distance from their opponent(s) where they will be first to every ball played behind them but close enough
  1. to intercept any inaccurate or underhit passes; then, if not possible,
  2. to *challenge* strongly for the ball; then, if not possible,
  3. to *jockey*, to delay the opponent, by retreating to take up the space between the opponent and the goal.

I have listed the three responses in priority order although I still find some coaches teaching jockeying first. To intercept should be top priority. If that is not possible then the defending player should still be in a position to challenge and possibly dispossess. Jockeying should be the concern only of a defending player who has been caught out of position or is outnumbered by opponents and needs to delay until help arrives.

Confined to Base—A Six-a-Side, Conditioned Game

Purpose. To develop defensive positioning.

Procedure. Each team has a goalkeeper, three defenders, and two attackers (figure 8.3). The goalkeeper and the three defenders are restricted to the defensive half of the field while the two attackers can play only in the attacking half of the field. Only the attackers can score. Players can pass the ball backward or forward across the halfway line. The object of the game is to get the ball quickly and accurately to one of the two attackers.

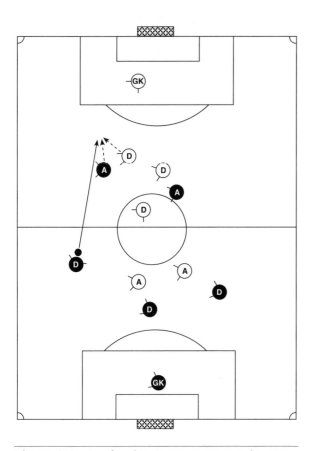

Figure 8.3 Confined to Base—a six-a-side, conditioned game to develop defensive positioning.

Coaching Points.

• Have the three defenders adopt a defensive shape of two defenders marking on a player-to-player basis with the third defender taking on the role of a covering player (sweeper).

• Try to get the players to establish their defensive shape when their attacking teammates are in possession and are attacking the opponent's goal. The defenders should not wait for their team to turn over the ball before thinking of defensive positioning.

• When their team is in possession of the ball the defenders should deliver early, accurate passes to their attackers.

• Insist that the goalkeeper help organize the defense so that it maintains an optimum defensive shape.

Understanding Defensive Responsibilities

The sweeper, marking backs, and forwards all have defensive responsibilities. The sweeper and marking backs should understand the need for defending in a triangular shape. The forwards must realize that their defensive actions dictate the actions of the rest of the team.

Triangle

The optimum defensive shape for the sweeper and the two marking backs is a triangle with the free defender—the sweeper—forming the apex of the triangle (figure 8.4). Defenders should ensure that they can get into a good defensive shape before their attackers lose the ball. Too often, we find defenders watching the game, waiting until their team turns over the ball before organizing their defensive positions. Usually, this is too late. Much of the focus in the initial stages of this small-sided, conditioned game will be on the defense of the team with the ball. Do they take up good support positions if the attackers choose to pass the ball backward? More important, do they organize themselves into a defensive shape whereby it is very difficult for their opponents to mount a counterattack? The goalkeeper and the sweeper should, of

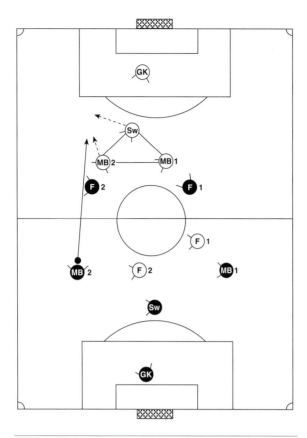

Figure 8.4 The defensive triangle.

course, take most of the responsibility of organizing the two marking backs into an optimum defensive shape.

I usually concentrate on coaching all the players in the team without the ball to think defensively. Without question, the first line of defense in the above activity is the two attackers. Once they lose the ball they should immediately focus on winning back the ball or forcing the play into their team's defensive strength. Forwards should understand that they are the first line of defense. All marking and covering positions behind them are dictated by the forwards' defensive posture (or lack of it).

The decision of whether to try to win back the ball immediately is a judgment call for the two attackers. They should calculate whether to risk going after the ball or whether to drop goalside of the ball. In all events they should learn how to work as a defensive pair; if they decide to try to win back the ball they are much more likely to succeed if they work together. A forward chasing after the ball on his or her own is unlikely to win back the ball without the support of his or her teammates.

Forwards should recognize that the way in which they force the play dictates to a large extent the positions (angles and distances) that their defenders take in marking and covering. For example, in figure 8.5 the two white forwards have forced black marking back 1 to play the ball down the right side of the field. This makes it easy for white marking back 1 and the white sweeper to mark and cover the left side of their defense. Since it is unlikely that black marking back 1 can pass the ball to black forward 2, it is easier for white marking back 2 to work the marking position (distance and angle). It would be very risky for black marking back 1 to pass the ball to either the black sweeper or black marking back 2.

In the small-sided, conditioned game outlined in figure 8.6 the white sweeper can concentrate on whether to double-team or not. If the receiving opponent has received the ball in a position where he or she cannot see a teammate and is heavily pressured by a marking defender, then it is an ideal opportunity for the sweeper to double-team. Double teaming is much more effective if the cover-

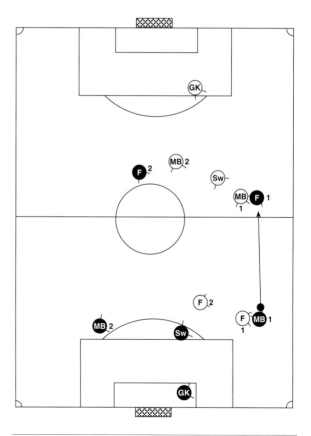

Figure 8.5 Forcing the play down a channel.

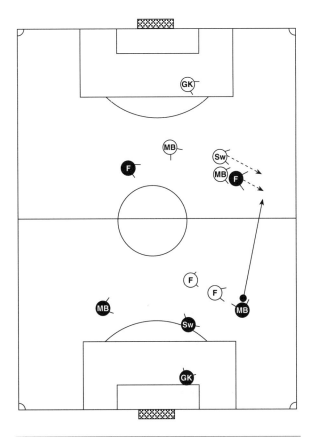

Figure 8.6 A double-teaming situation.

ing defender—the sweeper—communicates with the challenging defender and encourages the defender to win the ball. The mere fact that there is communication allows the challenging player to be more risky and aggressive in trying to win the ball, as the sound of the sweeper's voice has indicated roughly where the sweeper is likely to be.

Distances and Angles

The distance and angles between the challenging player and the covering player in a double-team situation are critical. If they are too far apart then it is possible for the opponent to evade the challenger, even stumble, but still have time to recover and take on the covering player.

Conversely, if the distance between the challenging player and the covering player is too tight, then it is possible for the opponent to beat both players with the same move or dribble.

Of course, the sweeper (covering defender) has a bigger role in the team than merely double teaming. The sweeper's biggest prob-

lem arises when an unmarked opposing midfield player has the ball and is running at the defense (figure 8.7). The white sweeper can resolve this crisis in one of two ways, either by coming forward to challenge the opposing midfielder or by instructing one of the marking backs to step forward to challenge while the sweeper steps up to mark. In figure 8.8 white marking back 1 goes to meet opposing black midfielder 1 while the white sweeper steps up to mark black forward 1.

Limited Freedom—A Seven-a-Side, Conditioned Game

Purpose. To develop defensive responsibilities of midfield players and sweepers.

Procedure. Each team has a goalkeeper, three defenders, and two attackers. The goalkeeper and the three defenders are restricted to the defensive half of the field while the two attackers can play only in the attacking half of the field. In addition, each team has one extra player who can play anywhere on the field without restriction.

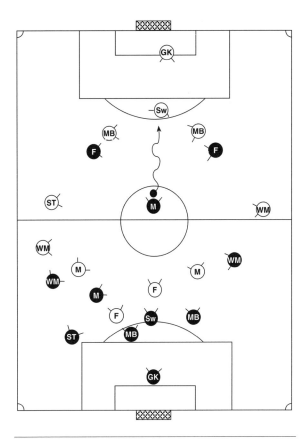

Figure 8.7 A crisis situation for the sweeper.

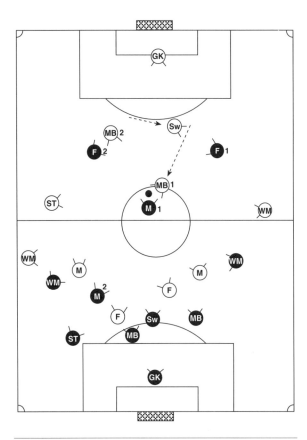

Figure 8.8 Resolving the crisis by stepping forward.

Coaching Points.

• The covering player (sweeper) and the goalkeeper should ensure that the two marking backs take up a position goalside and on the inside line of their immediate opponents before the opposing defense plays the ball forward. Additionally, they should communicate with their unrestricted player (the midfielder) to ensure that he or she will decide whether it is prudent to go forward or safer to remain in a defensive position, depending on what is happening on the ball and the position of other players.

• The midfielder who is repeatedly caught on the wrong side of the ball and has to make recovery runs to get goalside of the opponent causes problems of crisis proportions for himself or herself, for the marking backs, and for the sweeper. For instance, in figure 8.9 the white sweeper might have to step up to meet the black midfielder and try to delay the play until the white midfielder has recovered into a covering position. In reality the white midfielder has now become the sweeper and, until the ball is cleared, must remain in this position.

It is likely that the defenses in the six-a-side game outlined in figure 8.3 will have prevailed, particularly if all five field players learned to play together as a defensive unit by forcing the play and double teaming. But the addition of a player on each team who can cover the whole field means that it is likely that the smarter and more skillful player of these two will dictate the game.

The smarter player of these two players will decide when it is prudent to go forward and when it is safer to remain in a defensive position, depending on what is happening on the ball and the positions of other players. For instance, in figure 8.9 the white team had been on attack, and the white midfielder had entered the black team's half to support the attack. Reading early that the white team was going to lose possession, the black midfielder drifted toward the halfway line. Black indeed gained possession and quickly played the ball to the black midfielder. The white midfielder is caught upfield. A dangerous situation has developed because the white sweeper must step up to meet the

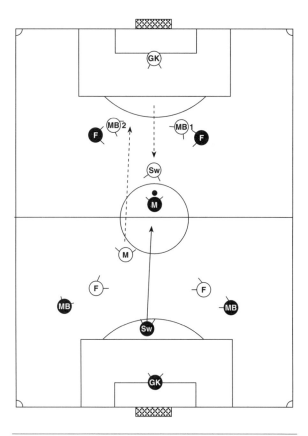

Figure 8.9 Stepping up to meet the challenge and interchanging positions.

opposing midfield player and try to delay the play until the white midfielder recovers into a covering position.

Almost Free—An Eight-a-Side, Conditioned Game

Purpose. To develop the defensive responsibilities of the team.

Procedure. Each team has a goalkeeper, three defenders, and two attackers. The goalkeeper and the three defenders are restricted to playing in the defensive half of the field while the two attackers can play only in the attacking half of the field. In addition, each team has two extra players who can play anywhere on the field without restriction.

Coaching Points.

• You should focus your attention on the activities of the four players who can play anywhere on the field without restriction. The smarter, more skillful, more disciplined combination of players in the two-versus-two situation will probably dictate the outcome of the game. When their team loses ball possession, or is likely to lose it, you must insist that they do the following:

a. Take up marking or covering positions behind their forwards depending on what is happening on the ball. Insist that the forwards give immediate chase when they lose the ball.

b. Challenge the player on the ball and force the play to one side of the field.

c. Cut off the passing lanes to the opposing forwards.

d. Cover each other and communicate with each other.

e. Track down any opposing midfield player who runs into the space behind them and who might receive the ball.

f. Delay opponents when outnumbered.

In figure 8.10 you can see that the players have successfully carried out coaching points a, b, c, and d. All black players upfield from black marking back 1 are marked goalside and inside by their white opponents. The angles and distances are about correct. White forward 1 is pressuring black marking back 1. Also note that white forward 2 has taken a position so that a pass to the black sweeper or black marking back 2 is dangerous. The excellent marking and positioning of the white players allows black marking back 1

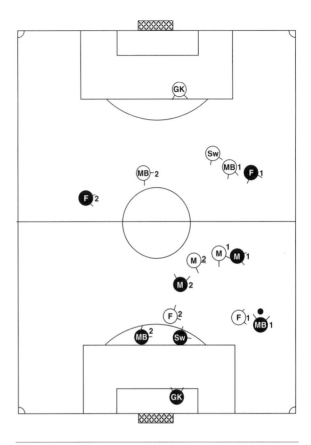

Figure 8.10 Forcing the play to one side of the field.

only two options—to play the ball to black forward 1 or to black midfielder 1. White marking back 1 and the white sweeper anticipate the first option and are ready to intercept, challenge, and if necessary double-team black forward 1. Similarly, white midfielder 1 is in a good position to close down black midfielder 1 if the second option is taken.

In figure 8.11, point e is satisfied when white midfielder 2 tracks down black midfielder 2, who is attempting to run into the space behind the white midfield. In figure 8.12, point f is satisfied. White midfielder 2 has to mark space and delay until white midfielder 1 gets back into a marking position against black midfielder 2. Note white midfielder 2's marking position. Should black marking back 1 play the ball to black midfielder 1, white midfielder 2 can close down and delay black midfielder 1 until white midfielder 1 has recovered. Should black marking back 1 attempt to play to black midfielder 2 (white forward 1 will probably prevent that), white midfielder 2 can close down black midfielder 2.

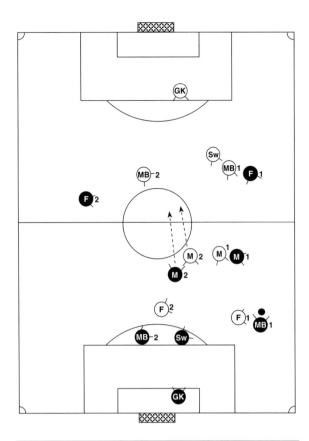

Figure 8.11 Tracking down.

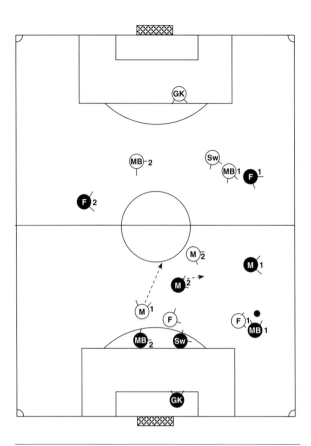

Figure 8.12 Delaying the opponents when outnumbered.

It is not only the two white midfield players in the two-versus-two situation in the previous conditioned game who will have greater difficulty in making successful defensive decisions. It now becomes more difficult for the white sweeper to decide when to double-team and when not to double-team, which covering angle to take, when to step up and when to stay, and when and what to communicate.

It also becomes more difficult for the white marking backs to determine their optimum marking position (distance and angle). For example, in figure 8.13 they can mark differently—shoulder to shoulder, and on the inside line—when the ball is too far away to be kicked into the space behind them. Similarly, the sweeper's covering position will be much closer in this situation.

Free at Last—An Eight-a-Side, Conditioned Game

Purpose. To develop defensive decision making for defenders and midfielders.

Procedure. Each team has a goalkeeper, three defenders, and two attackers. The goalkeeper and the three defenders are restricted to

playing in the defensive half of the field while the two attackers can only play in the attacking half of the field. In addition, each team has two extra players who can play anywhere on the field without restriction. You also allow one of the three defenders to go forward into the opponent's half of the field when his or her team is attacking. Normally, you would expect a defender other than the one who passed the ball to be in the best position to go forward (figure 8.14).

Coaching Points.

• In figure 8.14, black marking back 2 has passed the ball to black forward 2, but it is black marking back 1 who is in the best situation to go forward since this player will probably get in behind the line of vision of the white defenders who are facing the action on the ball.

• It becomes a judgment call by black marking back 1 whether to go forward or stay in a defensive position in his or her half of the field. Black marking back 1 will have to consider whether the ball is likely to get to him or her from black forward 2, or following

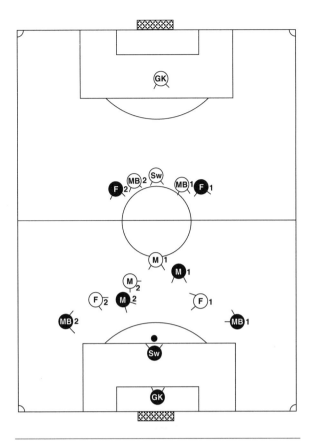

Figure 8.13 Marking shoulder to shoulder.

a pass from black forward 2 to another teammate. Black marking back 1, if going forward, must also consider how and when the black sweeper and black marking back 2 will readjust their marking positions. Normally, the sweeper should encourage the marking back to go if the chances of getting the ball are good, and to stay if the risk of losing the ball is great. If the sweeper encourages the marking back to go, the sweeper should immediately step up and mark white forward 1 (figure 8.15). Black marking back 2 should also readjust marking position relative to white forward 2.

• If the ball is lost and goes out of play for an opposition goal kick or throw-in, then black marking back 1 has time to get back into the usual marking back role. If the ball is lost in transitional play, however, the marking back might have to make a recovery run, into a defensive covering position, at speed. The marking back has now effectively changed roles with the sweeper, who in the meantime is performing the role of a marking back.

It becomes obvious from the preceding analysis of some simple events that occur

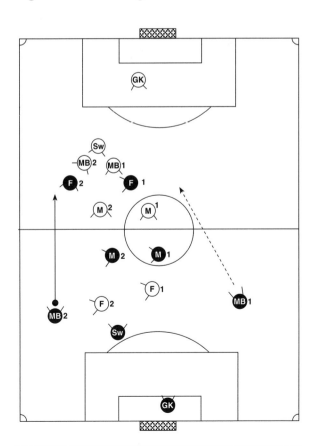

Figure 8.14 Attacking on the blind side.

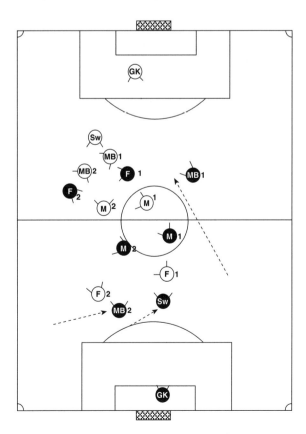

Figure 8.15 Readjusting the defensive shape.

repeatedly in soccer that all players must understand and perform the defensive roles and responsibilities of all positions. At any given time in the game a player will have either to mark or to cover, and players must learn to communicate with each other so that they form the best possible defensive combinations. The following are some ideas and guidelines that will help you develop defensive techniques and skills.

Tips for Teaching Defensive Techniques and Skills

You should
- constantly reinforce the belief that some of the world's greatest soccer players have been defenders—Bobby Moore, Franz Beckenbauer, Franco Baresi, Paulo Maldini, Carlos Alberto, and so forth,
- insist that all players take their part in any defensive plan,
- spend at least 50 percent of practice time on defensive skills and tactics,
- introduce practice activities and competitions whereby the winner(s) is the one who does the best defensively (e.g., concedes the fewest goals), and
- reward players and teams who have been the most successful in accomplishing defensive tasks.

Defensive Skills and Techniques Activities

I have refrained from describing the following activities as drills. The word suggests a military situation in which instructors condition recruits to respond to their commands. Rather, we should think of practice time as not only a fun-filled occasion but also an opportunity for lots of activity through which players learn from their decision making. We cannot produce creative, imaginative, or skillful soccer players through drills.

The following are some suggested activities that you can use to develop defensive techniques and skills.

Continuous One-Versus-One

Purpose. To develop defensive techniques and skills of marking players.

Procedure. A goalkeeper guards each goal and a team of players lines up behind each goal, with the goals placed 40 yards apart. The first player in the black team comes out and when he or she crosses the midline, the first player in the white team attacks with the ball to try to score on the black goalkeeper. If the ball goes out of play or if either goalkeeper gets the ball, the game ends. Then, immediately, the next player in the white team comes out and crosses the midline, and the second player in the black team advances to try to score on the white goal, and so on.

Coaching Points.
- Ask the defender to come out at speed but in the final five yards or so to get into a sideways-on, jockeying position (figure 8.16).
- The defender should take a position to force the attacker to go the way the defender chooses.
- Get the defender to use fake challenges to upset the attacker's balance.
- Explain how the defender should lean slightly away from the attacker so that the

Figure 8.16 A sideways-on jockeying position.

defender can push off the front foot vigorously to accelerate into the space behind him or her.

• The defender should always attempt to get into the space between the attacker and the ball when it is pushed past him or her.

On Guard

Purpose. To develop the defensive techniques and skills of the last defender.

Procedure. A goalkeeper guards the goal and a team of players lines up on each side of that goal. The coach (or a player) stands some 40 yards from the goal with a supply of balls. The coach plays a ball into the space between himself or herself and the penalty box (18-yard line). When the coach plays the ball, the first player in each team races out to get to the ball and then tries to score a goal. The player without the ball acts as the defender.

Coaching Points.

• Demonstrate that the defender should prevent the opponent from turning with the ball and facing the goal.

• The defender should take a position just far enough away from the attacker (about an arm's length) so that he or she can see the ball (figure 8.17).

• The defender, however, should avoid using the arm to push the opponent, which would give away an unnecessary foul.

Continuous Two-Versus-Two

Purpose. To develop defensive techniques and skills of marking backs.

Procedure. Both of the preceding practices (activities) can be played with two defenders and two attackers.

Coaching Points.

• All the previous coaching points would apply to the defender challenging the ball.

• The covering defender should take up a position dependent on the position (distance and angle) of the challenging defender.

• The covering defender should communicate with the challenging defender and encourage him or her to win the ball, particularly when the passing lane to the second attacker has been cut off.

• The distance between the covering defender and the challenging defender will, in general, decrease the nearer the ball gets to shooting distance.

Figure 8.17 The white defender takes up a position just far enough away from the attacker—about an arm's length.

One-Versus-One Plus One

Purpose. To develop the technique and skill of forcing the play and covering.

Procedure. Mark two 10-yard squares out at the top of the penalty box (18-yard line). A defender guards each square and is not allowed to play outside that square (figure 8.18). A line of attacking players, each with a ball, waits to attack the defense. The attacker can take a shot on goal from anywhere inside either square or anywhere inside the penalty box. The immediate attack is over once the defenders have cleared the ball out of the two squares or the penalty area or the goalkeeper gets it.

Coaching Points.

• The first defender should go forward to meet the attack and adopt a sideways-on position to force the play to one side.

• The first defender should not commit to a tackle unless 100 percent sure of winning the ball.

• The first defender should stay with the opponent and force him or her into one of the back corners of the first square.

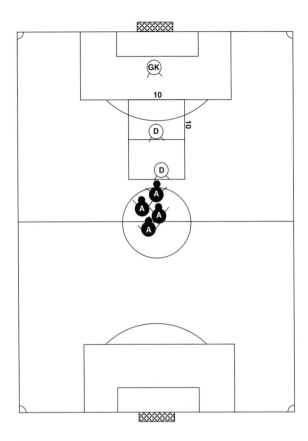

Figure 8.18   One-Versus-One Plus One—an activity that develops the technique of defensive covering.

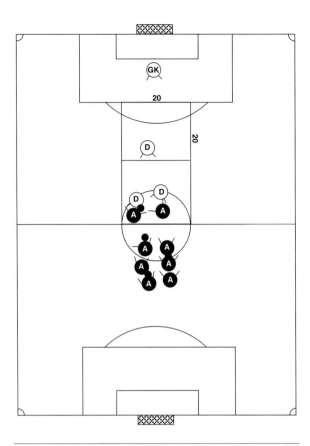

Figure 8.19   Two-Versus-Two Plus One—an activity that develops the understanding between the sweeper and the marking backs.

• The covering defender should communicate with the challenging defender and encourage the challenger to keep forcing the attacker to one side.

• The covering defender should play as far forward as possible in the second square and take up a covering angle depending on the play of the challenging defender.

• This is an excellent activity for practicing double teaming.

Two-Versus-Two Plus One

Purpose. To increase the level of understanding between sweeper and marking backs.

Procedure. Mark two 20-yard squares out at the top of the penalty box (18-yard line). Two defenders guard the first square and one defender guards the second square (figure 8.19). The attacking players form up in pairs on the halfway line and attempt to score a goal by shooting from inside either square or from inside the penalty box. The immediate attack is over once the defense has cleared

the ball out of the two squares or the penalty area or the goalkeeper gets it.

Coaching Points.

• The defensive player nearest the ball goes forward and takes up a sideways-on challenging position. This player should take a position to either cut off the pass to the second attacker (figure 8.20) or cut off the dribble into the space behind him or her.

• The nonchallenging defender in the first square must take up a position that considers the position (distance and angle) of the challenging defender and the movement of the second attacker.

• The third defender must communicate with the first two defenders and encourage them to force the play to the sides. The third defender plays as far forward as possible in the second square and anticipates the most likely direction of any successful attack.

• The goalkeeper's distance and angle from the goal will depend on the action on the ball.

The goalkeeper should play as far forward as possible without running the risk of having the ball kicked over him or her into the goal.

• Sweepers will benefit from this activity.

Tackling

An opponent receiving the ball should be under immediate pressure. If interception is not possible, the defender should at least prevent the attacking player from turning with the ball. However, there are many times in the match when a defending player may be caught out of position and the opposing, attacking player receives the ball cleanly, turns with it, and starts a run at the defending player. The defender must close down the attacking player immediately but with caution. Closing down means to get to and challenge the attacker from four to six feet away, sideways-on, in balance, with a low center of gravity, and with the body in a position to deny the attacking player the space he or she would like to attack.

Now is the time for the defending player to start looking for tackling opportunities. The pressure is on the player with the ball. The attacker must be creative but is slowed down by the defender, operates in restricted space, and sees the passing lanes being closed by the defender's teammates. Under these circumstances, it is highly likely that the attacking player will make a mistake. Until then, all the defending player has to do is wait patiently and then strip the attacker of the ball.

In some cases, when both the attacking and the defending player go for the ball, the defender should use a front block tackle. This kind of tackle requires the player to go in low, in balance, and with determination. If tackling with the right foot, the player should drop the right hip and bend the right knee so that on contact as much of the lower right leg as possible is behind the ball. After making contact the foot must keep pressure on the ball to squeeze it by the opponent. Whoever applies the tackle correctly will win the ball. Applying a front block tackle may involve some physical contact. Many players don't like that kind of contact and instead of blocking the ball with the lower leg will reach for it with the foot. That is ineffective and will result in ball loss.

A slide tackle can be effective, although it must be considered a last-ditch effort to dispossess an opponent of the ball. The

Figure 8.20   Cutting off the pass.

drawbacks are obvious—if the tackle fails, the opponent has the ball with the defender beaten and on the ground. If the player misapplies the tackle a direct free kick may result, or if it occurred in the penalty area, a penalty kick. The defender should execute the sliding tackle with the leg farthest from the opponent. It then becomes the upper leg (the leg closest to the opponent is under the tackling leg). The players can use the slide tackle to play the ball by using the instep to control the ball over the touchline, by passing to a teammate, or by controlling the ball with the instep and standing up with the ball in possession.

Tackling is timing. It takes a lot of practice. Practice slide tackling on a grassy wet field. If that's not possible, have your players wear old pairs of jeans.

Goalkeeper Skill and Technique Instruction

Goalkeepers play a significant part in winning and losing matches. The goalkeeper can make it difficult for the opponent to score, and through distribution of the ball can start attacks effectively. It is important that you take ample time to instruct the goalkeeper(s). Always work on hand technique and safety (protecting the ball). Allow no sloppiness in the practice—it will carry over into the match.

Progression of Skills and Techniques

The simplest distinction between skill and technique is to consider *technique* to be how to perform a movement or activity; *skill* is when, where, and which technique to use.

To develop skills and techniques, we recommend that you proceed from unopposed activities to opposed activities. It is much easier to succeed when unopposed. This success develops the necessary composure and confidence required when playing against opponents.

The simplest and most reassuring situation for any goalkeeper is having the ball safely tucked up in the arms. Warm-up activities for goalkeepers should always include numerous opportunities for them to tuck the ball away in their arms.

Tips for Teaching Goalkeeper Skills and Techniques

- Make sure that the goalkeeper is wearing the necessary injury prevention equipment, particularly to protect the thighs, knees, and elbows.
- Consider the ground conditions when choosing the content of your goalkeeping practice activity. Do not expect the goalkeeper to perform superbly on hard, sun-baked fields or in icy conditions. The body can absorb only so much jarring when the goalkeeper is practicing diving techniques.
- Prepare special practice areas for goalkeepers. Look for areas with a lush carpet of grass to place your portable goal, or water the area if it is sun-baked.
- Put down the field markings for a 6-yard and 18-yard box to help with goalkeeper positioning.
- Remember that the goalkeeper is both different and special in the team. The goalkeeper's performance will usually affect the outcome of a game.
- Encourage the goalkeeper to put in some extra training at the end of each practice. Make the goalkeeper feel special.

Goalkeepers should then progress to a situation in which they catch the ball with the hands behind in the classic W shape and have it immediately available for distribution.

Goalkeeper Practice Activities

Basically, the goalkeeper has four jobs: stop shots at the goal using any part of the body, cut out crosses, direct the defense, and start the attack. To stop shots at goal the goalkeeper must know how to catch a ball safely, deflect it, kick it, or punch it. You must train the goalkeeper in diving and jumping. The goalkeeper must know how to handle one-on-ones. But more than anything else the goalkeeper must know positioning—where to be and when. Cutting out crosses is the most stressful job. For that the goalkeeper needs a good starting position, swift judgment, and ability to jump, catch, punch, or deflect. The goalkeeper must communicate with the defense. When distributing the ball, the goalkeeper should place it so that a teammate receives it in an advantageous situation.

Practice activities for the goalkeeper should include all the techniques and skills mentioned above.

Protect Your Territory

Purpose. To develop goalkeeper technique in catching the ball.

Procedure. The coach marks out an area about 10 yards square, stands about 5 yards away with a supply of balls, and throws them one at a time so that they would land inside the square. The goalkeeper tries to catch each ball to prevent it from touching the ground inside the square.

Variation. The coach adds a 10-yard-by-5-yard space behind and adjoining the 10-yard square. The coach stands about 5 to 10 yards away with a supply of balls and throws them one at a time so that they would land inside the 10-yard-by-5-yard space. The goalkeeper must remain inside the 10-yard square and catch every ball.

Coaching Points.

• Make sure that the goalkeeper is in the basic set position before the server throws the ball.

• Insist that the goalkeeper, when in the set position, gets off the heels and has weight forward.

• Make sure that the goalkeeper's feet are still immediately before the throw. Never should the feet be moving just before the ball is thrown.

• Ask the goalkeeper to get both hands behind the ball when making the catch.

• Immediately after catching the ball the goalkeeper should pull it into the safety of the arms.

Rapid Fire

Purpose. To develop goalkeeper technique to deal with low shots.

Procedure. Place two large cones 8 yards apart on a soft, grassy area. Two players, each with a supply of soccer balls, line up some 15 to 20 yards on each side of the cones. A goalkeeper guards the space between the cones. One player uses up his or her supply of balls by taking successive low shots at the goal. Then the goalkeeper goes to the other side of the cones, and the second player fires a succession of low shots. The shooting players should allow the goalkeeper to recover into the basic set position before each shot.

Coaching Points.

• Make sure the goalkeeper's feet are still immediately before the shot. Never should the feet be moving when the shot is taken.

• Insist that the goalkeeper in the set position gets off the heels and has weight forward.

• Do not allow the goalkeeper to sit down and make himself or herself small.

• Instead, the goalkeeper should be prepared to go sideways and slightly forward to cover as much ground as possible.

• It is better for the goalkeeper to remain in the set position than to sit back. It is uncanny how many shots hit the goalkeeper if he or she stands up (big) in front of the shooter.

• Make sure that when diving sideways the goalkeeper gets the chest toward the ball rather than toward the ground.

• The hands and arms should form a window through which the goalkeeper can follow the flight of the ball.

• After catching the ball the goalkeeper should pull it into the safety of the arms.

• If unable to catch the ball the goalkeeper should fully extend the arms and fingers to divert the ball wide of the goal, keeping a stiff wrist to prevent the power of the shot from bending back the arm.

Low Shots
Straight at the Goalkeeper

Purpose. To develop technique to deal with low shots straight at the goalkeeper.

Procedure. A number of players, each with a ball, stand in the arc just outside the penalty line facing the goal. One at a time they shoot at the goal, aiming to hit the goalkeeper with a strong, low shot.

Coaching Points.

• Make sure the goalkeeper gets the hands behind the ball.

• The goalkeeper should also get some other body part (legs or trunk) behind the hands in case the ball slips through.

• The goalkeeper should bend at the knees and waist to get more body mass behind the ball.

Long Shots, High Shots

Purpose. To develop goalkeeper techniques and skills in dealing with long, high shots.

Procedure. A goalkeeper stands midway between the 6-yard line and the penalty spot (12 yards). A number of players, each with a ball, stand on a line between two cones 30 yards from the goal. One at a time they push the ball forward and immediately shoot at the goal with their second touch. They must shoot before the ball reaches the arc at the top of the penalty box.

Coaching Points.

• Since the shot on goal will be from a distance of about 25 yards, the goalkeeper's set position should be slightly more upright with fingers facing upward and backs of hands in front of chest. The goalkeeper should bend slightly at the knees and waist (figure 8.21).

• If the shot is high to one side the goalkeeper should lean to that side, drop the hands, and then throw them upward toward the ball. The goalkeeper should push vigorously through ankles, knees, and hips to obtain lift in the jump (figure 8.22).

• The goalkeeper should try to get both hands behind the ball in the classic W shape.

• The goalkeeper must understand the difference between the body shape of the shooter using the chip shot and the body shape of the shooter using the power shot. In particular, there will be no follow-through of the kicking foot by the shooter who is chipping the ball.

• When the goalkeeper recognizes that the shooter is going to chip the ball, he or she must decide to which side the ball is likely to go. The goalkeeper retreats to that side by turning sideways, thus being able to run diagonally backward at speed.

• The goalkeeper should always keep eyes on the ball.

• If, in going diagonally backward, the goalkeeper cannot catch the ball, he or she should help it on its flight and push it over the crossbar (figure 8.23).

One-Versus-One in Breakaway Situations

Purpose. To develop goalkeeper techniques and skills in dealing with one-versus-one breakaway situations.

Procedure. Two players stand one yard apart facing each other 40 yards from the goal with

Figure 8.21   The goalkeeper should bend slightly at the knees and waist for long, high shots.

Figure 8.22   Catching a long, high shot.

Figure 8.23   The goalkeeper should help the ball on its flight and push it over the crossbar.

feet wide apart and parallel to the end line. The player with the ball pushes the ball through the defending player's legs and goes for the goal while the defending player must start from this disadvantageous position to chase the attacking player.

Coaching Points.

• From the first touch on the ball by the attacking player, the goalkeeper must determine which angle the attacker is most likely to take.

• The goalkeeper must take a quick glance out of the corner of the eye at the near post to make sure he or she is in the correct position.

• From the attacker's second touch of the ball, or likely second touch of the ball, the goalkeeper must establish proper distance off the goal line. This will depend on several factors:

a. Can the goalkeeper get to the ball first?
b. Is the attacker likely to chip the ball?
c. Is the attacker likely to take a long power shot?

Crosses

Purpose. To develop the goalkeeper's skills and techniques in dealing with crosses.

Procedure. A line of players, each with a ball, forms up on each side of the field, about 30 yards from the goal line. Each player has two touches on the ball, one to pass it forward and the second to cross the ball from the space at the side of the penalty box into an area 12 by 20 yards immediately in front of the goal, marked out with flat cones. Play alternates from side to side. Two attacking players, who each may touch the ball only once in every attack, and who must make every touch inside the area, try to score goals. A goalkeeper guards the goal and may play only inside the area.

Coaching Points.

• The goalkeeper should get the chest facing the direction of the cross.

• The goalkeeper's feet should be placed one in front of the other to allow optimum opportunity to sprint forward to a near-post cross or to cross legs and get over to the far post.

• The fingers should point upward with the backs of the hands in front of the chest.

• The goalkeeper should take a position so that a mis-hit cross would not beat him or her at the near post.

• Never should the goalkeeper cheat and anticipate the cross by leaving the goal line too early.

• The goalkeeper should try to get to the ball first at the near-post area, and at its highest point in front of goal and at the far-post area.

Summary

This chapter highlights the following points to help you be a better teacher of defensive skills and techniques.

• Give special attention to positioning. This is the most important aspect of all defensive play.
• Use small-sided, conditioned games. They are the simplest and most effective way of teaching the defensive skill of positioning (marking and covering).
• Coaching in the game is the most effective method of coaching during small-sided, conditioned games.
• Instruct your players regarding their defensive positioning immediately before or as the play develops and help your players' decision making by identifying the cues in the play as it develops.
• Coach players off the ball. It is far more successful than trying to coach the players on the ball.
• Freeze the play to get across a general point. Use this tool sparingly.
• Emphasize that *all* the players on the team without the ball should think and act defensively.
• Make it clear to the forwards that they are the first line of defense. Teach them to work in groups of two or three rather than on their own.
• Work with midfield players to show when it is prudent to go forward and when it is safer to remain in a defensive position, depending on what is happening on the ball and the positions of other players.
• Make it clear that all players must learn to understand and perform the defensive roles and responsibilities of all positions.

Chapter 9

Teaching Defensive Tactics

When teams are almost equally matched it is more than likely that the team using the better tactical plan will win the match. The most successful soccer coaches are the ones who are best at preparing an appropriate tactical plan for each match. It is even possible for them to win matches against teams with superior players if they implement a well-conceived tactical plan.

 UNDERDOGS PREVAIL

In the 1989 Under-17 World Cup finals in Scotland the USA was drawn to play Brazil in its opening match. The Brazilian players were wonderfully gifted and artistic, with great individual technical skill. I decided, from having

watched many previous Brazilian national teams at all different age levels, that it was most likely that their two center backs (usually #s 4 and 6) would be the least likely to venture upfield with the ball. We instructed our two strikers, A.J. Wood and David McGuire, to go wide whenever the Brazilian defense secured the ball and thus prevent their two offensive-minded outside backs (#s 2 and 3) from receiving possession. We asked our midfield, which included the skillful Baba brothers and Claudio Reyna, to press the Brazilians in their half of the field. These tactics helped to frustrate the Brazilians and destroyed their mental equilibrium. Not only did we force the two Brazilians with the weakest technical skills to receive the major share of ball possession, we also challenged the Brazilians deep in their half of the field, a tactic that they were unaccustomed to. The 1-0 result in favor of the USA sent shock waves throughout the soccer world.

Just as in other team sports, such as basketball and hockey, the tactics of soccer are based on defending a certain target area—the basket or goal—and attacking a similar target area at the other end of the court or field. We have to recognize that in soccer it is much more likely that an attacking player will score a goal if in possession of the ball (or if the ball comes to the player) inside the shaded scoring area (figure 9.1). Only a very small percentage of goals are scored on shots taken from outside this shaded scoring area. An analysis of the goals scored in all the World Cup finals from 1962 (Chile) to 1994 (USA) proves this theory valid.

Soccer coaches should, therefore, base their strategies and tactics on the following:

1. Defending—how to prevent the opposition from getting the ball to one of their players inside the shaded scoring area

2. Attacking—how to get the ball to an attacking player inside the shaded scoring area near to the opponent's goal

It becomes apparent that the team most successful in achieving both objectives is likely to win the match. Virtually all tactics, strategies, team formations, systems, and so forth in soccer are based on the simple principle of either getting the ball into the shaded scoring area or preventing the opponent from doing the same. But there is also a second major consideration. The area outside the shaded attacking scoring area can be regarded as the preparation area (figure 9.2). A pass or a dribble could conceivably be made from anywhere inside the preparation area to get the ball into the scoring area. It is, however, much more likely that a player will make the final pass or dribble into the scoring area from that part of the preparation area known as the setup area (figure 9.3).

If you have the opportunity to analyze why a goal was scored, either through watching

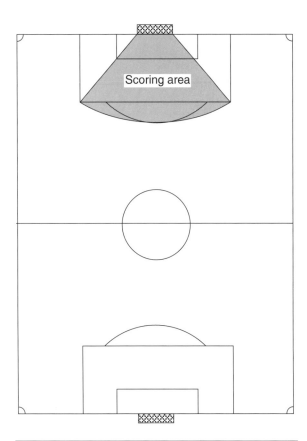

Figure 9.1 Most goals are scored from shots taken from inside the shaded scoring area.

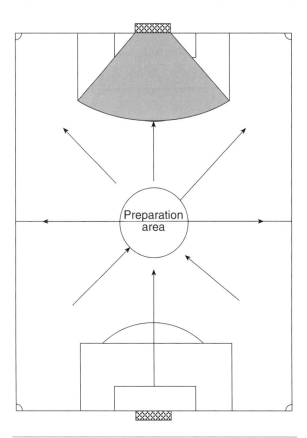

Figure 9.2 A pass or a dribble from inside the preparation area can get the ball into the scoring area.

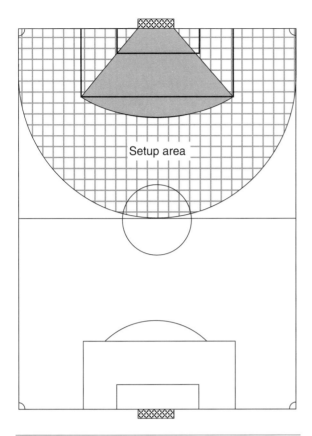

Figure 9.3 The passes or dribbles that lead to goals most likely originate from the setup area.

film or videotape, or through observation during a match, you will notice that in most instances a player will have been allowed to pass or dribble the ball from the setup area into the scoring area.

This pass from the setup area into the scoring area could take one of many forms. Some examples could be a throw-in, a corner kick, a free kick, an overlap followed by a cross, a give-and-go just outside the scoring area, or simply a long hopeful kick deep into the scoring area. It could also be a combination of a pass and dribble or simply a run onto a pass over the top of a square-lying defense.

The issue at stake is that any team that allows its opponent good possession in the setup area nearest its goal is in deep trouble. Conversely, a team that can secure good possession in the setup area nearest to the opponent's goal is in a commanding position to win the match.

Command of the setup area, therefore, becomes the key component of defensive or

attacking tactics. How to achieve command of the setup area remains the most difficult, but most stimulating, tactical challenge for any soccer coach.

Goalkeeper and Defensive Tactics

Probably the most important single player in determining defensive strategy and tactics is the goalkeeper. There are two general types of goalkeepers:

1. The *line goalkeeper* is basically a shot stopper and plays most of the match near to the goal. Dino Zoff, the great Italian goalkeeper, was a classic example of a line goalkeeper.
2. The *sweeper-keeper* plays farther away from the goal, almost as a second sweeper behind the regular sweeper. The sweeper-keeper often plays outside the penalty area and is confident and competent when playing the ball with the feet or controlling it with the body. Rene Higuita, the flamboyant Colombian goalkeeper, is an excellent example of a sweeper-keeper. So is Jorge Campos, the diminutive but colorful Mexican goalkeeper.

A team that has a line goalkeeper must be concerned with the distance between the goalkeeper and the last defender. If, for example, a team sets out to press the opposing team in the opponent's half of the field, then that team will be extremely vulnerable to a ball played into the space behind its defense. It will be even more vulnerable if its last line of defense is slow.

Some teams attempt to compromise by playing a sweeper behind the other defenders, but tactically aware opposing strikers can undo this by pushing up to the line of the sweeper and creating space between the sweeper's defense and the midfield.

If the sweeper continues to drop off behind the defense then a tactically aware striker will continue to push up onto the line of the sweeper, taking the marking defenders along and thus further increasing the space between the defenders and the midfield (figure 9.4).

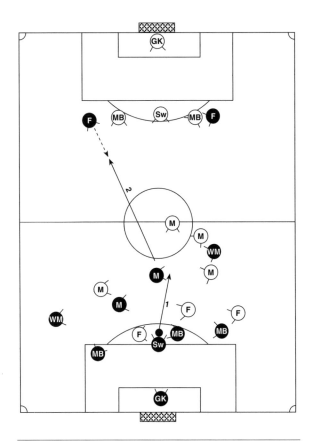

Figure 9.4 Pushing up on the line of the sweeper.

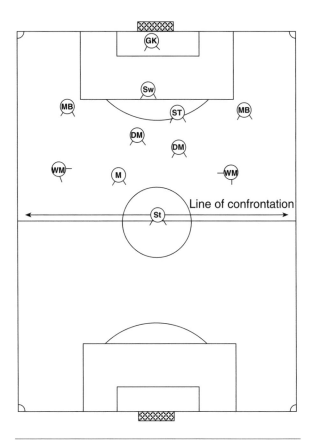

Figure 9.5 Falling back deep to draw up the line of confrontation.

Line of Confrontation

The Italian World Cup champion team of 1982 solved the problem of having a line goalkeeper by falling back deep into its own half of the field to draw up its line of confrontation. The *line of confrontation* is an imaginary line taken across the field from sideline to sideline at a point where the farthest forward players in the team without the ball will challenge for the ball. The remainder of the defensive team will take up covering positions behind these challenging players (figure 9.5). This meant that the Italians could challenge every possession in the setup area nearest to its goal.

The highly successful Liverpool team of the late 1980s could afford to pressure opposing teams in their half of the field since they had Bruce Grobbelaar (a sweeper-keeper) and speed in defense. They drew up their line of confrontation about 30 yards from the opponent's goal (figure 9.6).

Of course, the reality is that both Zoff and Higuita are extreme examples of a line goalkeeper and a sweeper-keeper, respectively. The great majority of goalkeepers would fall

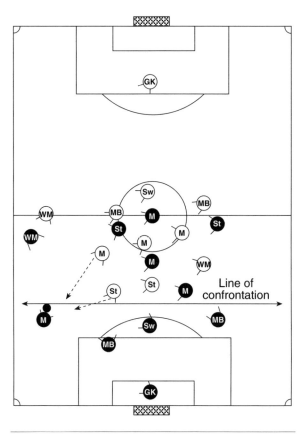

Figure 9.6 High pressure.

somewhere between these two extreme examples. The coach must fully understand the distance from the goal at which the goalkeeper is most comfortable. It is no good asking a line goalkeeper to play as a sweeper-keeper.

Defensive Formations

After deciding where to draw up the line of confrontation, the coach can choose a defensive formation. The coach must consider the strengths and weaknesses of both his or her players and those of the opposing team. The coach must, for example, have fully prepared the team if one or more opponents are to be marked on a player-to-player basis. A typical lineup against a team using a 4-4-2 formation is illustrated in figure 9.7.

I have assumed that the goalkeeper is a line goalkeeper and there is no great speed in the defense. Two white defenders (marking backs) mark the two opposing black forwards on a player-to-player basis, while a third white defender (the sweeper) provides them with cover. Two white wide midfielders match up against the opposing black wide midfielders. Two white stoppers (or two de-

fensive midfielders) and a white playmaker (attacking midfielder) make a triangle of players in the center of the five-player midfield. Two additional white strikers make up the remainder of the team using this 3-5-2 formation.

It should be obvious that if the opposition persists in keeping four players in defense (in its 4-4-2 formation), then the team using a 3-5-2 formation will have the luxury of an extra player in center midfield and thus an excellent opportunity of commanding the setup areas.

A typical lineup against a team using a 4-3-3 formation is illustrated in figure 9.8. This time I have assumed that the goalkeeper is a sweeper-keeper and there is above-average speed in the defense. Three white defenders (marking backs) mark the three opposing black forwards on a player-to-player basis, while a fourth white defender (the sweeper) provides them with cover. The three opposing black midfielders can be marked up in a variety of ways:

1. zonally, with a covering (defensive) midfielder

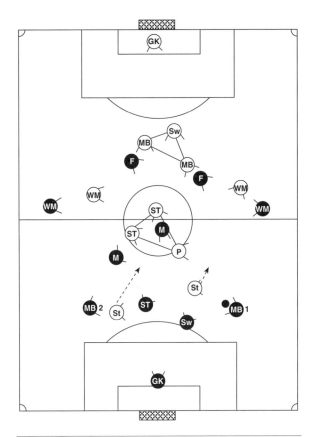

Figure 9.7 A typical lineup against a team using a 4-4-2 formation.

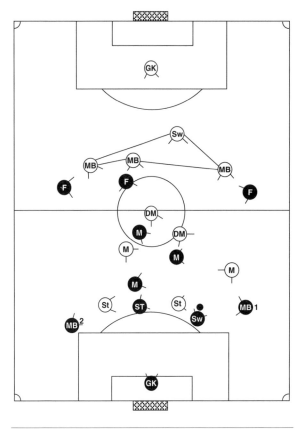

Figure 9.8 A typical lineup against a team using a 4-3-3 formation.

2. player-to-player, leaving free either

  a. the white playmaker,
  b. the white defensive midfielder, or
  c. one of the white wide midfielders

Most opposing teams, however, will not be so naive as to keep four players in the defensive line. Invariably you will find that the outside defenders (the right and left fullbacks or wing backs) will join in on the attack. You must be prepared for this and brief your extra midfielder about this possibility.

I have found by experience that by far the most effective way of teaching defensive tactics is through small-sided, conditioned games. Whichever team formation or defensive lineup you decide upon, you can evaluate its strengths and weaknesses in small-sided game situations. It is sometimes difficult, if not impossible, to analyze the capabilities of a defensive lineup in an 11-a-side match on a full-size field. There are too many players involved, presenting too many variables, and the tactic or situation that concerns the coach may hardly ever occur.

A conditioned game means that the coach imposes one or more extra rules or conditions on the game that are likely to produce repetitive situations of the type that the coach wishes the players to experience. I have already discussed the importance of small-sided, conditioned games in chapter 8. I need to reinforce the belief, though, that coaching in the game in small-sided, conditioned games is by far the most effective coaching method of developing skills and improving tactical understanding in soccer.

It is unlikely that any other method of coaching will have as much effect on the development of skills and the improvement of tactical understanding. You should structure the training program so that the problems encountered in match situations are presented and encountered in training situations. As a coach you must help your players solve these tactical problems successfully. To do that you will need a keen awareness of defensive principles.

Understanding Defensive Principles

To better teach defensive tactics, you can categorize the coaching points into five key defensive principles:

- Compactness
- Depth (cover)
- Delay
- Balance
- Patience

Compactness

At halftime or after a match you can frequently hear forwards complaining that the midfield didn't provide support. At the same time the defense may complain that the midfield didn't come back quickly enough. Obviously, there is something wrong here. If you take another look at the match you will find that, in most cases, the midfield wasn't at fault at all. Instead, it was the forwards who didn't execute their defensive responsibilities, or the defense that didn't push up when on attack. Both actions stretched the team from end to end, thereby giving the opponent a dangerous amount of space in the preparation area and perhaps even in the setup area.

By far the most important defensive principle is compactness. You have only to watch some of the world's best teams, such as Brazil, Argentina, Germany, and Italy, to realize that they will invariably manage to outnumber any opponent in possession of the ball.

It is generally recognized that any team on defense stretched out longer than 30 to 35 yards from its first defender (remember that when the ball is lost, all your players are defenders, thus the first defender could very well be one of your forwards) to its last defender is likely to have defensive problems. There will be abundant space between its players for the attacking team to exploit. The best defensive teams, such as AC Milan, seldom allow more than a 35-yard space to develop between their first and last defenders.

Of course, it will be a judgment call by the coach where to draw up the line of confrontation, and the decision will depend on the strengths and weaknesses of both team's players. As explained previously, the goalkeeper will be a major deciding factor on where the last defender plays. The speed of the last defender is also important.

Top defensive teams will compact (shorten) not only the distance from the first to the last defender to about 30 to 35 yards but also the space between players across the field, thus denying the attacking team the opportunity to switch the play from one side of the field to the other (figure 9.9).

Perhaps your team has become stretched out from its defensive line to its forwards in its previous match or matches mainly because the forwards did not come back and defend. Here's a small-sided, conditioned game that will help your team address this weakness.

Strategic Withdrawal

Purpose. To improve the team's understanding of where, when, and how to defend.

Procedure. Two teams of seven-a-side play on an 80-by-50-yard field. They play a regular game with all the rules, plus the condition that when the opposing goalkeeper has the ball then the entire team without the ball must withdraw into its own half of the field. During the play in this small-sided, conditioned game, the coach should find opportunities to make the following coaching points through the coaching-in-the-game method as, or immediately before, the play develops.

Coaching Points.

• All players on the team without the ball are defenders.

• The activity of the defending player nearest the ball determines the defensive posi-

tioning (marking and covering) of the other defenders.

• Players who must make recovery runs into defensive positions must do so immediately and at speed to limit the opposing team's counterattack opportunities.

• Players on the defensive team must communicate.

• When a team has possession of the ball some of its players must still think defensively and take up positions to prevent a quick counterattack.

• The other players on the team take up their marking and covering positions using the cues given by the defender nearest the ball and by the movement of opponents.

• The defender nearest the ball forces the play to either side and does not allow the ball to be played across the field (figure 9.10).

If, on the other hand, your team is stretched from end to end because the back four or back three are ball watching, lazy, or cautious, and don't push up on your team's attack, then the following small-sided, conditioned game will be of benefit.

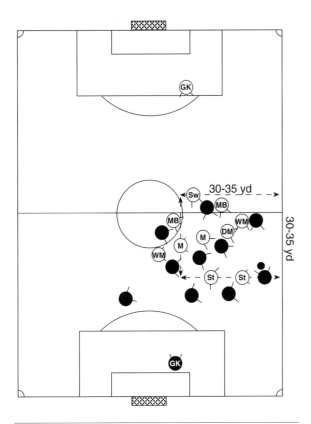

Figure 9.9 Compactness across the field.

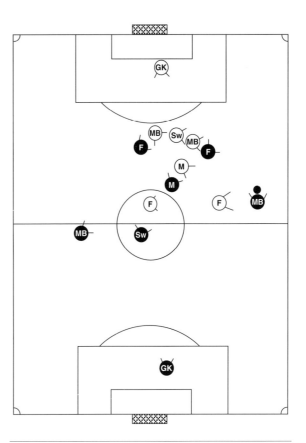

Figure 9.10 Withdrawing into your half of the field and forcing the play down channels.

High Pressure

Purpose. To improve players' understanding of how to play high-pressure defense.

Procedure. This activity uses the same procedure as the Strategic Withdrawal activity except that to score a goal a team must get all its players except the goalkeeper into the opponent's half of the field. This will force the defensive line of the team to push up and not leave any space between the defense and the midfield. It will probably mean that the team is likely to play a high-pressure defensive game in the opponent's half of the field. This will mean that the last line of defense will repeatedly find itself square across the halfway line. The defenders—marking backs and sweeper—must learn to function as a unit playing square across the field.

Coaching Points.

• When the ball is lost the player nearest the ball must give immediate chase and prevent a forward pass.

• If the player nearest the ball has managed to close down the opponent with the ball, then teammates must immediately move into supporting defensive positions to prevent easy advancement of the ball by the opposition.

• Whenever there is a good chance of regaining possession by immediate chase and pressure, have the supporting covering players verbally encourage those who are involved in the chase.

• Make sure that the supporting covering players push up in support of the front players.

Once all players understand the importance of compactness you can entrench and unify their newfound tactical awareness by using the following small sided, conditioned game.

Low Pressure, High Pressure

Purpose. To develop a team's understanding of when to play low- or high-pressure defense.

Procedure. It is possible to place more than one condition on a game. For example, we might ask a team to (a) withdraw all its players into its own half of the field when the opposing goalkeeper collects the ball, and (b) advance all its players, except for its goalkeeper, into the opponent's half of the field when one of the team's players takes a shot on the opponent's goal.

Coaching Points.

• The outcome of the above two conditions being simultaneously imposed on a game would be for all players in each team to play much closer together in tight defensive units.

• You should insist

   a. that the teams maintain a maximum distance of 30 to 40 yards between the first and last field players,

   b. that the first player force the play to one side of the field so that the supporting and covering players take up better angles in their marking positions, and

   c. that teams communicate from back to front.

Depth (Cover)

It is important that players challenging for the ball have support. Thus teams cannot play in straight lines on defense. This is particularly true when the sweeper has been put in a position of commitment, leaving the attackers with equal or greater numbers of players than the defenders. For instance, if two players attack two defenders, one of the defenders must challenge for the ball. The other defender, even though he or she may be a marking defender, must support the challenging defender first. If there is no support, the attacking player has a one-on-one opportunity. Also, the attacking player with the ball could play the ball in the space behind the second defender for the second attacker to run onto. The second defender must provide depth (cover or support) to pick up the player with the ball should the first defender be beaten and to guard against a through pass or wall pass. The second defender must do that from a position that allows him or her to close down the second attacker should the first attacker play the ball to the second attacker.

Defenses can push up and play flat across the back only when

• their attackers are in possession of the ball,

- the opposing player in possession of the ball is facing away from his or her goal, or
- there is immediate pressure on the opponent in possession of the ball, forcing the player to look down at the ball.

When a team loses possession, a well-organized defense will not push up and become flat across the back unless there is pressure on the ball. If the opponent in possession of the ball is unchallenged and can play the ball behind the defense, it is dangerous for the defense to push up. The opposing forwards or midfielders need only time their runs into the space behind the defense to receive a pass and have a clear run on goal. Defenses that play flat across the field are easily beaten by such a pass, or even by a dribble (figure 9.11).

The number of players required to provide depth and cover on defense will depend on the number of forwards the opponent is using. Here is an ideal small-sided, conditioned game to train defenders in these situations.

Four-Back or Three-Back Defense

Purpose. To prepare the team to play against an opponent using two or three forwards.

Procedure. If you know that your next opponent will play with three forwards, you can use a conditioned game to test the four-back defense. Figure 9.12 shows a typical situation in the game. Here the white team uses three marking backs and a sweeper. If, on the other hand, you know that the next opponent will play with two forwards, you can use the conditioned game to test the three-back defense. Figure 9.13 illustrates a typical situation in the game. Here the white team uses two marking backs and a sweeper.

Coaching Points.

- You should insist that your defense line up with a marking back against each of the opposing forwards.

- Your sweeper—the covering player—should ensure that all opposing forwards are marked on a player-to-player basis.

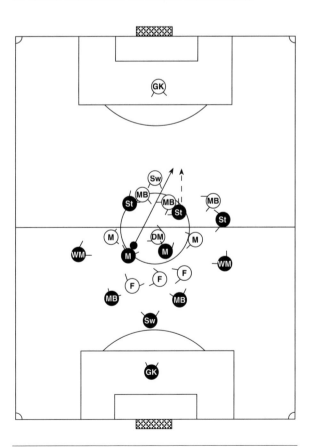

Figure 9.11 Defenses that push up when there is no pressure on the ball are easily beaten.

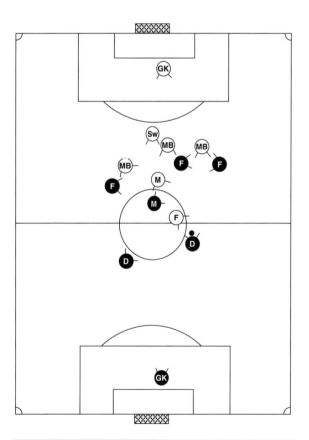

Figure 9.12 Playing against three forwards.

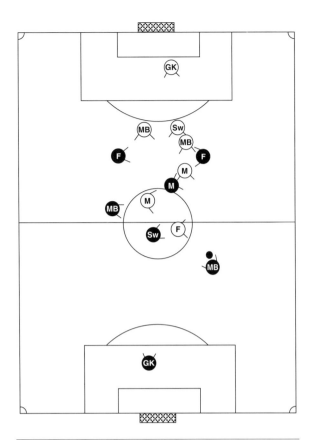

Figure 9.13 Playing against two forwards.

ond defender provides cover so that he or she can pick up the player with the ball in case that player beats the first defender. However, the second defender's angle and distance of cover must be such that he or she can close down the second attacker in case the first attacker passes to the second attacker. Should that happen the player who was the first defender must provide cover for the defender who is then putting pressure on the ball.

At first, to get the defending players accustomed to providing cover at the proper angle and distance, play the game without allowing the attacking players a shot at goal. Once the defenders become more proficient, the attackers may shoot at goal at any opportunity after entering the penalty area.

Coaching Points.

• The defender, without overcommitting, should put immediate pressure on the player with the ball.

• The angle and distance of support (cover) provided by the second defender must be such that he or she can pick up the opponent with the ball should that player get by the first defender, but not so deep that the second defender can't get to the second attacker should the second attacker get the ball.

• If the first defender's body position takes away the attacking player's passing option, the second defender may shorten the angle and distance from the first defender.

Delay

Occasionally a player or a group of players in a team will find themselves outnumbered by a quick counterattack. In such a situation the nearest defensive player to the ball must decide whether to

• challenge and win the ball, or
• delay the opposing player(s) until additional defenders get back into defensive covering positions.

Of course, challenging and winning the ball is ideal. Challenging and not winning the ball could spell disaster. In most cases the defender nearest the ball will prefer to delay and prevent the opponent from doing any-

• The goalkeeper can be an extra pair of eyes and ears for the sweeper in ensuring an optimum defensive shape.

There are many other conditioned games that you can use to teach defensive skills and tactical understanding. Good defenders will cover each other so that they can do the following:

• Cut off through passes.
• Confront an opposing dribbling player.

Here is a game to practice cover provision in its simplest form.

Quick-Cover Game

Purpose. To practice the second defender's covering position.

Procedure. Two attacking players start the game from just outside the penalty area. Two defenders are in the penalty area. The player with the ball enters the penalty area and is challenged by a defending player. The sec-

thing creative with the ball, such as dribbling into a good position in the scoring or the setup area, executing a good pass into the scoring area, or getting off a shot at goal.

The simplest form of delaying an opponent is to get into a jockeying position to slow down the opponent. The body position (goalside and inside) of the jockeying player can prevent the attacking player from entering dangerous space, making an effective forward pass, or getting a clean shot at goal. The delay will allow colleagues time to recover into covering defensive positions.

Here is a very simple activity that teaches delay.

Five-Second Delay

Purpose. To develop patience and delaying tactics when challenging.

Procedure. Create an area 40 yards long and 20 yards wide with a small goal on each end. Several players station themselves beside each goal. From the halfway line a ball is played in to one of the goals. One player, the attacker, receives the ball. The attacker's job is to try to score on the other goal. The moment the ball is played, a player from the other goal, the defender, goes out to meet the attacker. The defender's job is to delay the attacking player. After five seconds a second defender leaves the same goal as the first defender did. The second defender's job is to provide cover, communicate, and encourage the first defender to tackle the ball away. After gaining cover, the first defender should make a serious effort at tackling the ball away. Ideally, after the tackle the two defending players should be in possession of the ball and should attack the other goal while the lone attacking player tries to prevent that.

After awhile, when the game goes well, you can add a second attacking player who leaves the line when the second defender does.

Coaching Points.

• The first defender must close down the attacker quickly. The defender should give the attacker as little distance into the field as possible.

• The defender, when approaching the attacker, should be under restraint and balanced to avoid overrunning the attacker or being caught flat-footed.

• The defender, particularly in the last few strides, should approach sideways, preferably facing the closest touchline.

• By jockeying and through body position the defender should be able to slow down the attacker, force the attacker outside, and contain him or her there.

• Once covered, the defender should force the attacker to make an error and tackle the ball away.

A defensive player or a group of defensive players that is frequently outnumbered by opposing attackers must learn to recognize early when such situations are likely to happen. Early recognition of such situations should enable them to organize their defense earlier and prevent counterattacking opportunities.

Balance

One of the greatest dangers for any defensive player or group of defensive players is for one or more of them to be caught ball watching and allow opponents to get into space behind them. Good defensive players will take up defensive postures whereby they can see as many opponents as possible.

Defenders who communicate with each other and alert each other to possible danger are much more likely to present a balanced defense that can withstand any attacking threat. This is true even in a case where the defense has momentarily lost its advantage of outnumbering the opposing forwards. That may happen when, on attack, one of the marking backs, or even the sweeper, has seen an opportunity to make an effective run or dribble into the opponent's half. The defender may have even ventured into the attacking third to provide support for the player with the ball or may have taken a position to offer depth or width for an outlet pass or cross. When a defender participates in the attack, the remaining defenders will have to adjust and cover. The situation becomes somewhat ticklish when the team loses possession. The attacking defender must now recover to the marking position if he or she has time. In most cases however, the attacking defender would recover behind the other defenders and assume the role of sweeper.

Use the following small-sided, conditioned game to practice this tactic. I use this game for many other purposes, some of which I will discuss later.

Three Zones

Purpose. To develop understanding of defensive tactics.

Procedure. Another conditioned game, played with any number of players from five-a-side to eleven-a-side, uses a field divided into three zones (figure 9.14). A field 90 by 50 yards is divided into two end zones of 35 by 50 yards and a middle zone of 20 by 50 yards. With nine players on a team use one goalkeeper, three defenders, three midfielders, and two forwards. Each player is restricted to a zone. The object is for the goalkeeper, defenders, and midfielders to get the ball to their forwards so they can score.

Variations. A defender may move forward into the middle zone if a defender on the same team passes the ball to one of its midfield players. When the team loses the

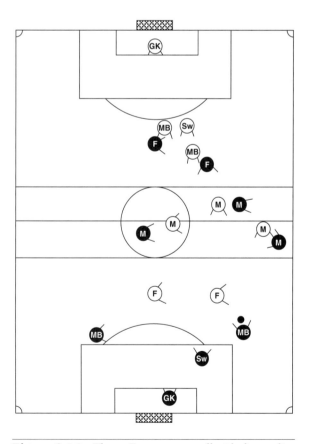

Figure 9.14 Three Zones—a small-sided, conditioned game to develop defensive tactics.

ball the defender must recover immediately into the team's end zone. Similarly, a midfield player may move forward into the attacking zone on the same conditions.

Coaching Points. Several critical decision-making situations continually arise in the above conditioned games. As a coach you must be prepared to help your players in solving some difficult problems:

- *Is it prudent for the defender to advance into the middle zone? What happens if the team loses the ball?* The defender should be confident that the team will retain ball possession and that the remaining defenders will cover for him or her.
- *Which defender goes forward? Why should it be that player? How do they communicate with each other?* Usually the defender on the blind side of the opposing defense should go forward since that player is much more likely to catch the opposition unawares.
- *How do the remaining two defenders mark up if the third defender has gone forward?* They should mark on a player-to-player basis, goalside and on the inside line of their immediate opponent.
- *How does the defender who has advanced into the midfield zone exploit the extra-player situation?* This player should get into a supporting position where he or she can receive the ball and then immediately deliver an early, accurate pass to the forwards.
- *How do three midfield defenders play against four midfield attackers? Can they cut off the pass to the forwards?* They should not allow an opposing midfielder to get ball possession in the space behind them; instead, they should keep the play in front of them, forcing the opponents to play long passes to their forwards.
- *How does the defensive midfield player who wins the ball or cuts off an intended pass effect a counterattack?* This player should immediately deliver an accurate pass to one of the forwards.
- *Where should the defender make the recovery run? When the ball is lost how does this player reestablish contact with the two defensive partners?* The recovering defender should take a position behind the defense where he or she can see both fellow defenders, the two opposing for-

wards, and the ball, but close enough to double-team if possible.

- *If a midfield player gets the opportunity to go forward into the attacking end zone, how do the three defenders now combat the three-versus-three situations?* They should play on a player-to-player basis with the sweeper challenging the opposing midfield player.

Further variations, using both of the above conditions, might see (a) four defenders, four midfielders, and two forwards in each zone or (b) four defenders, three midfielders, and three forwards.

There are many other conditioned games that you can use to teach defensive skills and tactical understanding. You can design your own conditioned games as long as you keep in mind that they must duplicate match situation problems you want to correct.

Patience

All too often, defenders who are in good defensive positions lose patience and allow opponents to reestablish the initiative. An example of such loss of patience is illustrated in figure 9.15, where white marking back 1 is in a good defensive position to contain black striker 1 and prevent the ball from being played across the face of the goal. But in haste to win the ball, the marking back fouls black striker 1 and gives away a penalty kick. In figure 9.16 white marking back 1 does a much better defensive job. Here, black striker 1 has received the ball facing away from the goal; white marking back 1 closes down and does not allow black striker 1 to turn with the ball so that it can be played into the scoring area.

The example in figure 9.15 is severe because it resulted in a foul and a penalty. Defensive players should be patient. Challenges from a bad angle or distance are bad, but committing to the ball at the wrong time can spell disaster, or at least give the opponent an advantage. The opponent can't glue the ball to his or her foot. The defender can force the attacker to make a mistake—all it takes is patience.

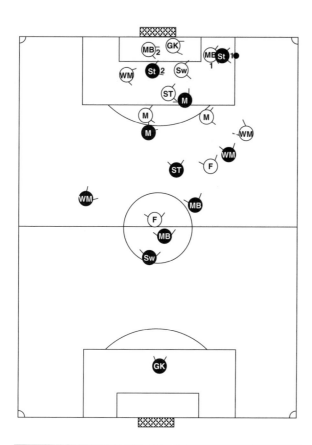

Figure 9.15 Losing patience in defending.

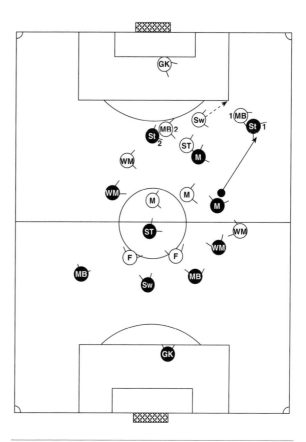

Figure 9.16 Maintaining patience in defending.

Developing Better Defensive Teamwork

Without question, you can establish better defensive teamwork only by placing players in repeated situations that they are likely to experience in the match situation.

Phases of Play

Phases of play can be likened to a piece of film that shows a problem that occurred during a match. In practice, on the field, you can duplicate the phase. You can then play it repeatedly, but you have license to move some of your players into more advantageous positions until they consistently solve the problems posed by the opposition.

A typical example is shown in figure 9.17, where the black midfielder has unopposed possession of the ball on the halfway line. The white marking backs, the white sweeper, and the white midfielder must learn to defend against such a situation. Several options are available:

- The white sweeper and white marking backs retreat while the white midfielder chases down the black midfielder.
- The white sweeper steps up to challenge the black midfielder while the white midfielder makes a recovery run into the sweeper position.
- White marking back 2 steps up to challenge the black midfielder while the white sweeper moves up to mark black forward 2.

It is possible for the players to practice this phase of play repeatedly until the defenders become adept at preventing a goal-scoring opportunity.

A common problem for most teams playing with a three-player defense in a 3-5-2 formation is balls played into the space behind the wide midfielder for forwards to run onto (figure 9.18). Here, white marking back 1 should prevent black forward 1 from turning on the ball. White marking back 1 should keep the opponent facing the touchline and

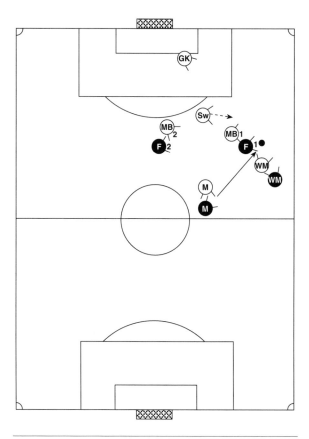

Figure 9.18   Solving the problem of balls played into the space behind the wide defensive midfielder.

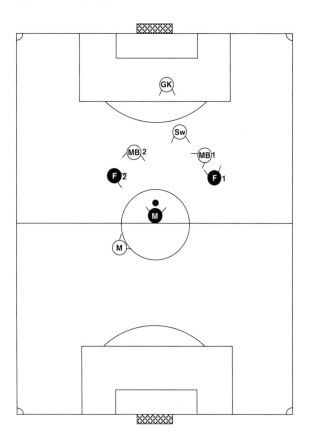

Figure 9.17   A typical phase of play.

thus isolated from black forward 2. At the same time the white sweeper should calculate whether white marking back 1 has closed down black forward 1 sufficiently to permit a double team. The white wide midfielder should also close down black forward 1 from the front and make a sandwich of that player with the sweeper, but the white wide midfielder should be careful that black forward 1 does not pass off the ball to the black wide midfielder.

You can easily recognize phases of play. Analyze situations in a match that your defenders have trouble dealing with and practice them repeatedly.

Defensive Set Plays

Defensive set plays fall into the following categories:

- Corner kicks
- Direct free kicks
- Indirect free kicks
- Throw-ins

The key to success when defending at set plays is organization. All players should know their roles and respond quickly. If the team must set a wall, the goalkeeper calls for the number of players needed in the wall, and the players should know who goes in the two-player wall, three-player wall, and so on. A field player should be assigned the duty of setting up the wall.

There are two problems with practicing set plays. One, it is a time-consuming, tedious job. Two, in most cases the defending team knows what the attacking team is going to do. To overcome the first problem, I like to get all the players involved in critiquing the play. Thus, directly after the attacking team has made its play, we ask all players to comment on what was right and what was wrong with the play. Furthermore, rather than standing around and going through the same routine repeatedly, you can play an 11-a-side match in which you are the referee and call imaginary corners, fouls, and throw-ins every minute or so.

To overcome the second problem, that of the defense knowing exactly what the offense is going to do, you can give the attacking players various options. On attack, we use no more than three simple set plays for each of the restarts. We do most of our set plays on attack with the same players. Directly before a practice of defense at set plays, we give the attacking players some new options. In other words, now the defense doesn't know what will happen.

 SETTING UP THE WALL

There are still those who feel that the goalkeeper should set up the defensive wall. That can be costly. Remember that on a direct free kick the referee doesn't have to restart the match. The opposing team may take the kick at any time the ball is placed on the spot where the infraction occurred and if the ball is not moving.

Portland played Notre Dame in the women's NCAA championship match in 1995. It was the longest championship match ever. The teams had battled to a 0-0 tie in regulation time. The match was still scoreless after two overtimes. In the early stages of the first sudden-death overtime, Portland defender Kristen Eaton fouled Notre Dame's Michelle McCarthy just outside the Portland penalty area. While Portland goalkeeper Erin Fahey was lining up the wall from the near post, Notre Dame's Cindy Daws took the kick and shot through the wall toward the far post. She scored and Notre Dame was the NCAA Division I champion.

 CONFIDENCE THROUGH ORGANIZATION

In the 1991 Under-17 World Cup finals in Italy we, along with Argentina, were drawn in the same group as the host nation. Confidence and morale in our players were low as they expected to lose the matches against these two international powerhouses.

In the buildup to the World Cup finals we played a series of friendly matches, mainly against college or men's teams, and we did not concede a single goal from a set play in these matches.

FIFA had decided to experiment with the offside law in the finals, and we made a tactical change to accommodate this change in the law. We now found that we were impregnable in defense and rarely conceded a goal.

We went on to defeat both Argentina and Italy, without conceding a goal, and headed our group on the way to the quarterfinals.

Corner Kicks

From a corner kick the most dangerous areas for the ball to be crossed into are

1. the near-post area, and
2. the far-post area.

To defend at corner kicks, you must recognize this and place defenders in these areas. A competent goalkeeper should be the firm favorite to win any ball crossed into the 6-yard box in the area immediately in front of the goal. The goalkeeper should not be expected to win any ball crossed more than 6 to 10 yards from the goal line. Teams have adopted two main methods of defending the areas outside the goalkeeper's range: zonal marking and player-to-player marking.

A typical zonal marking defense might line up as follows when defending at corner kicks. In figure 9.19, for example, you might instruct players to attack the ball in the sector immediately in front of them. White midfielder 1 would join white wide midfielder 1 if the opponent plays a short corner kick.

Other teams assign players to mark the near- and far-post areas but then mark up the remaining opposing forwards on a player-to-player basis. Some teams have adopted a combination of zone and player-to-player marking.

ORGANIZATION

In 1983-84, while I was the director of the Umbro Soccer Education Division, I helped develop the Furman University soccer program in Greenville, South Carolina. Since it was a new scholarship program, and the team was made up largely of freshmen and sophomores, it was decided to concentrate heavily on set-play organization. I had a particular corner-kick play that I favored, and we used it to great advantage in our earlier matches. This play was especially successful against teams whose coach had not bothered to scout us, and we managed to win matches by the narrowest of margins simply because of our set-play organization.

Direct Free Kicks

The critical decision in defending against direct free kicks is whether it is likely that an opponent can score directly from the kick. If so, the goalkeeper might demand a wall of players to help protect the goal. A simple decision-making chart to help determine the necessity of a wall is shown in figure 9.20.

In area A, you might use a wall of two players, whereas in area B, you might use

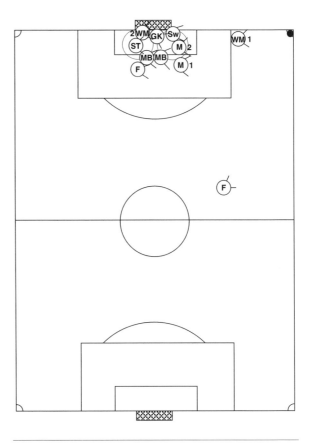

Figure 9.19   Zonal defense at a corner kick.

four players. I have avoided using walls of three or five players because too many wall variations can confuse players, and too large a wall can obstruct the goalkeeper's view of the ball. Defend a direct free kick from area C as you would a corner kick.

Players in the wall should stand with feet slightly apart (about six inches or so) and about six inches from the next player in the wall. Players should hold hands with arms straight down in front of their bodies. Their chins should be on their chests and their neck muscles clenched. They must resist any temptation to move when the opponent takes a shot (figure 9.21).

The goalkeeper should be the player to decide whether a wall is required and whether it should be a wall of two or four players. Players should form the wall about 10 yards from the ball. Assign one player from the defending team, usually a forward, to line up the wall. The player should do so from a point about 10 yards from the ball and arrange it so that a straight line could be drawn connecting the player, the ball, the second player

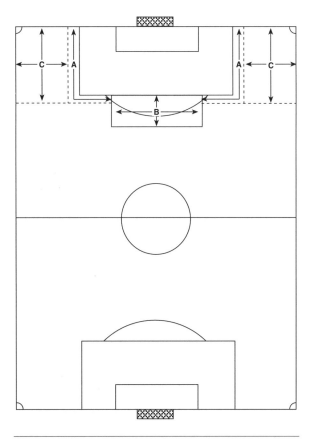

Figure 9.20 A chart used when deciding on defensive walls at free kicks.

in the wall, and the nearest goalpost (figure 9.22).

Normally, midfield players will make up the wall, allowing the remaining defenders to mark on a player-to-player basis. Notice that the defending players line up on a line parallel to the wall. It is the goalkeeper's responsibility to get first to any ball played into the space behind the wall.

The forward detailed to line up the wall, after completing this duty, should take a position about 10 yards from the ball to prevent any short square passes that will create more advantageous shooting positions.

The goalkeeper should always concentrate on the ball. The goalkeeper should have sufficient confidence in the forward detailed to line up the wall that it is unnecessary for him or her to go to the near post to check the alignment. The goalkeeper should take a position slightly to the open side of the wall where the ball is always visible.

All ten field players should defend at direct free kicks when a wall of four players is required. One forward can remain upfield only when a wall of two players is used. Direct free kicks taken from a point on the

Figure 9.21 Player posture in a defensive wall.

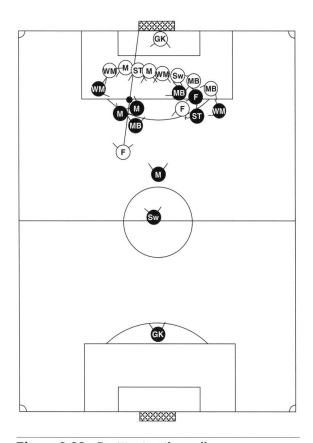

Figure 9.22   Positioning the wall.

field where it is very unlikely that a goal can be scored demand that the defense be on the alert against a quickly taken free kick, that the defense be quickly organized, and that the defense mark up all opponents who have entered the scoring area and the setup area. The defense should line up so that if the opponent plays the ball over the top, the goalkeeper is expected to deal with it. It would be very difficult for a goalkeeper to deal with the situation if the defenders retreated into the goal area.

Indirect Free Kicks

Indirect free kicks can be divided into two types:

- Where a short pass can lead to a shot at goal
- Where the kick is taken at a point too far from the goal to present a shooting opportunity from a short pass

Most indirect free kicks in the first category are given against the goalkeeper who, for instance, might have taken too many

steps when carrying the ball or picked up the ball from a back pass from a defender. Such infringements of the laws of the game lead to an indirect free kick from inside the penalty box. Of course, this is a very dangerous situation for the defending team, and an indirect free kick from a point less than 10 yards from the goal demands desperate defensive measures (figure 9.23). Notice that all ten field players form a wall along the goal line with the goalkeeper positioned in front of them.

Players should defend as they would against direct free kicks when the offense was committed in either area A or B, and as they would at a corner kick when the infringement took place in area C (see figure 9.20 on page 125).

At all free kicks, defensive players should take special care that an opponent's quickly taken free kick does not exploit their defense. They must become disciplined to organize themselves quickly, and the goalkeeper and sweeper must take extra responsibility to

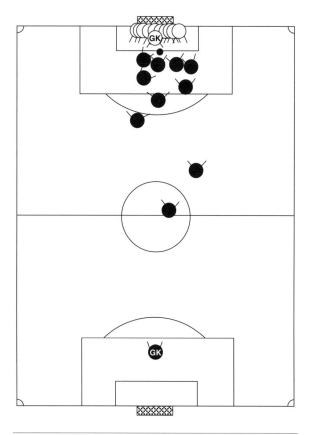

Figure 9.23   An indirect free kick from a position less than 10 yards from the goal.

ensure that no one in the defending team is slow to take up a defensive role.

 THE RIGHT EQUIPMENT

In the 1991 Under-17 World Cup finals in Italy, Nelson Vargas and Temoc Suarez were the two players who orchestrated our offensive free kicks and corner kicks. In our training program leading up to the finals we would usually allocate the last 10 to 15 minutes of each training session to such set plays. Very often, some of the players not immediately involved in the set play would complain, especially if we asked them to stand in defensive walls.

When we arrived in Monte-Catini we discovered that plywood cutouts of walls of three, four, and five players had been made available for our use. Nelson and Temoc were overjoyed and would stay behind for an hour or so each day to practice their free kicks.

Throw-Ins

Without question, the most frequently recurring set play is the throw-in. The ball will go out of bounds over the touchline between 30 and 60 times during a match. Teams must be well organized defensively to guard against a set-play opportunity that occurs so frequently.

A simple chart of throw-ins indicates that a team will have different objectives for throw-ins from different parts of the field (figure 9.24). In quarter A of the field, the emphasis should be on complete safety of ball possession. In quarter B of the field, the emphasis can shift to comparative safety of ball possession with some risk. In quarter C of the field, there will be some risk of ball possession with some degree of safety. In quarter D of the field, the emphasis should be on high risk leading to goal-scoring opportunities. Good defensive teams will be well organized against all four objectives but particularly against a throw-in that can be thrown into the scoring area.

The objective of the defensive team should be to clear the ball out of their end of the field and prevent opponents from receiving the ball in front of the goal or helping it into the area in front of the goal. It is likely that the defending team will have a numerical advantage because one opponent has to throw the ball in and teams will usually keep an extra player in defense to prevent a counterattack. In figure 9.25, for example, notice the mark-

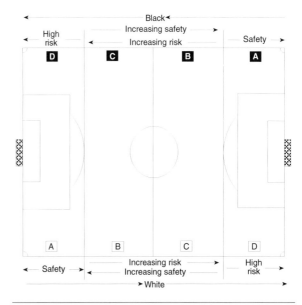

Figure 9.24 Different objectives for throw-ins from different parts of the field.

ing position of white wide midfielder 1 nearest the point of the throw-in. This player takes a position midway between three opponents so that it becomes risky to throw the ball to black wide midfielder 1 or black

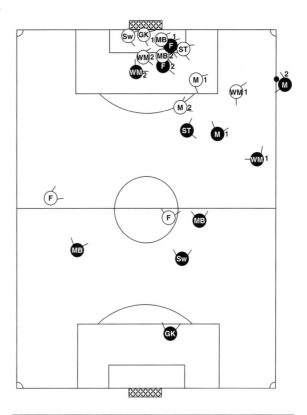

Figure 9.25 Defending against long throw-ins into the scoring area.

midfielder 1. This defender can also cut off any return pass to black midfielder 2.

Notice also the marking positions of white marking back 1 and the white stopper. They have managed to sandwich black forward 1, the intended target for the throw-in, so that it becomes very difficult for this player to receive the ball. Notice also the marking positions of white midfielder 2 and white marking back 2, who are shoulder to shoulder with their immediate opponents.

Summary

As you work on teaching defensive tactics to your team, consider the following points:

- Command of the setup area is the key component of any tactical plan. Helping your players achieve this is your most difficult, but most stimulating, coaching challenge.
- Evaluate the strengths and weaknesses of all your players, as well as the strengths and weaknesses of the players on the opposing team, before deciding on a tactical plan.
- Decide where to draw up your team's line of confrontation. It is important in any tactical plan.
- Demand that all of your players be part of the defensive tactical plan.
- Decide on your tactical plan before working out systems of play and team formations.
- Make sure all players understand their roles in a defensive tactical plan, whether they play sweeper, marking back, stopper, any of the midfield positions, or forward.
- Design small-sided, conditioned games. It is the most effective way of developing defensive skills and improving tactical understanding.
- Present identical problems in training to those encountered by players in the match situation.
- The key defensive principles are compactness, depth (cover), delay, balance, and patience.
- The most dangerous areas for the ball to be crossed into from a corner kick are the near-post area and the far-post area.
- The critical consideration in defending against free kicks is the likelihood that an opponent can score directly from the kick or after a short pass.
- Teach the team that when a wall is demanded by the goalkeeper, they should know how many players go into the wall, who those players are, who lines up the wall, and what the other players do.
- The most frequently recurring set play is the throw-in. Teams must organize defensively to guard this frequently occurring set-play opportunity.

Part IV

Coaching Offense

Chapter 10

Basic Offensive Skills and Positions

For every defensive aim or objective there will be an equal or opposite aim or objective by the offense. Every player should have a role to play in the offensive aim or objective of the team. It may be that you should require the team's principal defenders—goalkeeper, sweeper, marking backs, and stoppers—to deliver early, penetrative passes over and behind the opposing defense that is pushing up too far and playing square across the field. This will allow the team's forward(s) or attacking midfielder(s) to run onto the passes in the space behind the opposing defense.

On the other hand, it may be that the team should look for overload situations along the wings in which the wide midfielder(s) takes on the opposing player in one-versus-one confrontations; or it might be that the central midfielder(s) overlaps on the wide midfielder(s). Such situations should create numerous opportunities to cross the ball across the face of the opponent's goal.

Probably the most overwhelming offensive aim or objective is to control the setup area nearest the opponent's goal to create frequent goal-scoring chances.

Since all your players have attacking responsibilities when your team has ball possession, it's prudent to take a look at the general and position-specific skills and attributes needed to launch a successful attack.

Forwards

Teams will use three, four, five, or six players to try to control the setup areas. This will usually mean that they will play with three, two, or one forward(s).

Most successful teams will have a primary striker and a withdrawn striker. When a team plays with one forward he or she will be regarded as a primary striker. A team with two primary strikers and no withdrawn striker will have difficulties in developing attacking combinations. Similarly, a team with two withdrawn strikers and no primary striker will have difficulties in penetrating the opposing defense.

A team playing with only one forward will probably use either a 4-5-1 or a 3-6-1 formation. The 3-6-1 formation is illustrated by the white team in figure 10.1.

Forward Skills and Attributes

Here are some of the skills and attributes of successful forwards:

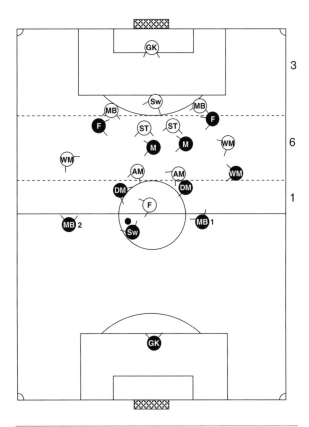

Figure 10.1 The 3-6-1 formation.

- They have the creative genius to work out any weakness—bad marking, poor covering, lack of speed, and so forth—in the opposing defense and exploit it.
- They can play with their backs to the opponent's goal yet know precisely the position of every player on the field.
- They have great ball control.
- They are wonderful dribblers.
- They have a burning desire to score goals.
- They have the nerve of a bullfighter and are icy cool when in goal-scoring positions.
- They gamble on getting in behind the opposing defense.
- They have an uncanny knack of timing runs to escape their markers.
- They can shoot accurately with either foot.
- They are good headers of the ball.

The primary forward is often regarded as the most important player on the team. He or she is expected to lead the offense and score the majority of the team's goals. When a team has a successful primary forward, it usually will enjoy great results. The primary forward needs to be able to:

- stay up on the line of the opposing sweeper,
- look for runs behind the opposing defense,
- recognize opportunities to exploit one-versus-one situations,
- recognize when he or she is outnumbered and hold up the ball to bring the midfielders into the play,
- be quick with excellent ball control,
- anticipate well and have an eye for goal chances, and
- form the first line of defense and force the play to one side of the field.

Let's look at each of these points in greater detail.

Stays Up on the Line of the Sweeper

Probably the easiest way to beat any defense is to make a penetrative pass into the space behind the opposing defense. The forward(s) who does not stay up close to the line of the sweeper will be handicapped in the race for any through pass into the space behind the opposing defense. The forward should seek to gain every possible advantage by playing in an almost-offside position. No matter how many defenders are deployed in the opposing team's defensive lineup, the forward will be required to outrun only the one farthest back, usually the opposing sweeper.

In figure 10.2, although the black team is on the attack, the white forward has taken a position on the line of the black sweeper, thus forcing black marking backs 1 and 2 to play square across the field. This allows the white forward not only to come to the ball in space A, but also to have a good chance of getting to the ball if it is played into space B behind the black team's defense.

 ONLY ONE FORWARD

Before the 1994 Snickers USYSA National Under-16 finals held in Blaine, Minnesota, I decided to change the attacking formation of my team, the Texans Soccer Club. My reasoning for the change was based on the fact that I had three outstanding forwards, but not one of

them was prepared to do much defending. I asked two of them to become attacking midfield players but at the same time pointed out that I expected midfield players to defend.

The change from a 3-4-3 system to a 3-6-1 system produced the desired results. In our final matches we scored a total of seven goals on our way to the national championship. Our two attacking midfield players played their part in bolstering our midfield defense and controlling the setup area.

Makes Runs Behind the Defense

The forward should practice making runs for the ball on northwest, northeast, southwest, and southeast directions.

The forward should avoid running in east or west directions (across the field) as the defenders remain goalside in such situations and the forward will end up receiving the ball while facing the touchline.

The forward should also avoid running directly north since it would be very difficult for a teammate to pass accurately to the forward or for the forward to keep eye contact with the ball passer. Running directly south, or straight at the ball passer, also presents difficulties because the forward will have his or her back to the defender and thus have greater problems choosing the next move.

The best forward players will bend their runs before heading in northeasterly, northwesterly, southeasterly, or southwesterly directions (figure 10.3).

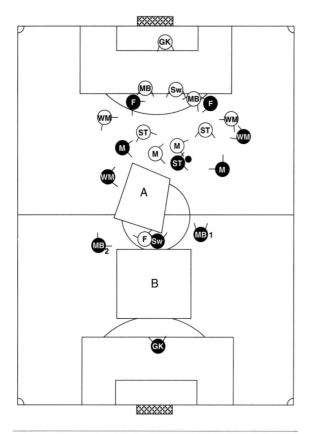

Figure 10.2 Pushing up on the line of the sweeper.

Figure 10.3 Direction of forwards' runs.

By being able to keep eye contact with the ball passer and by being aware of the movements of the nearest players, they will be much better informed to make the next decision in the play. In figure 10.4, black forward 2 has bent the run on a southwesterly direction. By taking the ball with the foot farthest away from white marking back 2, black forward 2's line of vision takes in sector A. Black forward 2 notices the possibility of black forward 1 making a run in behind white marking back 1. This attacking possibility would have been missed had black forward 2 come straight to the ball on a southerly direction.

The directional terms used—southwesterly, southerly, and so forth—are for the coach's information and won't be used in discussion with players.

Probably the most difficult run to make is the one in behind the defense. It should begin with a slow jog across the face of the defense and then a sudden sprint into the space diagonally behind the defense just

before the ball passer plays the ball. The forward should always maintain eye contact with the ball. Never should the forward turn his or her back to the ball passer. The key is to be able to run diagonally into the space behind the defense while turning the head to view the ball.

Exploits One-Versus-One Situations

Very often a forward who stays up on the line of the sweeper and comes to the ball on a southwesterly or southeasterly bent will get the opportunity of one-versus-one situations. These opportunities come in two main forms:

1. In figure 10.5, the black forward has come to the ball on a bent southwesterly run. Both the white marking back and the white sweeper have come with the forward but have allowed him or her the chance to turn to face the goal while they remain flat. Effectively, the forward has a one-versus-one opportunity against the white marking back since the white sweeper does not give any real cover.

2. In figure 10.6, the black forward has come to the ball on a bent southwesterly direction and the white marking back has come with the forward while the white sweeper remains in a loose covering position. Here the forward has the opportunity of a one-versus-one against the white marking back since the white sweeper is too far away to make it one-versus-two. Of course, if the forward gets past the white marking back, he or she will then have another one-versus-one against the white sweeper.

Avoids Being Outnumbered

Forwards who are able to get a quick glance over the shoulder when coming to the ball will be better informed to make the next decision because they will be able to see the exact positioning of the defenders.

In figure 10.7, black forward 1 has bent the run in a southwesterly direction to receive a pass from the black midfielder and has recognized that he or she will be heavily double-teamed by white marking back 1 and the white sweeper. Black forward 1 takes the ball with the right foot (the one farthest away from the defenders and the one nearest to the

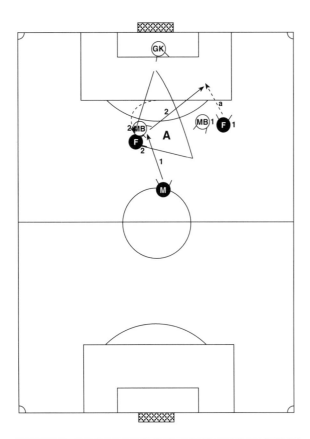

Figure 10.4 Improving the forwards' spatial awareness.

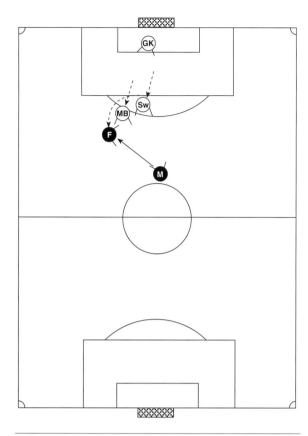

Figure 10.5 Recognizing one-versus-one opportunities.

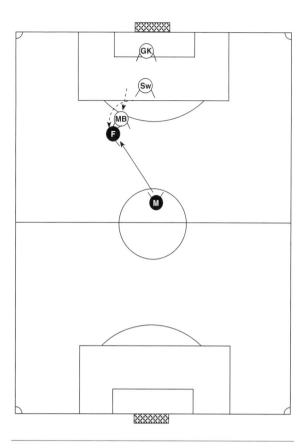

Figure 10.6 Recognizing another one-versus-one opportunity.

ball). Black forward 1 holds the ball until challenged by white marking back 1 and then lays it off to black forward 2, who is in a supporting position.

Shows Quickness With Excellent Ball Control

One of the most important attributes and skills of good forwards is that they are quick with good ball control. They need not be fast over 40 yards or more but should be extremely quick from a stationary position to a point 5 to 10 yards away. They will need good ball control to go with a burst of acceleration, and they must learn to ease into a ball-receiving position and decelerate to maintain a good balanced posture. In figure 10.8 the player has accelerated into the space diagonally behind the defense and has eased into a comfortable, composed receiving position.

Anticipates Well

Without question the single most important attribute of good forwards is that they antici-

pate well and have an eye for goal chances. Many forwards stand and wait for their goal-scoring chances, while the best forwards go to the ball and make their chances.

In figure 10.9 the black forward has recognized that the black wide midfielder will just about be able to cross the ball before being tackled by the white defender. The black wide midfielder will have to reach for the ball to be able to get in the cross. The black forward anticipates that the cross is likely to be low and thus unlikely to get to the far post. The black forward makes a strong near-post run and gets to the ball before the white marking back.

Represents the First Line of Defense

Very often I find that players think the role of forwards is over when their team loses ball possession. On the contrary, the forwards should consider themselves the first line of defense. If the opportunity arises for them to regain ball possession by immediately and aggressively challenging the opposing play-

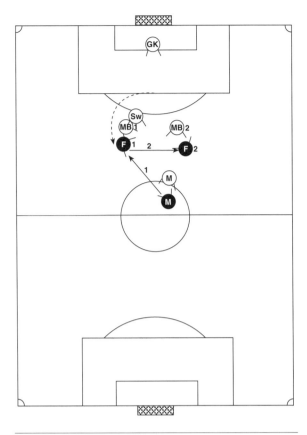

Figure 10.7 Recognizing double-team situations.

ers, they should do so. However, when heavily outnumbered by three or four opposing players, it may be futile to chase after the ball. In such situations forwards should force the opponents to direct their attack into the strength of the team's defense.

  ANDY FOR ENGLAND

From 1967 to 1971 I coached a team called Skelmersdale United, which became the amateur champion of England. Several of the players were highly skilled and were drafted to play for England's national amateur team. The crowd's favorite player, however, remained unrecognized by the national team selectors, and soon the chant "Andy for England" went up at home matches. Andy had won over the fans because of his fitness and prowess in giving immediate chase whenever his team lost the ball deep in the opponent's half of the field. A sliding tackle often climaxed these chases, and Andy would then initiate an immediate counterattack. There was always drama and excitement whenever Andy was near the ball. Andy was finally rewarded in 1970 when he was drafted onto the England national squad and went on to gain four England caps.

In figure 10.10, the white team has lost the ball and has withdrawn to its area of con-

Figure 10.8 Easing into a comfortable, composed receiving position.

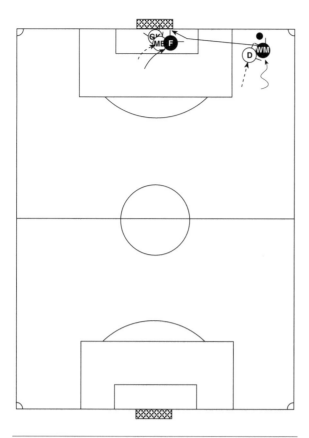

Figure 10.9 Anticipating near-post crosses.

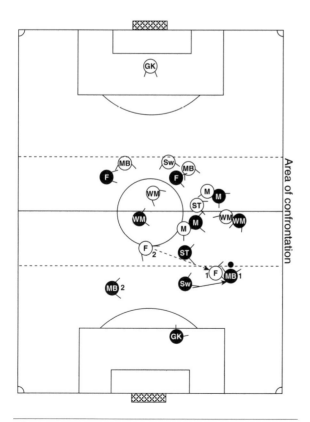

Figure 10.10 Forcing the play to the side of the field.

frontation, which is roughly 15 yards each side of the halfway line. The black sweeper has passed the ball to black marking back 1. White forward 1 takes a position so that it will be dangerous for the black marking back 1 to pass to either the black sweeper, black marking back 2, or the black stopper. Black marking back 1 will be forced to play the ball down the field into the defensive strength of the white team.

Withdrawn Striker

It is no coincidence that some of the most famous players in the history of soccer were withdrawn strikers. Pele, Maradona, Platini, Baggio, DeStefano, Puskas, Keegan, Dalglish, and Cruyff are but a few that have played as withdrawn strikers. The demands of playing the role of a withdrawn striker are extremely high, but a player emerging with the talent to play this role is usually stunningly successful.

Withdrawn Striker Skills and Attributes

The attributes and skills required of a withdrawn striker are as follows:

- The withdrawn striker must be totally aware of all other players, teammates, and opponents, not only in the line of vision but also in the space behind him or her.
- The withdrawn striker will attempt to exploit the space behind the opposing team's midfield.
- He or she must have an uncanny knack of timing runs to positions where and when teammates can pass the ball to him or her. The withdrawn striker is likely to be heavily marked (figure 10.11).
- The withdrawn striker must be able to turn quickly over either shoulder and accelerate, usually preceding the turn with a fake (figure 10.12).
- The withdrawn striker must be a supreme ball passer.
- He or she should be a good dribbler and able to hold up the ball in crowded situations.
- The withdrawn striker should be an accurate shooter.

Figure 10.11   Heavy marking of the withdrawn striker.

Figure 10.12   Faking, turning, and accelerating.

- He or she must recognize one-three opportunities, often called third player running combinations.

A one-three is a situation in which the first player passes the ball to a second player who then passes to a third player running into a space behind the defending players.

In figure 10.13 the black primary striker has received the ball from the black withdrawn striker but is heavily marked by the white sweeper and marking back 1. The black primary striker lays the ball off to the black midfielder, who has the opportunity of playing a one-three to the black withdrawn striker, who is running into the space behind white marking back 2.

Midfielders

There are several attributes required of midfield players, and it is unlikely that any player will adequately fulfill all the require-

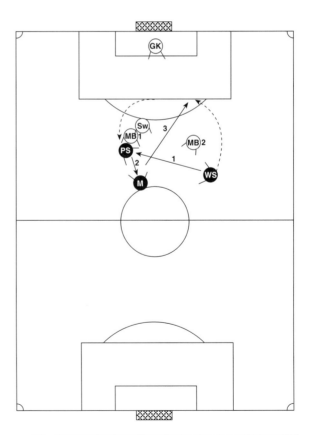

Figure 10.13   A one-three.

ments. In a 3-5-2 system the midfield might play with two stoppers (or defensive midfielders) and one attacking midfielder (playmaker), or they might play with one stopper (defensive midfielder) and two attacking midfielders (playmakers).

The demands made on a single stopper are different from those made on a stopper playing alongside another stopper. Similarly, the demands made on a single attacking midfielder are different from those made on an attacking midfielder playing alongside another attacking midfielder. The demands made on the wide midfielders are fairly consistent no matter how the center midfield is organized.

Stoppers

Any sweeper or marking back faces enormous problems when an opposing midfielder takes possession of the ball in front of the defense and can either play penetrative passes into the space behind the defense or run at the defense with the ball at his or her feet. The stopper's primary role is to prevent such a situation from developing. He or she does that by defending the space in front of the marking backs while providing defensive cover to the midfield. Obviously, effective stoppers are alert and anticipate dangerous developments early. Much will depend on the stopper's performance because the stopper is in a position to be constantly involved in the heart of the game.

Skills and Attributes of a Single or Double Stopper

All the attributes of the single stopper should be present in the double stopper. Furthermore, a double stopper should learn to play with his or her co-stopper and share defensive and offensive responsibilities.

- The stopper should have good positional sense to cut off the passing lanes to the opposing forwards (figure 10.14).
- The stopper should be a good leader and must communicate with players in front of him or her to ensure that the team takes a good defensive shape.
- He or she should relish defensive responsibilities and be prepared to anchor the

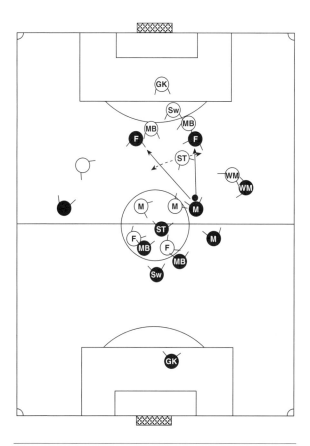

Figure 10.14   Positioning to cut off the passing lanes.

midfield. In figure 10.15, the white stopper has stayed in a defensive position to prevent any possible black counterattack.

- The stopper should be a good header of the ball.
- He or she should be a good, safe ball passer.

    NOBBY

One of my most enduring memories of the 1966 World Cup was of Nobby Stiles, the English stopper, dancing in front of the TV cameras with the World Cup held aloft. Nobby was an unlikely looking soccer player. He was small and slight, and his uniform looked too big for him. He was exhausted after the effort required in playing extra-time against the West Germans. His socks were rolled down; his thin, sparse hair was plastered on his head with perspiration; and his face was beaming in a wide grin that showed his missing upper teeth.

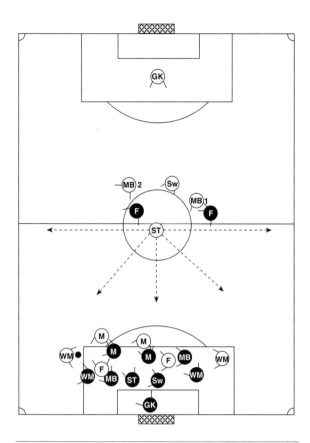

Figure 10.15   Anchoring the defensive shape.

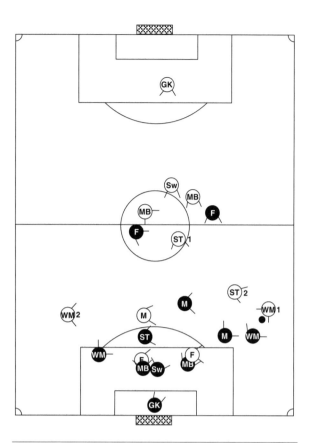

Figure 10.16   The roles of twin stoppers.

You underestimated Nobby at your peril. He was a great ball winner and had the annoying habit of always being in the way when a midfield opponent wanted to pass to one of his forwards. Nobby also led by example, and he would die for the cause. He was one of the unsung heroes of England's one and only World Cup triumph.

In figure 10.16, white stopper 2 (one of the twin stoppers) has made an attacking run to support white wide midfielder 1; white stopper 1, the other twin stopper, has remained in a supporting position to prevent counterattack opportunities by the opposition.

The twin stoppers should learn to pivot on each other so that whenever one goes forward the other stays at home.

Attacking Midfielders (Playmakers)

Intelligent, skillful attacking midfielders are a nightmare to opposing defenses. Their daring one-on-ones can leave a defense outnumbered. Their accurate penetrating passes into the scoring area can create scoring

opportunities galore. They are the generals of the attacking forces. Fans love the excitement and thrills they bring to the match. They also can adjust to the demands of the position should the system of play change.

In a 3-5-2 formation a team might play with either one (figure 10.17) or two (figure 10.18) attacking midfielders.

In a 4-4-2 formation one of the two central midfield players will be designated as the attacking midfield player or they will pivot on each other and share defensive and offensive responsibilities.

Attacking Midfielder Skills and Attributes

No matter which formation or system of play you use, attacking midfielders should have the following attributes:

- They should be incisive front-foot, outside-of-the-foot passers of the ball into the areas behind the opposing defense.
- They should be able to turn quickly, using feints and changes of speed. It is more than likely that these players will

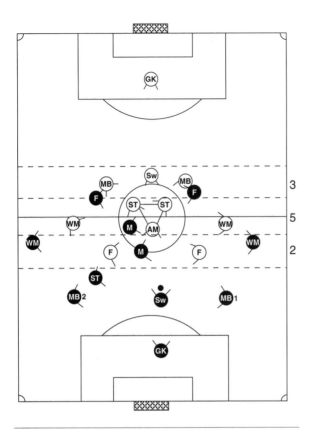

Figure 10.17 A 3-5-2 formation with one attacking midfielder.

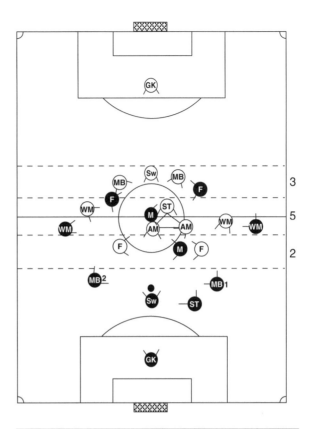

Figure 10.18 A 3-5-2 formation with two attacking midfielders.

be below average in height, with low centers of gravity.

- They should possess a good shot from either foot.
- They should be good dribblers of the ball and should always be prepared to go at the opposing defense.
- They should be adept at playing one-twos or give-and-goes.
- They should have the ability to ghost in behind defenses (figure 10.19).
- They should be good communicators, and when possession is lost they should instruct the players in front of them to force the play to a particular side of the field.

Wide Midfielders

Wide midfielders are the workhorses of the team. They usually attack and defend in a relatively narrow area of the field, but the area is ever so long, from goal line to goal line.

In reality the wide midfielders in a 3-5-2 system have to play three positions during the same match depending on what is happening on the ball. They might have to play

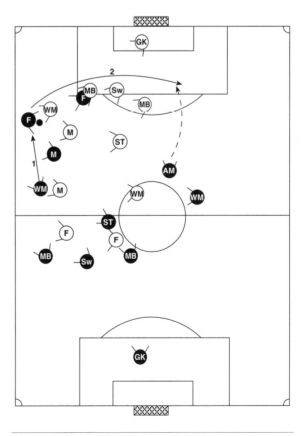

Figure 10.19 Ghosting in behind a defense.

Figure 10.20   Crossing the ball.

fullback, wide midfielder, or winger, depending on who has the ball, where the ball is, and what is likely to happen next.

Wide midfielders in a 4-4-2 system do not have such stringent demands placed on them since they have the luxury of having a defender in the space behind them.

Wide Midfielder Skills and Attributes

The main attributes of wide midfielders are as follows:

- They should take up good marking positions depending on where the opponent is and where the ball is.

- They should instruct their forwards where to force the opposing defense when they are in possession of the ball.
- They should have the speed and endurance to cover the length of the field.
- They should be able to cross the ball well (figure 10.20).
- They should relish opportunities of running their immediate opponent in one-versus-one situations.
- They should anticipate runs to the far-post area for any long crosses.

Summary

Success on offense depends on the entire team's ability to understand, develop, and execute basic offensive technical and tactical skills. In addition you must work with individual players to develop the offensive skills needed in their specific positions. The summary will give you some hints about what to look for and what to work on.

- Teach forwards to stay up on the line of the opposing sweeper, to look for runs behind the defense, and to recognize and exploit one-versus-one situations.

- Work with the forwards to further develop explosive speed, ball control, and ability to anticipate what's going to happen next.
- Spend extra time with your withdrawn striker(s). Emphasize improving vision, improving awareness, and exploiting the space behind the opponent's midfield.
- Develop the positional sense of your stopper(s). Make sure the stopper communicates constructively. Work on heading and passing skills.
- Contribute to the effectiveness of your attacking midfielder(s) by developing his or her awareness and leadership skills. Also work on dribbling, passing, and shooting.
- Teach the wide midfielders to recognize transition early—when to abandon the attacking role in favor of defensive positioning. Show them how to provide far-post width on attack. Work on their long and short crosses, and one-versus-one skills.

Chapter 11

Teaching
Offensive Skills

In the modern game of soccer, at the highest level, the distance from the last defender to the primary forward is usually about 30 to 35 yards. It is necessary, therefore, to develop attacking players who can play their way through or around compact defenses. To do that successfully you must take the time to constantly provide practices that further develop the team's technical abilities in the areas of passing, shooting, heading, screening, receiving and turning with the ball, dribbling, and playing off the ball. For most of these offensive techniques and skills, you need to design small-sided, conditioned games that will improve the effectiveness of each technique and skill.

Once the players have recognized the need for developing particular skills, through involvement in conditioned games, you should introduce skills in unopposed form. When players obtain success in unopposed activities, increase the level of difficulty through reduction of time and space and an increase in the number of opposing players. Thereafter, you must continually expose your players to playing against compacted defenses so that they become familiar with playing in limited time and space.

Offensive Skills and Techniques

Just as all players must understand their defensive responsibilities and apply their defensive skills when the ball is lost, so must all players have a clear understanding of their offensive responsibilities when their team is in possession. Therefore, all players need to develop their offensive skills and techniques.

Passing

Your athletes can't play the game successfully if they constantly serve passes that are too soft, too hard, inaccurate, or badly timed.

If players are to succeed in the modern game they must become good passers of the ball in confined situations. Remember that a good pass has five distinct qualities: accuracy, speed or weight, controllability, disguise, and timing.

The pass must be accurate, for obvious reasons; it must have the proper speed, often called weight, to avoid interception; the receiver should have no difficulty controlling the ball; it must be disguised to gain time for the passing player or the receiver; and the pass must be well timed. The timing depends not only on the passer but also on the timing of the run made by the receiver.

Let me share with you some of the small-sided, conditioned games I like to use to develop passing skills with my players.

Pin Ball

Purpose. To develop the technique of give-and-go.

Procedure. Players can work in give-and-go situations as shown in figure 11.1. Black midfielder 1 passes to black midfielder 2 (solid line 1) and follows the pass (dotted line a). Black midfielder 2 lays the ball off to the incoming black midfielder 1 (solid line 2), who immediately plays a first-time pass to the black striker (solid line 3). Black midfielder 1 follows the pass (dotted line b) and runs onto the black striker's lay-off pass (solid line 4) for a first-time shot (solid line 5).

Coaching Points.

• The movement of black midfielder 1 should not be at a constant speed. Instead,

---

Tips for Teaching Passing

• Teach players to move to the ball and into the path of the ball.
• Show that the simple pass is often the most effective.
• Instruct players to pass quickly. The player who hangs on to the ball will come under pressure. In addition, the opposing team will close the passing lanes.
• Make sure players know that the first priority is to pass the ball forward. However, the ball can also be passed square across the field or backward. There is obviously a greater element of risk in square or back passes and accuracy should be a high priority. The passing player should be alerted to the danger of a possible interception by an opponent.
• Direct players to pass the ball, in most cases, to the feet of the receiving player in the defensive and midfield thirds of the field.
• Emphasize the importance of disguising the pass.
• Discourage long, optimistic, inaccurate passes.

---

black midfielder 1 should accelerate immediately after passing the ball and decelerate to receive it.

• Try to get black midfielder 1, if possible, to strike the pass from a point about 12 to 15 inches in front of him or her.

• It is much more comfortable and accurate if the player uses the outside of the foot to strike the ball by turning the foot slightly inward.

Off the Wall

Purpose. To develop the techniques and skills of give-and-go short passing.

Procedure. Black attacker 1 has the ball, and the objective is to get the ball to the black target player from inside the shaded area (5 by 15 yards). The white defender defends outside the shaded area (figure 11.2). Black attackers 2 and 3 are available for black attacker 1 to bounce the ball off them (as in a wall pass). Black attackers 2 and 3 move with the play but can only play on the outside of the shaded space; they are restricted to

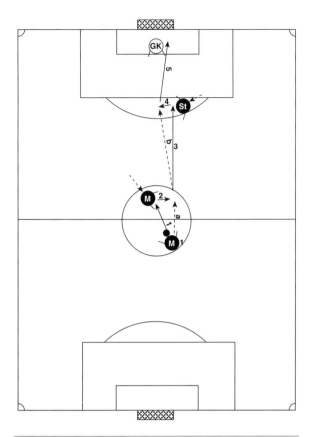

Figure 11.1 Pin Ball—an activity that develops the give-and-go.

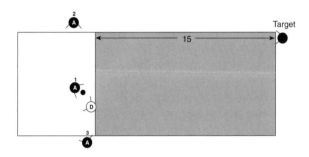

Figure 11.2 Off the Wall—an activity that develops the give-and-go.

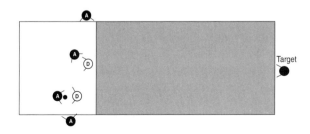

Figure 11.3 Off the Wall variation—another activity that develops the give-and-go.

one touch of the ball and they are not allowed to pass to the black target player.

Variation. The preceding practice can be developed to include two-versus-two inside the longer area (figure 11.3). Give-and-goes or wall passes can be played between the attacking players, either inside or outside the longer area.

Coaching Points.

• Have the player with the ball attack the defender; the ball should be about 20 to 30 inches in front of the player.

• The side players should move with the play and take up positions alongside the defender and facing the ball player.

• The ball player should strike the pass off the front foot and immediately accelerate on the blind side into the space behind the defender for the return pass.

Through the Minefield

Purpose. To develop passing skills against high-pressure defense.

Procedure. A team of three white players plays against four black defenders in each of two 20-yard squares, which are separated by a 5-yard corridor (figure 11.4). Position a solitary white player in this 20-by-5-yard corridor. The object of the game is for the white team to advance the ball through the solitary player to its other three players to get it to the white target player. Restrict the solitary player to three seconds on the ball, but the player can pass the ball both forward and backward into the corridor.

Coaching Points.

• Encourage the ball player to keep the head up so that he or she is aware of the position of teammates and opponents. In particular the ball player must be alert to any possibility of getting the ball to the solitary white player in the 20-by-5 corridor.

• Get the attacking players off the ball to adopt support positions where the ball can be passed to them without fear of interception by the opponents.

Shooting

I would be a rich man if I had received a 10-dollar bill every time a coach said to me, "We play well and we can get into the scoring area, but we can't finish." Shooting! It is

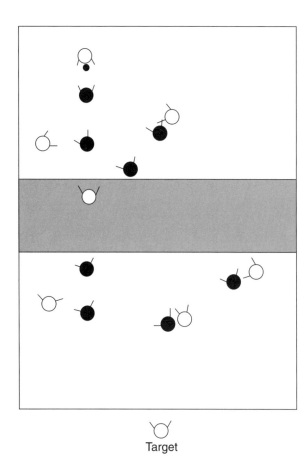

Target

Figure 11.4 Through the Minefield—an activity that develops passing skills against a high-pressure defense.

frustrating to a team to work hard playing out of the back through the midfield and into the scoring area with a good opportunity to score, and then the player on the ball blows the shot by blasting it over the goal, outside the post, or straight at the keeper. Part of every practice should involve a realistic small-sided game that practices shooting.

Shooting on goal is a combination of power and accuracy. Most young players go for too much power and too little control, while the great finishers choose the right blend of power and accuracy. Somehow, these great finishers have found the knack of "passing" the ball into the goal using the maximum degree of accuracy. Too often we find the inexperienced striker blasting the ball high or wide from a good goal-scoring position.

Think of the field as a golf course. The area outside the scoring area is the fairway, from which you can shoot with power to gain

distance. The scoring area is the green, where you delicately blend force and accuracy to put the ball into the cup.

Many paragraphs have been written about the mechanics of shooting. They talk about placement of the nonkicking foot, knee bend over the ball, eye on the ball, follow-through, and so forth. That's all well and good in ideal situations. But the player in front of the goal seldom receives an ideal ball in an ideal position. True, the player should anticipate the ball and move into its path—if there is time. However, time is not a luxury that the shooter often has, and if the shooter takes the time to set up the shot, the scoring opportunity will be gone. Rinus Michels, the famed former Dutch national coach, compared the match to an action movie. The frames move fast and every frame is different. What was available to the shooter in the first frame may not be there in the next frame. In the next frame the goalkeeper may be positioned, or a defender may have moved between the ball and the goal. The shooter must take advantage of what is offered in the

Tips for Teaching Shooting

- Allow players to take chances in the scoring areas.
- Use praise to entrench the thrill of success.
- Teach the players to go for the early, quick shot. The quick touch or poke at goal while the goalkeeper is out of position and the defense is trying to recover pays off. Bending back the leg for the hard shot takes time.
- Force players to take the responsibility for a shot when they have it. Some, for fear of failing, will pass when they shouldn't.
- On the other hand, you must also coach them to pass the ball when another player has a better shot at goal.
- Make them aware of the goalkeeper's vulnerabilities. A goalkeeper moving across the goal may be out of position and leave part of the goal unprotected.
- Caution the players always to follow their shots. They should always look for the "garbage" goal.

first frame. That means that the shooter must be able to shoot any ball received in any position. The accuracy comes not so much from how the shooter hits the ball, but from where the shooter hits the ball. In the end it comes down to what area of the foot should hit what area of the ball to make this shot accurate. Obviously, that makes shooting an art of instant, instinctive decision making. That is why shooting accurately is difficult and requires endless hours of positive, successful practice.

There is another area of concern. When a player shoots at goal there can be only one of two results, success or failure. I feel that most players fear failure so much that it stresses them to the point where they can't really take an effective shot at goal. With the imagined embarrassment of missing each additional shot the fear of failure gets more entrenched. Again, it is up to you to design small-sided, conditioned games that allow a high rate of success, have the benefit of your keen observation and correction, and, most of all, your constant praise for successful attempts. Give them opportunities to memorize success rather than failure. It takes self-confidence to be a successful finisher.

 ULTIMATE CONFIDENCE

During the 1995 season I had the pleasure of coaching Adrian Reyes, a player from Mexico. Adrian is a prolific scorer. He can shoot hard and accurately with either foot, can chip an out-of-position goalkeeper, can bend balls, and can head. Simply said, Adrian is good.

During shooting practices I like to observe the shooting player from as close as possible without being clobbered. One day, while Adrian was making a series of fabulous shots, I noticed something. Just before he took each shot I heard him mutter to himself. I stopped and asked him what he was saying. It turned out that before Adrian takes any shot he says to himself, "It's in."

It was refreshing to hear that since throughout my coaching career I have had to deal with players whose last thought before shooting was, "Oh, please don't let me miss."

Again, I would like to give you some of the small-sided, conditioned games I use with my players to improve shooting.

Run and Shoot

Purpose. To improve shooting technique.

Procedure. In groups of three, players combine to shoot at goal (figure 11.5). Black midfielder 1 passes to black midfielder 2 (solid line 1), who turns and immediately feeds the ball to the black striker (solid line 2) to shoot on goal. Black midfielder 2 should concentrate on feeding the pass onto the run that the black striker makes (dotted line). Limit the black striker to one or two touches with a minimum of time involved between touches.

Coaching Points.

• The black striker should begin the run just as black midfielder 2 has executed the turn. If the black striker begins the run too early he or she will end up too wide or possibly in an offside position. If the black striker begins the run too late then the chance is lost.

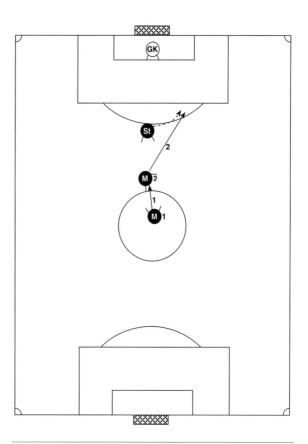

Figure 11.5 Run and Shoot—an activity that improves shooting techniques.

• When making a run to the right, the black striker should turn the head to see over the right shoulder. The opposite, of course, will apply on a run to the left.

• The pass from black midfielder 2 should allow the black striker to move onto the ball at speed in no more than four or five strides.

Cross and Finish

Purpose. To improve shooting on goal from crosses.

Procedure. The black winger rounds the cone and crosses for the black striker to shoot on goal (figure 11.6). Restrict the black striker to one touch.

Coaching Points.

• The black striker should time the run to meet the ball going forward at speed.

• The black striker should read the cues from the black winger's approach to the ball. If the ball is rolling quickly as the black winger approaches it, then it is likely to be a

low cross. On the other hand, if the ball is almost stationary as the black winger approaches it and he or she gets the plant foot close up to the ball, then it is likely to be a high cross.

• If in doubt, the striker should attack the space in front of the first post.

• You should encourage the striker to bend the run in a loop toward the ball. This is much more effective than running in a straight line diagonally toward the ball.

Spin to Win

Purpose. To improve the technique of turning and shooting on goal.

Procedure. In pairs, one player passes to a partner who almost has his or her back to the goal. The receiving player turns and in not more than two steps shoots on goal. Allow the shooter only one touch for receiving and turning and one touch for shooting.

Coaching Points.

• You should encourage the receiving player to get into position to see both the ball and the goal. This is easier to achieve if the player turns his or her back to one of the sidelines.

• The first touch should set up the ball about two to three yards diagonally behind the player on the side to which he or she turns. If shooting with the right foot the player should turn over the left shoulder.

• Encourage your players to move to the ball but to ease up just before ball contact.

• They should use the large surfaces on the outside and inside of the foot to effect the turning touch.

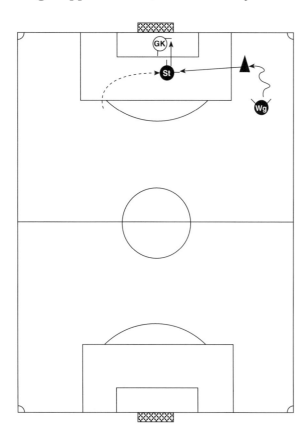

Figure 11.6 Cross and Finish—an activity that improves shooting on goal from crosses.

   THE SAINT AND GREAVSIE

A soccer TV program that enjoyed great popularity and viewing audiences in Britain was *The Saint and Greavsie Show.* The program was named after two outstanding former players— Ian St. John and Jimmy Greaves—both prolific goal scorers. One of the main reasons for the popularity of their show was their quick wit in giving out one-liners on virtually any soccer topic that arose. It was as if they were on a constant high, living on the edge, but with sharp, crystal-clear minds. In fact, their type of personality and mind-set might have been the main reason for their soccer goal-scoring success. They were clinical in their finishing and rarely spurned a chance.

Platform for Success

Purpose. To improve control of high passes leading to shots on goal.

Procedure. Standing, facing the goal at a distance of 25 yards, and holding a ball, the player punts it about 20 to 30 feet in the air. The player controls it with either chest or thigh and immediately shoots on goal. The ball should not bounce more than once after the chest or thigh control. The shot can be either a volley (figure 11.7) or half volley (figure 11.8).

Coaching Points.

• Encourage the player to get to the place where the ball will land and be in a ready, balanced position.

• The player should have both feet planted firmly on the ground about 12 to 15 inches apart.

Figure 11.8 A half volley shot.

Figure 11.7 A volley shot.

• The player should use the receiving surface—chest or thigh—to hit the ball upward and forward.

Heading

Few players have difficulty with a defensive, clearing header that plays the ball high and far. That is probably true because the ball is hit below its center and feels more natural. But one of the most poorly executed skills in American youth soccer is heading in attack. With realistic practices that teach heading to clear, control, score, and pass, you can do much to improve on this weakness. Few players can outjump the defense at the far post and come over the ball to head it powerfully down into the goal, or get to an air ball first at the near post and redirect it, with outstretched neck, past the goalkeeper.

Even those who can get up and over the ball may fail when opponents challenge them.

It takes a courageous player with a love for body contact to get up high in a crowded penalty area to meet a hard-driven ball, get over it, and head it down powerfully without consciously thinking of an incoming challenger. Players who can do that are worth their weight in gold.

The mechanics of a powerful header are not that difficult when you remember that the entire body from the feet to the head contributes to the power. To get a feel for body involvement in the header, ask your players to place their right foot sideways about 24 inches behind a forward pointing left foot. Now have them rock back, then forward, as if heading a ball without leaving their feet. All the muscles used for that rocking motion are used in a powerful header.

One of the better ways the team can learn the mechanics of heading is by viewing videos in slow motion of players capable of heading with power to score. One of my favorites is former Dutch national team player Ruud Gullit.

During the next small-sided, conditioned games, observe and see if the players are using the proper mechanics.

Use Your Head

Purpose. To improve heading on goal.

Procedure. Groups of three players play together. One player has the ball in a wide position and from the second touch must cross the ball in the air to the area in front of goal. The other two players each have one touch on the ball to score. One of these touches must be a header, and the header can go directly into the goal or be used as a pass to the partner.

Coaching Points.

• Inform the player delivering the crosses that he or she can get a high, accurate cross more often by kicking the ball just before it stops after the first touch. This allows the player more time to place the plant foot adjacent to the line of the ball, thus allowing a full swing of the kicking leg.

• Have the players in front of the goal make looped runs to the ball, one covering the front post and the other the back post.

• Allow the receiving players to make decisions on whether to head for goal or make a headed pass depending on the amount of power and accuracy they can get on the ball and the positioning of the goalkeeper and the teammate. Players should head for goal if they think they can score.

Heading in the Right Direction

Purpose. To improve heading on goal.

Procedure. Groups of players line up facing each other at a distance of about 30 yards on a line drawn diagonally through the middle of the goal (figure 11.9). The players behind the goal each have a ball and, in turn, they serve the ball in the air over the crossbar to the player immediately opposite them. Goals can only be scored off a header with both feet off the ground.

Coaching Points.

• Ask your serving players to kick the ball so it will land in the space some 5 to 10 yards in front of the heading players.

• Get your heading players to attack the ball and hit it hard with their heads.

• Players should look at the ball at the moment of impact.

Flick-Ons

Purpose. To improve the technique of flick-on heading.

Procedure. In groups of three, one player with a ball stands at the top of the arc, the second player stands on the six-yard line, and the third player stands behind the goal. The third player takes a throw-in toward the second player, who must flick-on the ball with the head for the first player to catch.

Tips for Teaching Heading

• Ask the players to judge the path of the ball early. They should move to meet the ball, even if that means taking a step back first.

• Instruct players to jump off one foot.

• Players should not lose sight of the ball.

• Teach players to bend the body backward to form a bow and to release the bow just before contact.

• The feet and lower legs come forward, the lower body moves back, and the upper body, neck, and head snap forward.

• Use plyometrics to increase the vertical jumps of your players.

• Ask the third player to throw the ball in a flat trajectory straight at a point just above the second player's head. Insist that the player not deliver a high, lobbed throw.

Always use hand-stitched leather balls when practicing heading. You can let some air out of them when introducing heading to beginners.

 OH! MY HEAD

I held a coaches' clinic in Houston, Texas, in June 1983, and I was asked to give a heading-on-goal demonstration. I asked a colleague to cross some balls so that I could demonstrate the heading technique. As the first cross was delivered I made the appropriate run to the expected arrival area and took off so that I could get my head slightly above the ball to head it powerfully downward toward the goal. At the last moment the ball knuckled and hit me high on the forehead. I fingered the indentations left on the top of my forehead by the ball. This was my first encounter with a molded ball, and the manufacturer left its imprint on my head.

Screening

One of the skills I look for when first viewing a player is the ability to maintain possession of the ball while under pressure of one or two opponents. The player must be able to screen the ball, play out of trouble, or delay until help arrives. Alas, too many of our players lose the ball one-on-one, try the impossible shot, make a hopeless pass, or lose the ball over the touchline or goal line. The ability to maintain possession while under pressure takes the confidence and determination that only numerous successful practices can instill.

Probably the greatest mistake that players make in screening the ball is that they turn their backs to their opponent. They are thus at a disadvantage as they form only a narrow screen, and the defender can get at the ball easily. Moreover, the screening players have difficulty in predicting the movement of the defender if there is no body contact. Instead, they should screen sideways-on and play the ball with the foot farthest from their opponent. This not only gives them a wider screen but also allows them to see the movements of the defender (figure 11.10).

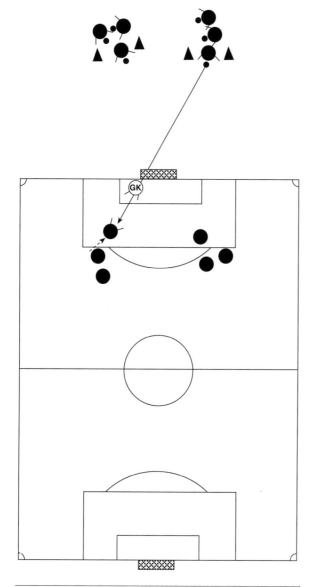

Figure 11.9 Heading on goal.

The second player should come to the ball, and just before the ball would hit his or her forehead, the player should lift the chin so that the forehead forms a backward angle. The ball should skip off this angled surface into the hands of the first player.

Coaching Points.

• Ask the second player to move to the ball to get into a position where he or she could head the ball forward while standing at full height. Just as the ball is about to make contact with the forehead, the player takes the head back to offer an almost horizontal forehead surface to the ball.

I like using the following small-sided, conditioned games to practice screening.

Keep It Safe

Purpose. To improve ball protection.

Procedure. A group of players, each with a ball, plays in an area about 30 by 30 yards. Three players without a ball individually attempt to get possession of any ball. Players with a ball can run away with the ball or screen the ball from an opponent. An opponent who wins the ball now becomes the possessor and dribbles or screens. A player who has lost a ball is not allowed to attempt to win back the same ball.

Coaching Points.

• Ask your ball players always to be aware of all players in the area, particularly the ones without a ball.

• Insist that they turn away from defenders rather than trying to dribble past them.

• Your better players will have the ball on the side farthest away from the defender and take a sideways-on screening position.

Figure 11.10   The sideways-on screen.

Tips to Teach Screening

• Teach *all* players to screen effectively. Even defenders in possession may have their passing lanes blocked momentarily.

• Work on weight distribution. Most players would benefit if they were to bring their center of gravity down a bit, especially when screening the ball.

• Coach players to turn around the opponent if they are screening and to attempt to beat the opponent. Turning into the opponent and showing the ball often results in loss of the ball.

• Emphasize that before turning around the opponent, the player with the ball should fake the opponent. The player with the ball should get the opponent thinking that he or she is going to do something and then do something else.

• Point out that when a player with the ball screens well, the defender may for an instant lose sight of the ball and panic. This may cause the defender to do something foolish on which your player can capitalize.

• Your weaker players will probably screen the ball with their backs to the defender. This is too small a screen, and the defender can easily steal the ball.

Keep to Shoot

Purpose. To improve ball protection.

Procedure. Divide two teams into several one-versus-one groups. All the players in the white team have possession of a ball while their immediate opponent tries to dispossess them and force the ball out of the 30-by-30-yard area. The player who keeps possession for 15 seconds is allowed a free setup pass of no more than five yards and then a shot on goal.

Coaching Points.

• Ask the white players to get sideways-on to their opponent and to control the ball with the foot farthest from the opponent. If they wish to change direction they should immediately pivot to get the opposite shoulder against the opponent in the sideways-on position and control the ball with the opposite foot.

• Insist that they turn away, rather than into, their opponent.

Noah's Arc

Purpose. To create goal-scoring opportunities when heavily marked.

Procedure. A defender marks an attacker inside the arc. A second attacker passes the ball into the arc, and the first attacker has five seconds to get off a shot on goal. The ball should remain inside the arc in possession of the attacker until the shot is made. If the ball goes outside the arc, then the defender has won the game.

Coaching Points.

• Get your attacker to take up a position where he or she can see both the defender and the second attacker just before receiving the ball.

• Encourage the attacker to develop a repertoire of turns, fakes, and touches to set up a shooting opportunity.

• Have the attacker shoot on goal whenever there is a chance to do so.

Receiving and Turning

Receiving the ball, under pressure or not, is another technique at which U.S. players do not excel. Receiving the ball and turning with it is an essential tool for every player, but especially for attacking players, who often receive the ball with their backs to the goal. Under screening I mentioned that the first question we ask when looking at a player is, "How well does the player maintain possession under pressure?" The second question we ask is, "How is the player's first touch on the ball and is it in preparation for the second touch?"

The speed of the game has increased so much over the last few decades that players receiving a ball are almost immediately pressured by an opponent. The era of comfortably trapping the ball and then deciding what to do with it is long gone. In fact, the term "trapping" is antiquated. Today's players must know what is going on around them *before* they receive the ball. Before receiving the ball, players must be able to fake the opponent. Players receiving the ball must control it, change its direction, and turn with it all in one motion.

There are two main methods of receiving and turning with the ball. In the first, players come to the ball in a slightly sideways-on position and take the ball with the inside of the back foot. As the ball makes contact with the foot, players drag it back so that the ball ends up two or three yards diagonally in front of them after they have turned. Players rotate on the supporting foot (figure 11.11).

The second method usually involves a preliminary fake. Players look as if they are going to receive the ball with the inside of the back foot but instead take it on the outside of the front foot. Again, the touch should set up the ball two or three yards diagonally in front of them after they have turned (figure 11.12).

Use the following small-sided, conditioned games to practice receiving and turning.

Relay Turns

Purpose. To improve the techniques of receiving and turning at speed.

Procedure. Several teams in groups of four or five players line up about 15 yards apart (figure 11.13). Teams race against each other to move the ball through the middle players to the end player and back to the starting player five times. End players can have only

---

Tips for Teaching Receiving and Turning

• Allow players to practice without pressure at first. Thereafter slowly increase pressure until you are practicing under match conditions.

• Watch to see that players are well balanced when receiving the ball.

• Make sure that players' first touch on the ball has an unpredictable result. That is, they must fake to cause the defender to believe that they are moving the ball to their left and instead move the ball to their right. At first most players will control the ball directly in front of themselves. That is very predictable. Skilled opponents will read that and play off the player who is receiving the ball.

• Observe to see that players receiving the ball are aware of players around them, both teammates and opponents.

Figure 11.11   Turning with the ball.

Figure 11.12   Faking and turning with the ball.

one touch, while the middle players have one touch for the turn and one for the pass.

Coaching Points.

• Get your players to understand that if they pass the ball quickly and accurately to the next player, then it will be easier for that player to make a quick turn on the ball.

• The inside receiving players should move to the ball but just before the point of contact they should ease into a relaxed, balanced position. The feet should be about 20 inches apart, one foot in front of the other, with the chest at about a 45-angle to the passing player.

• The simplest turn is to take the ball on the inside surface of the rear foot while pivoting over the rear shoulder. Players should drag the ball back to a point about a yard or two immediately behind them. From this position players can get off the next pass immediately.

Pass, Turn, Shoot

Purpose. To improve direction and timing of runs into scoring positions.

Procedure. As illustrated in figure 11.14, in groups of three players, the player with the ball passes to the second player in front of the center circle (solid line 1). The third player makes a run to receive the ball in a scoring position (dotted line a). The second player must receive and turn with the ball in one touch and immediately play the pass to the third player (solid line 2), who has one touch to shoot (solid line 3).

Coaching Points.

• Try to get the third player to understand when, where, and how the second player can pass the ball to him or her.

• If the third player runs for a pass before the second player has controlled it, the third

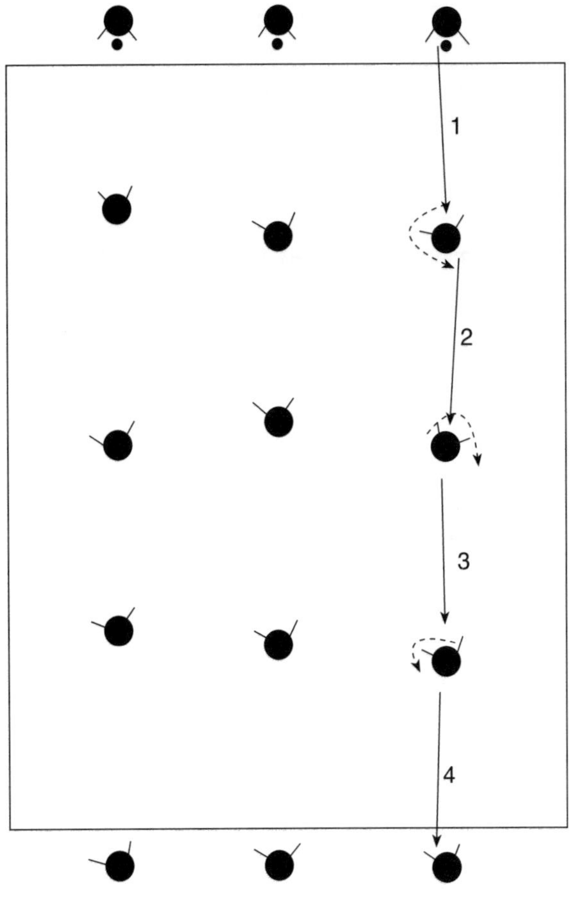

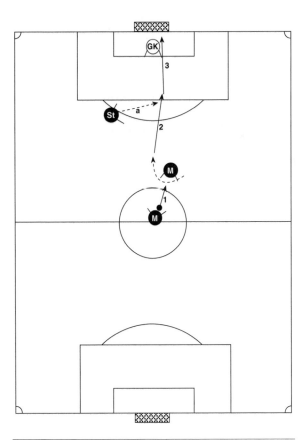

Figure 11.13 Relay Turns—a relay race for receiving and turning.

Figure 11.14 Pass, Turn, Shoot—an activity that improves the timing of runs into a shooting position.

player is likely to make too long a run or be in an offside position.

• Get the second player to turn with one touch and deliver the pass with the second touch. This will make it easier for the third player to time the run.

• Have your third player make a looped, diagonal run. Remind the second player that the challenge is to deliver the pass into the stride path of the third player's run.

Dribbling

Dribbling is not a dying art; it is the technique players need to play out of trouble, to create space for themselves or teammates, or to create scoring opportunities. Unfortunately, most of the offensive emphasis in the modern game is placed on passing. You should recognize that dribbling skills are also vitally important.

Dribbling is also a skill that excites players, coaches, and fans. It is about the unexpected or the inventive, and when used in the opponent's half of the field it can destroy that team's defensive shape and balance.

When dribbling is mentioned, most people think of intricate moves and turns with the ball. While ball manipulation should certainly be part of every player's arsenal of weapons, it is not the only skill that contributes to effective dribbling. In our haste to teach the intricate stuff we sometimes overlook the simpler, yet equally effective, means to an end.

Dribbling means running with the ball, away from an opponent or at an opponent. If the run is away from the opponent, especially if going toward the goal, then speed and maintaining control of the ball is everything. But, if the run is at an opponent, nothing unsettles that opponent more than sudden changes of pace. It's a simple skill, but often overlooked. Some players have explosive speed. When they come at an opponent slowly but then suddenly explode with the ball into the space behind the opponent, they may leave the opponent standing. Another change of pace is for a player to come at an opponent at speed, slow down, and speed up again, which may cause the opponent to stumble or at least be caught on the wrong foot.

Another tactic that can leave defenders in an awkward position is for a player to take on an opponent at speed and suddenly change direction. This can be particularly effective if the player can change direction several times. These are two simple ways of unsettling a defender.

All players should practice the more intricate tools of dribbling and faking. The tricks can be as simple as pretending to go to the left, and going instead to the right, or vice versa; faking to kick, but kicking over the ball; faking to pass the ball one way, but instead stepping over the ball and turning the other direction; faking to heel kick the ball, but instead stepping over the ball and playing it with the other foot to the side; and so forth. There are numerous ways of manipulating the ball.

Here are a few of the small-sided, conditioned games I use for dribbling practices.

To and Fro

Purpose. To improve quickness in turning with the ball.

Procedure. Mark two parallel lines three yards apart. Players line up with one foot on the

---

Tips for Teaching Dribbling

• Encourage dribbling in the attacking third.
• Discourage dribbling in the defending third, especially when under pressure.
• Have players each show their favorite move with the ball. Then, if you approve of the move, ask all players to duplicate it and practice it.
• Practice various moves designed to beat an opponent in one-versus-one situations. If the move is successful the player may finish with a shot at a goal protected by one of the goalkeepers.
• Teach players that when a dribble has successfully beaten an opponent they should explode into the space opened up by the dribble. Players too often create an opening and continue at the same pace, allowing the defender to recover. They shouldn't have to beat a defender twice.

ball on the first line. They race to find which player can move the ball over the second line and back over the first line five times, finishing with the foot on the ball on the first line. Restrict players to two touches—one touch to turn and the second touch to move the ball.

Coaching Points.

• Explain to the players that they must develop a forward touch on the ball so that they get to it just as it crosses the line.

• Encourage them to use both the inside and the outside of the foot surface in making the turns.

• Show them that the best turns are made not when the ball is stopped but when it is dragged back in the opposite direction.

Run the Gauntlet

Purpose. To develop fakes, feints, and tricks in dribbling.

Procedure. Mark three 10-by-10-yard squares and place a defender in each square. A line of attacking players attempts to get through the space and shoot into the unguarded goal (figure 11.15).

Coaching Points.

• Get your attackers to go at the defenders with the ball at controlled speed.

• Encourage the attackers to develop fakes and feints on the ball.

• Remind the attackers that they can develop a larger repertoire of fakes, feints, and tricks on the ball if they dribble with the ball directly in front of them. When confronted by a defender, the ball should never be more than one yard from the front foot.

 SUPERSUB

During the NASL years Elson Seale played for the Portland Timbers. After the demise of the NASL, I coached him for a little while. Elson was an exciting dribbler and loved to take on players one-on-one. The Timbers used him as a substitute. The fans would frequently yell for the Timbers' coach to bring on Elson and they cheered when he came into the match. They wouldn't be disappointed. As soon as Elson got the ball he looked for an opponent to take on. After finding one he quickly proceeded to beat him. At that point you would have expected him to continue toward the goal, pass, cross, or

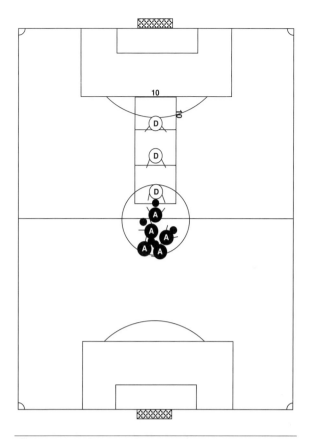

Figure 11.15 Run the Gauntlet—an activity that develops fakes, feints, and tricks in dribbling.

shoot. Not Elson; he loved the one-on-ones so much that he patiently waited for the beaten opponent to catch up with him so that he could beat him again.

Runs

Probably the most difficult skill for any attacking player to learn is the timing of runs. Players should always make their runs in the ball handler's line of vision. It simply does not make sense for players to make a run for the ball when the ball handler can't see them.

Badly timed runs can take two forms. The first is when the player makes the run too early and usually runs too far; the second is when the player makes the run too late. A well-timed run usually covers no more than 5 to 15 yards. The player initiates the run just as the ball handler makes his or her controlling touch. If the ball handler and runner wait until they establish eye contact, it is too late. The movement of the running

---

Tips to Teach Runs

- Watch if there was eye contact between the runner and the passer *before* the passer received the ball.
- Teach players to bend their runs so that when they receive the ball they are already facing the goal.
- Be ready to point out the effectiveness of the run to the player who made it but didn't get the ball. The player may be frustrated. Many goals are scored because the player making the run took defenders into poor positions, thereby creating space and time for a teammate.

---

player (body language) informs the ball handler where and when the running player wants the ball.

Here are some small-sided, conditioned games to help players improve their off-the-ball runs.

Big Ben

Purpose. To improve timing of runs.

Procedure. Groups of four players with one ball play pass-and-move with no opposition. Players must play the ball with one or two touches within two seconds. The players off the ball may sprint or walk only—no jogging. Players are not allowed to talk; they can communicate only through body movements. The ball can be passed only to a running player.

Coaching Points.

• Get your moving players to initiate their runs just as a player receives the ball.

• The moving players' runs should be in the receiving player's line of vision.

• The receiving player should deliver the pass to the space or spot at a speed dictated by the shape and direction of the moving player's run.

Five-Versus-Two

Purpose. To improve movement off the ball.

Procedure. Five play against two in the penalty area. A point is scored each time one of the five players can place a foot on top of the ball on one of the shorter (18-yard) lines of the penalty box. They must alternately attack one line then the other. The five offen-

sive players are restricted to two touches on the ball in each possession.

Coaching Points.

• Demonstrate to your players that the ball player should always have at least two teammates in positions where the ball can be played to them without interception by opponents.

• The ball player should deliver the pass before being closed down by an opponent.

• The two nearest supporting attackers should take up positions almost in a straight line, one on either side of the ball.

• Insist on high-quality, quick, accurate ball movement.

  OFF THE BALL

After we beat Brazil 1-0 in the 1989 FIFA Under-17 World Cup finals in Scotland, the Brazilian coach paid the American players the ultimate compliment during the postmatch press conference. He said that his team found it extremely difficult to regain possession of the ball after they had lost it. The skill level shown by the American players had been very high, and their movement off the ball outstanding.

It was no coincidence that the Brazilian coach should mention some of the topics that we had concentrated on during our training camps leading up to the World Cup finals. It was not only skill on the ball that made the likes of Claudio Reyna, Imad Baba, Nidal Baba, Joel Russell, and Jorge Salcedo so good; it was also their movement off the ball.

Games for Offensive Technique Development

The following small-sided, conditioned games that I have developed help players deal with most offensive challenges, and, in particular, with compacted defenses.

• Players in possession of the ball are limited to three seconds. If they take longer, award a free kick to the other team.

• To score a goal all of the attacking team, except the goalkeeper, must be in the opponent's half of the field.

• Whenever a goalkeeper takes possession of the ball all of the opposing players must withdraw over the halfway line before they can resume defending.

• Impose all the conditions simultaneously. Top-level teams compact their defense not only from back to front (down the length of the field) but also from side to side (across the field) (see figure 9.9 in chapter 9).

An enjoyable conditioned game that helps to develop switching play is to use four goals. Here, one team guards two goals while the other team guards the other two goals. This practice activity will help your goalkeepers improve their understanding of distance and angles.

Summary

It is a big thrill to watch a team play attacking soccer with confidence and flair. Before a team can do that, however, you must give attention to the development of the offensive techniques needed to mount effective attacks. The reminders that follow will help you develop those techniques.

- Require offensive players to break down a compact defense by either playing through it, over it, or around it.
- Continually expose offensive players to the problem of beating a compact defense in small-sided, conditioned games.
- Coach players to move the ball quickly, not only down the length of the field but oftentimes across the field before moving downfield.
- Work hard with the players so they become good passers of the ball in confined situations.
- Emphasize that shooting on goal is a combination of power and accuracy. The good finishers have found the knack of "passing" the ball into the goal using maximum accuracy.
- Practice heading a lot; it is one of the most poorly executed skills in American youth soccer.
- Teach the players to screen by turning sideways-on to the opponent and playing the ball with the foot farthest from the opponent.
- Spend time on developing players' ability to receive and turn with the ball simultaneously.
- Don't discourage dribbling in the attacking third; it is as much part of the game as the ball. Players who can beat their opponents by dribbling the ball past them can unsettle the opposing defense and carve open the way for a pass, a cross, or a shot on goal.
- Be patient when working on timing of runs. This is probably the most difficult offensive skill for any player to learn.
- Make sure that players make their runs in the ball handler's line of vision.

Chapter 12

Teaching
Offensive Tactics

The most successful attacking teams will usually have groups of two or more players that combine well. They will be able to find a way through the opposing defense, around the opposing defense, or over the opposing defense. The more opportunities that these groups of players have to play together in realistic soccer practices against groups of defenders, the more likely they are to find solutions to the problems presented by the defense.

The first requirement for finding solutions to problems is a thorough understanding of the five key principles of offense. The next project is to train your team to develop better overall offensive teamwork.

Set plays in your favor are scoring opportunities. You must capitalize on them and practice offensive set plays thoroughly. Both throw-ins and penalties need attention.

Understanding Offensive Principles

You can better teach offensive tactics if you categorize coaching points into five key offensive principles:

- Support (depth)
- Penetration
- Width
- Mobility
- Improvisation (creativity)

Every coach and every player should understand that when players and teams adhere to these offensive principles they are much more likely to achieve offensive success. If you analyze a team's offensive failure you will probably find that a player or players on the team did not observe one or more of these principles. On the other hand, successful players and teams will consistently adhere to the key offensive principles, resulting in a much more potent attack.

Support

A player in possession of the ball should always have one or more opportunities of passing the ball to other members of the team. This means that players off the ball on the team in possession should move into positions that allow the ball to come to them. Very often, however, we find that players off the ball wait for the ball to come to them, allowing defenders to get between them and the ball. This is most notable when players stand in lines either down or across the field.

The player in possession should ideally have the possibility of passing the ball forward, sideways (across the field), or backward to other players on the team. In figure 12.1, for example, black marking back 1 can pass to either his wide midfielder, his sweeper, his stopper, his midfielder, or even to one of his forwards.

In my 30 years of experience as a soccer coach I have found that by far the most effective method of getting players to better understand soccer tactics is to place them in small-sided, conditioned games.

The simplest, but probably most effective, small-sided, conditioned game that you can use to practice support goes as follows:

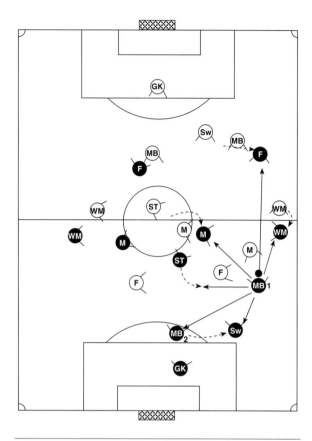

Figure 12.1   Support for the ball handler.

Confined to Base

Purpose. To develop forward play using two forwards.

Procedure. Two forwards play against three defenders and a goalkeeper in each half of the field. No player is allowed to cross over the halfway line, although the ball can be passed backward and forward over the halfway line. Only the forwards can score. Observe all laws of the game except the corner-kick law.

Coaching Points.

- Observe that most forwards want to come toward the ball. In the beginning stages they will tend to kill their space and position themselves near the halfway line (figure 12.2). Notice the position of the black forwards.

- They will be much more successful in receiving the ball if they push up on the line of the sweeper. This scenario makes it much easier for them to get the ball because they have more space to come to the ball, as well as an opportunity of running onto the ball in the space behind the defense.

• Forwards should time their runs to coincide with what is happening on the ball. They should move to the ball when their defender in possession receives the ball and when there is a clear path for that defender to pass to the forward.

• The two forwards should work harmoniously. If the first forward goes to the ball then the second forward should normally hold on the line of the opposing sweeper.

• If the first forward is able to turn on the ball then the second forward has three main options: (a) to make a diagonal run behind the defense, (b) to move away from the first forward allowing the latter to have a better one-versus-one dribbling opportunity, or (c) to offer himself or herself as a target for a wall pass.

• If the first forward receives the ball facing away from the second forward and is heavily pressured by an opponent, then the second forward should be alert to the possibility of the first forward passing backward as a prelude to a further penetrating pass. This

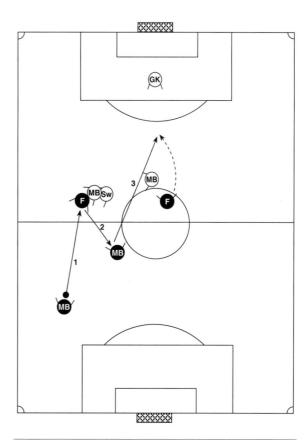

Figure 12.3   A one-three pass.

move might be described as a one-three (figure 12.3).

• Sometimes the first forward will move to the ball too early but will take a defender with him or her. This will allow the second forward to make a run into the space created by the first forward's movement.

• The forward who comes to the ball and is heavily pressured by an opponent should receive the ball with the foot farthest from the opponent (figure 12.4).

• However, the forward who is given the opportunity to make even a quarter turn should get the ball onto the front foot. The forward is then in a much better position to play a one-two or to dribble at speed.

Penetration

Whenever possible, the player in possession should pass the ball in a forward direction. The objective of the game is to score goals, and ultimately the ball must get into the scoring area (see figure 9.1 in chapter 9) if a team is to score goals. Experience has shown

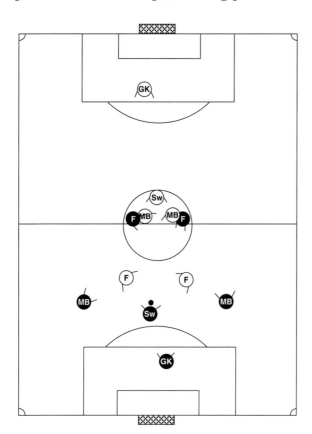

Figure 12.2   Black forwards have killed their receiving space.

Figure 12.4 Receiving the ball with the foot farthest from the opponent.

that the quicker a team plays the ball forward, the more likely it will be that the opposing defense is disorganized.

A successful team can play the ball quickly and accurately to its front players. This means that the runs of the front players allow the team the opportunity of playing over, around, or through the opposing defense.

A small-sided, conditioned game that helps develop quick penetration goes as follows:

Three-Pronged Attack

Purpose. To develop forward play using three forwards.

Procedure. The simplest way of preparing three forwards to combine is to play a realistic, small-sided, conditioned game. Three forwards play against four defenders and a goalkeeper in each half of the field. Restrict all players to their half of the field. Only the forwards can score. Players can pass the ball backward or forward over the halfway line. Observe all laws of the game.

Coaching Points.

• You should make certain that the forwards understand the coaching points made when only two forwards played against three

defenders. With the addition of another forward and another defender in each half of the field, the number of opportunities for combination play greatly increases. You can now focus on having one of the three forwards get in behind the defense. The offense will usually be unsuccessful if all three forwards persist in making runs toward the ball.

• If you wish to play with three forwards you may find it best to play with one advanced (primary) striker and two withdrawn (secondary) strikers. It is the responsibility of the primary striker to push up on the line of the sweeper while the two secondary strikers look for the ball in the space in front of the defense.

• If one of the secondary strikers or the primary striker receives the ball and is preparing to drop it to a supporting midfielder, then the other secondary striker should look to make a diagonal run into the space behind the defense (figure 12.5).

Once your players meet some success in the previous small-sided game, you can in-

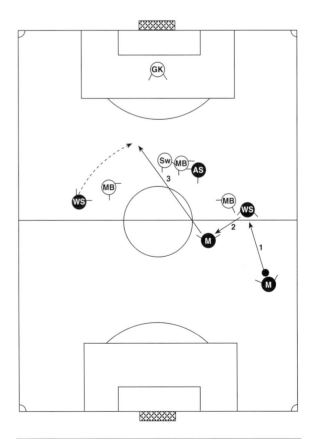

Figure 12.5 Getting in behind the defense.

crease the pressure on the forwards by adding an additional defender to each side. The following small-sided, conditioned game develops.

Penetrating With Three Against Five

Purpose. To further develop forward play using three forwards.

Procedure. Three forwards play against five defenders and a goalkeeper in each half of the field. Restrict all players to their half of the field. Only the forwards can score. Players can pass the ball backward or forward over the halfway line. Observe all laws of the game except the corner-kick law.

Coaching Points.

• Again, the coach should make certain that the forwards understand the coaching points made when three forwards played against four defenders.

• The addition of another defender in each half of the field makes opportunities for combination play more difficult to capitalize on. You should focus on getting one of the three forwards in behind the defense. The offense will usually be unsuccessful if all three forwards persist in making runs toward the ball.

Width

Modern-day defensive tactics aim to restrict the space in which the attacking team can operate. The defensive team will pressure the player on the ball and try to prevent him or her from playing the ball forward, sideways, or backward.

The priority of the defense will be to stop the ball from being played forward, and they will get many of their players in the area of the ball. This often means that it will be easier to play the ball backward or sideways before attempting a forward pass (figure 12.6). This tactic will usually be successful if the attacking team can retain some width in its attacking shape.

Three and One

Purpose. To develop forward play using three forwards and one midfielder.

Procedure. You can develop the previous small-sided, conditioned game into one that lends itself well to practicing width on of-

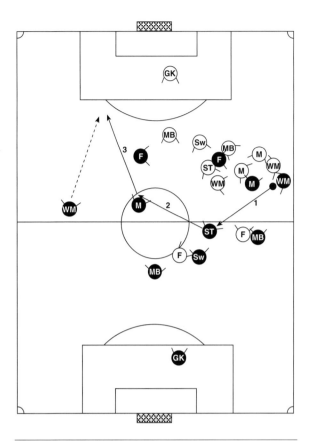

Figure 12.6   Switching the play.

fense. All you do is add another player to each team. These additional players play without any conditions and can cover the whole field.

Coaching Points.

• The addition of an extra unrestricted player on each team creates the opportunity of developing the concept of creating space for others. Also, players must now begin to think of taking defenders out of covering positions (figure 12.7) rather than taking them into covering positions (figure 12.8).

• In figure 12.7 the black advanced striker has moved away from the ball and the immediate defenders—white marking back 1 and the white sweeper—have followed. The movement by the black advanced striker has allowed black withdrawn striker 2 and black withdrawn striker 1 a better opportunity of dribbling or interpassing to get in behind the defense. In figure 12.8 the black advanced striker has run into the space behind white marking back 3. The defender, white marking back 2, has responded and gone with the black advanced striker. In effect, the black

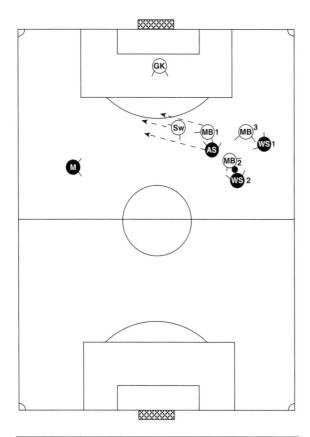

Figure 12.7 Taking defenders out of covering positions.

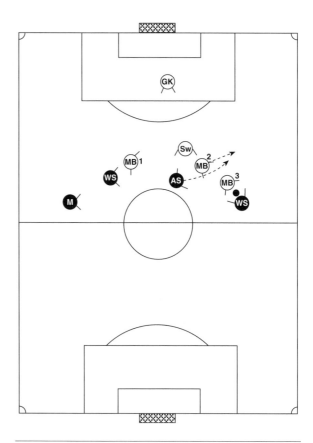

Figure 12.8 Taking defenders into covering positions.

advanced striker has taken white marking back 2 into a good defensive covering position.

Attack in Numbers

Purpose. To develop attacking play.

Procedure. You can develop the previous small-sided, conditioned game to include two or three unrestricted players on each team. Opportunities will be available for creating space for others, overlapping, running at defenses, and interpassing.

Coaching Points.

• When the ball is passed to a wide player there is always the opportunity of making a looped run to the outside of that player. This type of run will usually allow the offense to penetrate on the outside of the defense (figure 12.9) or, when the defense tracks down the overlapping player, will allow the wide player to cut inside (figure 12.10).

• It is also likely that one of the unrestricted players will manage to get possession of the ball in the space behind the opposing unrestricted players. This will allow the player to run at the opposing defense.

• There will also be numerous opportunities of combination play through interpassing. The key to success is to get quick, simple, but accurate ball movement. If the ball sticks with one player for longer than a couple of seconds, then it is likely that the defense will have sufficient time to reorganize.

Mobility

Probably the least understood offensive principle is mobility in attack. In America, we are far too position conscious. In many teams we see players who confine their activities to certain areas of the field. Probably the biggest culprits are the wide players—the wing fullbacks and the wide midfielders.

The reality is that a player who plays in a fixed position and remains in a certain area of the field is much more easily marked.

A player who plays with a degree of freedom and mobility will be much more difficult to mark. In figure 12.11, the black wide

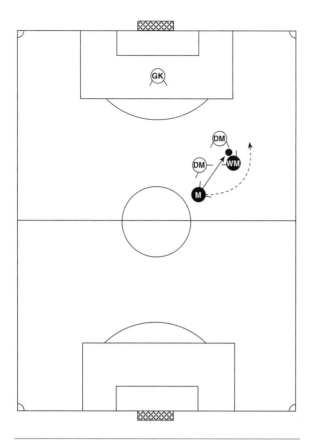

Figure 12.9   Overlapping.

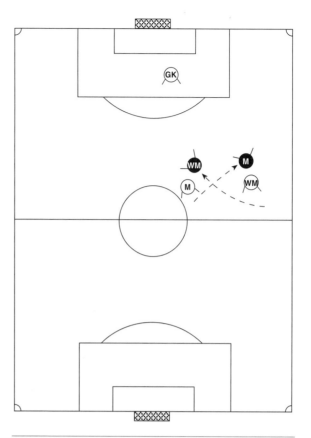

Figure 12.11   Switching positions.

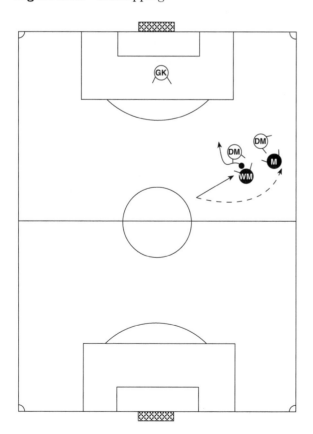

Figure 12.10   Cutting inside.

midfielder makes a run inside while the black midfielder moves to the outside. Effectively, the black wide midfielder and the black midfielder have exchanged positions so that now the black wide midfielder is playing in central midfield while the black midfielder is playing on the right side of midfield. What is more important, the exchange of positions has created problems for the defensive players, the white wide midfielder and the white midfielder. Do they stay in their positions or do they track down their immediate opponents?

Again, a forward who plays in a fixed position is easily marked, but by exchanging positions with other players the forward will create greater problems for the defense (figure 12.12). Does the white marking back follow the black forward? If he or she does, this creates an opportunity for the black midfielder to steal into the space.

The Triangle

Purpose. To develop the players' offensive understanding of the balance between risk and safety.

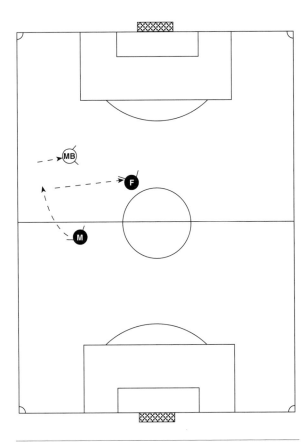

Figure 12.12   Mobility in attack.

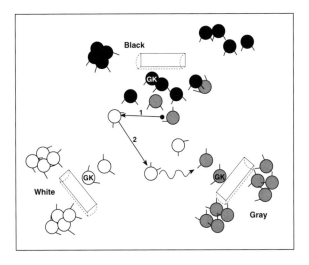

Figure 12.13   The Triangle—a three-goal game.

Procedure. This small-sided, conditioned game uses three goals set out in a 50-yard equilateral triangle. Three teams of four players line up against each other (figure 12.13). Each team defends one designated goal while it tries to score on either of the other two goals. A team may gang up with another team but they should beware of being double-crossed.

Coaching Points.

• In the initial stages teams will often neglect the defense of their goal. Too many players will go forward, leaving only one or two players to defend their goal.

• The smarter players will soon learn that to win they must get all their players goalside of the ball. When on the offensive, and in possession of the ball, the players must calculate the balance between safety and risk. If one or more players go forward on the offensive then the remaining players must organize themselves so that they are least vulnerable to a counterattack.

• The player in possession should also realize that an attack in one direction is easy to stop. Most often it is better to suddenly switch the point of attack and even go to another goal. The player in possession must also calculate whether it is prudent to pass the ball to one of the players in another team. How likely is a double cross?

• When their team is in possession, players without the ball also have many difficult decisions. "Do I stay in a defensive position?" "Do I move forward on the attack? If so, where do I go?" "Do I move into a supporting position behind the ball, do I advance in front of the ball, or do I take a wide support position?"

Improvisation (Creativity)

Whenever you observe a top-class team you will notice that they will move the ball quickly, simply, and accurately from one player to another. Occasionally, however, one of the players will make a move with the ball that not only will catch the eye of the spectators but also will unbalance the opposing defense. The player will do something that is completely unpredictable and unexpected.

This unorthodox activity might be a pass. In figure 12.14, the black forward, who is heavily marked by white marking back 2, receives the ball from the black midfielder. The black forward 1 is aware that there is space between white marking back 1 and the white sweeper for black forward 2 to run onto a through pass. While still facing the black midfielder, black forward 1 bends the ball off

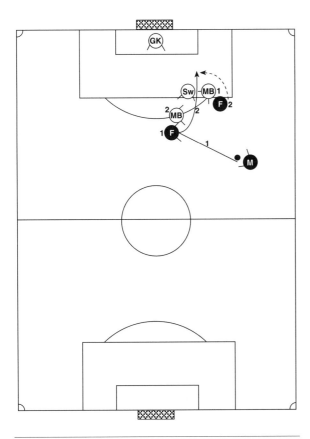

Figure 12.14 Doing the unexpected.

the outside of the left foot around white marking back 2 into the space between white marking back 1 and the white sweeper.

Usually, however, the unorthodox activity is a fake or dribble, particularly in the area near and inside the scoring area. Coaches should encourage players to be imaginative, inventive, and unorthodox in this space. The unexpected move or fake will often unbalance the opposing defense. Coaches should refrain from calling plays in this area and allow their players freedom of expression. Coaches who insist on calling the plays or drilling their players through patterns of play will produce dull, unimaginative, and mechanical players.

The key to producing creative and imaginative attacking teams is to find the player that fits the role of the playmaker. Usually this player will operate in the area near the scoring area and will be heavily marked, often facing away from the goal. However, the player's uncanny awareness of what is happening all around will allow him or her to pick out cues that other players will not even

see. It is no coincidence that some of the superstars of soccer operated in this space—Pele, Maradona, Platini, Cruyff, and others.

In figure 12.15 black forward 1, who is heavily marked by the white sweeper and white marking back 2, receives a pass from the black midfielder. Black forward 1 knows where black forward 2 is positioned, fakes to receive the pass, and at the last moment allows it to run through his or her legs to black forward 2.

Three-Cone Game

Purpose. To develop the offensive play of a pair of attacking players.

Procedure. Place three upright cones 20 yards apart in an equilateral triangle in one half of the field. Two play against two in a game to see who can knock down any cone with the ball. Mark out a boundary line, usually about half a soccer field.

Coaching Points.

• The player in possession of the ball often must screen the ball from a defender. The player in possession should take a sideways-

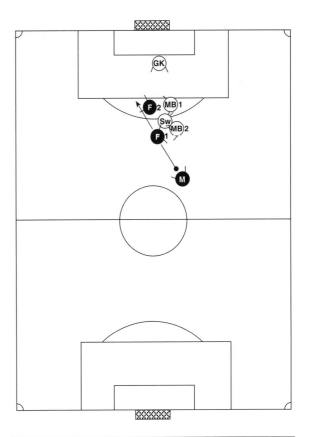

Figure 12.15 Faking to receive the ball.

on position so that he or she can see (a) the opponent, (b) the teammate and the second defender, (c) the ball, and (d) the cones.

• The player in possession will also have to run with the ball and protect it at the same time. This will often mean dribbling the ball with the foot farthest away from the challenging defender (figure 12.16).

• The dribbling player will have to effect sudden changes of speed and direction.

• In changing speed the player will usually perform a fake turn before sudden acceleration.

• A left-footed player drags the left foot over the ball and twists the hips so that it looks as if he might turn over the left shoulder. But, at the last moment, the player brings the inside of the left foot behind the ball and pushes it into the space in front. The player then plants the right foot facing forward to enable acceleration after the ball.

• If the defending player has anticipated this sudden acceleration and has moved slightly ahead of the attacking player, then the attacking player could execute a spin turn. Here, the attacking right-footed player takes the right foot over the ball and hits it with the outside of the foot some three to five yards into the space behind. Notice how the player plants the left foot across the field, allowing the hips and shoulders to pivot more quickly into a reverse position. The player should accelerate immediately out of the turn (figure 12.17).

• There are many variations of this turn, but the key point to all of them is for the attacker to keep his or her body between the defender and the ball. Usually, therefore, the attacker should spin away from, not into, the defender.

Developing Better Offensive Teamwork

Again, I must stress that the most effective way of developing an understanding of the key offensive principles is through small-sided, conditioned games. The following small-sided, conditioned games will provide many opportunities for developing all the key offensive principles.

Figure 12.16   Sceening while dribbling.

Figure 12.17   The spin turn.

Square Off

Purpose. To develop the offensive play of a group of three players.

Procedure. Place four upright cones in a 20-yard square inside half a soccer field. Three players play against three other players in a game to see who can knock down any cone with the ball. Mark out a boundary line, usually about half a soccer field.

Coaching Points.

• All the skills in the two-versus-two game will apply, but now there are considerably more opportunities to develop a passing game. In particular, one of the three players in the team in possession of the ball should take a position to be available for a pass inside the 20-yard square.

• Possession inside the 20-yard square will allow the ball handler the opportunity to move toward any cone. If cut off, the ball handler can spin toward a different cone.

Two-Goal Game

Purpose. To improve players' understanding of how and when to switch the point of the attack.

Procedure. One of my favorite small-sided, conditioned games that develops better offensive teamwork is the two-goal game. Place the goals on the corner of each penalty area with one goalkeeper defending both goals. Have six or seven field players play against a similar number attempting to score on either goal.

Coaching Points.

• The design of this game makes the ball handler look up and "switch the field" whenever possible. It improves the understanding of midfielders and defenders of when and where to make forward runs. It is usually much more successful to make forward runs through the back door or on the blind side of the opponents (figure 12.18).

Two Goals, Two Balls

Purpose. To develop players' understanding of when to attack quickly and when to retain possession.

Procedure. A fascinating development of the preceding game is to use two soccer balls.

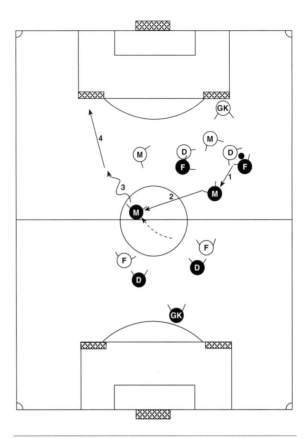

Figure 12.18 Switching play.

This helps to get the team in possession to understand the meaning of tempo. Sometimes it will be smart to hold the ball and keep possession, while on other occasions it will be necessary to develop sudden, quick counterattacks.

Coaching Points.

• In the beginning stages of this small-sided, conditioned game, you will usually find that too many players wish to attack at all costs, leaving their goal largely unguarded. I have found it useful to credit each team with five goals and to deduct a goal each time they are scored upon. The team to lose all five goals has to pay a penalty such as taking down the nets or picking up all the cones.

• As the players become more experienced in playing this game, they become smarter tactically. They very quickly begin to understand the numbers in a situation. If, for example, they get a two-versus-one situation or a three-versus-two situation, they realize that they must attack quickly to benefit from the extra player. On the other hand, if they are outnumbered defensively they learn to buy time to get more defenders in position.

Offensive Set Plays

The major set plays can be divided this way:

- Corner kicks
- Throw-ins for penetration
- Throw-ins for possession
- Direct free kicks near the goal
- Indirect free kicks near the goal
- Other free kicks

Offensive free kicks require organization and observation. The need for organization is obvious. All players should know their responsibilities and should have practiced their roles in the play. Sometimes we fail to observe the situation on the field. In our haste to execute a perfect set play, we may have overlooked that the particular set play we are executing is to the advantage of the opponent. The first rule of executing any set play is to observe what the opponent is giving away. Has our opponent set up the wall correctly? Is the wall tight? Can we lift the ball over the wall? Do they allow teammates who are not in possession to get behind the wall? Who sets up their wall? Is it set up quickly? In other words, look for a tactical advantage. If the opponent is giving something away, capitalize on it.

As stated earlier, practicing set plays has two drawbacks: they are tedious, and the team defending against offensive set plays knows the plays. You can overcome both drawbacks.

When practicing offensive set plays the burden is on the player serving the ball. If the service is faulty, the set play is unlikely to succeed. Thus, you should encourage servers to work on their own before and after regularly scheduled practices. It is true that for indirect and direct free kicks, especially close to the penalty area, they must learn how to beat the wall, but we don't really need a human wall. There are wooden cutouts on the market that you can use for a wall. I sometimes borrow the high jump standards and bar from the track and field department to make a wall. That combats some of the tediousness of practicing set plays.

The defense that tries to anticipate set plays can guess wrong, sometimes resulting in a goal. If you keep your set plays simple and keep the same players involved in variations, you minimize predictability.

A high percentage of all goals are scored as a direct result of a set play. When I was an instructor on the FA coaching courses, I remember that Charles Hughes, then the FA assistant director of coaching, would stress that 70 percent of all goals scored in the 1962-1974 World Cup finals originated from set plays. I have not checked his figures but I do know from experience that many goals are scored at corner kicks, free kicks, and even throw-ins. This suggests that every coach and every team should spend time in set-play organization.

Corner Kicks

By far the most important consideration in establishing any set play in a corner-kick situation is to find the player who can repeatedly kick the ball accurately to a designated area near the opponent's goal. It is unlikely that a team will develop a successful corner-kick play if the kicker's service is irregular and inaccurate.

The service not only must be accurate but also should possess a particular flight trajectory. If it is kicked too high the ball will tend to float and come down steeply, making it much easier for the goalkeeper to catch or punch the ball.

On the other hand, a ball that is driven hard across the face of the goal is much more difficult for the goalkeeper and presents greater opportunities for contact by an attacker.

The kicker should deliver an accurate service to either the near-post area or the far-post area. The goalkeeper is likely to win the ball served into the area immediately in front of the goal.

When the ball is to be served to the far-post area it is usually better for the kicker to use an "outswinger," a right-footed kick from the right-side corner with the ball swinging away from the goal (figure 12.19). This flight path allows the player attacking the ball to get much more power into the header. It is also more difficult for defenders to head the ball away with much power because the ball is going away from them.

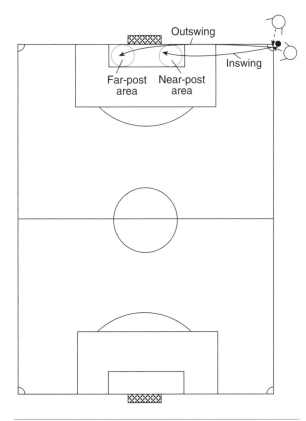

Figure 12.19   Corner kicks to the near- and far-post areas.

The ball served to the near-post area is usually best delivered by a kicker using an "inswinger," a left-footed kick from the right-side corner with the ball swinging in toward the goal. It is usually not necessary to require any great power in near-post headers as the aim is usually to deflect or redirect the ball. The inswinging, near-post corner kick is the most difficult for the goalkeeper to deal with, and statistics have shown that by far the greatest number of goals scored from corner-kicks originate from a near-post, inswinging service.

It is unusual to find a player who can deliver either an inswinging or an outswinging corner kick with either foot. It is far more common to find a player who can deliver an accurate right-footed outswinging service to the far-post area from the right-side corner and an accurate right-footed inswinging service to the near-post area from the left-side corner. The left-footed player would deliver an equally accurate but opposite service from the other corner positions. This usually means that both these right-footed and left-footed players should prepare to take any corner kick. In this way not only can they

keep the opposing defense guessing but they may get the opportunity of playing a short, quick corner kick.

The advantage of sending two players to the corner to take the corner kick is that it effectively requires two defenders to defend against it. If only one defender goes out to defend then the attacking pair has a two-versus-one situation. If, on the other hand, two defenders go out to stop the short corner kick, then an attacker can ghost into the space vacated by one of the defenders.

Throw-Ins for Penetration

Many players are now able to throw the ball into the scoring area, but the majority of these players can throw the ball only into the near-post area.

Probably the simplest and most effective long throw-in is for the receiving player to face the thrower, allowing himself or herself to be marked goalside. At the moment of the throw the receiving player moves in a straight line toward the ball and flicks it on into the space behind the defense for a teammate to run onto (figure 12.20).

Figure 12.20   A flick-on header.

The player taking the throw-in can make it easier for the receiving player to flick-on the ball by throwing it in a flat trajectory. A throw-in of this sort will also be difficult for the marking defender to get to, particularly if his or her marking position is directly behind (goalside of) the receiving player.

Throw-Ins for Possession

Throw-ins designed to keep possession are usually taken in the defensive half of the field. Most players will calculate on the side of safety in this area and avoid the risk of lost possession.

One of the biggest mistakes made by teams awarded a throw-in in their half of the field is to have too many players wanting to receive the ball. They attract their immediate opponents into the receiving space, making it extremely crowded. The central midfield players are usually the greatest culprits, and it is possible to see seven or eight players from each team attracted to the receiving space at a throw-in.

Probably the simplest and most effective throw-in to keep possession is one made to colleagues behind or square of the ball rather than ahead of the ball. There is obviously a degree of risk when a player throws the ball square across the field or back to a supporting defender, but an accurate throw-in to the feet of the defender (without bouncing) reduces the risk considerably (figure 12.21).

 SURPRISE! SURPRISE!

In the summer of 1988 the USA Under-17 team went on a tour of Scotland, where we played a series of friendly matches against Celtic, Rangers, Morton, and Scotland. In the opening minutes of our first match against Celtic, we were awarded a throw-in deep in their half of the field. Tony Hyndman, who had perfected the "headspring" throw-in, took the ball, and the Celtic defenders marked up in a solid defensive formation 5 to 25 yards from the point of the throw-in. To their surprise and consternation Tony launched himself into the headspring throw-in and the ball sailed over all the Celtic defenders to land at the feet of one of our players, who had ghosted in at the far post, for an easy goal.

A simple example of keeping possession at a throw-in is illustrated in figure 12.22, where black midfielder 1 makes a forward run and

Figure 12.21   A throw-in to the feet of the receiver.

Figure 12.22   Creating space for others.

takes white midfielder 2 along. The black stopper moves into the space created by black midfielder 1 to receive the throw-in. Another example would be to make a simple throw-in back to the supporting defender, black marking back 2.

Direct Free Kicks Near the Goal

Usually, the more complicated the plan and the more players involved, then the less likely it will be that the free kick will succeed. Keep all free kicks simple.

Just as in corner kicks, the key is to find both a right-footed and a left-footed player who can consistently hit the target from a one- or two-stride approach. Too often we find coaches who look for the player with the power shot who takes a five-to-eight-stride approach run. It is uncanny how many power shooters always seem to shoot either high or wide.

The simplest of all free kicks is illustrated in figure 12.23. A direct free kick has been awarded about 20 yards from the goal. The opposing team sets up a defensive wall of five

players lined up against the near post while three additional defenders mark up on the side of the wall. Two attacking players line up near the ball, one right-footed and the other left-footed. These two players decide who has the better chance of shooting into the goal, considering the position of the wall and the position of the goalkeeper.

Another simple ploy is to overload one side of the wall with extra attacking players. This will often mean that the narrow side of the wall is unguarded, and a player can run onto a pass made into this space (figure 12.24).

Indirect Free Kicks Near the Goal

Whenever a shooting opportunity occurs at an indirect free kick, the accuracy and direction of the first touch (or lay-off) are vitally important. The lay-off pass should be made so that the shooting player can move diagonally onto the ball without breaking stride. The pass should be a short one made diagonally sideways and backward. The direction

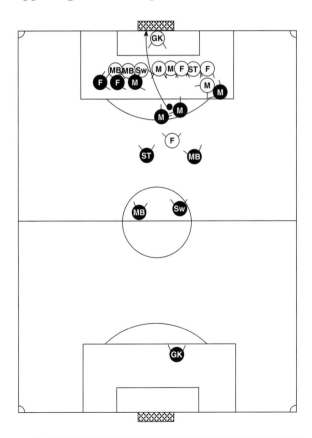

Figure 12.23 A simple offensive free kick.

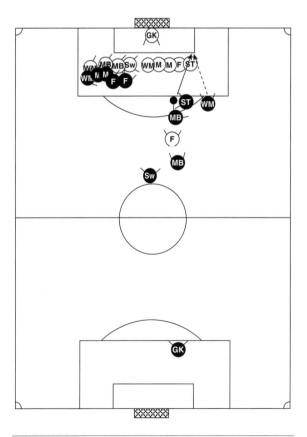

Figure 12.24 Overlapping on the weak side of the ball.

Figure 12.25   A lay-off pass for a left-footed shot.

of the lay-off pass for a right-footed shot is from left to right to the shooter's far (right) foot.

The approach run of the shooter should be short so that the goalkeeper gets little warning of the upcoming shot. The direction of the lay-off pass is reversed for a left-footed shooter (figure 12.25).

It will be obvious that if we are to fully utilize the possibilities offered by both a right-footed and a left-footed shooter, then a third player needs to orchestrate the play at an indirect free kick near the goal. The presence of a third player offers several additional options. Here are a few examples.

In figure 12.26, the black stopper passes to black midfielder 1, who is positioned about two yards away. Black midfielder 1 stops the ball for black midfielder 2, who steps up and hits a right-footed shot.

A variation on the set play above is to use the same setup, with the black stopper passing to black midfielder 1, who again is about two yards away. Now, instead of stopping the ball, black midfielder 1 lets the ball go through the legs for black midfielder 2 to hit with a right-footed shot (figure 12.27).

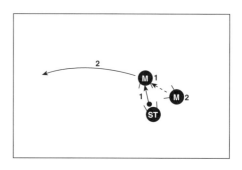

Figure 12.26   Setting up a right-footed shot at a free kick.

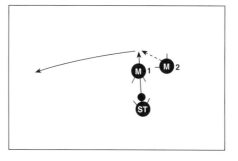

Figure 12.27   Another setup for a right-footed shot at a free kick.

One more variation is to have the black stopper pass to black midfielder 1, who is about two yards away. Black midfielder 1 immediately passes the ball back to the black stopper, who lets it go through the legs, allowing black midfielder 2 a left-footed shot at the goal (figure 12.28).

Other Free Kicks

In general, the quicker a team takes a free kick, the less likely it will be that the offending team will have time to regroup or reorganize. Quickly taken free kicks will often catch defenders unprepared and out of position.

If it is not possible to play the free kick quickly, then the team should revert to practiced free kicks. One such free kick is illustrated in figure 12.29. The offended team's midfield and forwards have all pushed up onto the opponent's penalty line (18-yard line). One midfield player comes to the ball, and the player who took the free kick moves to receive a return pass.

Another simple free kick would be to hit a long, high ball into the space diagonally behind the defense.

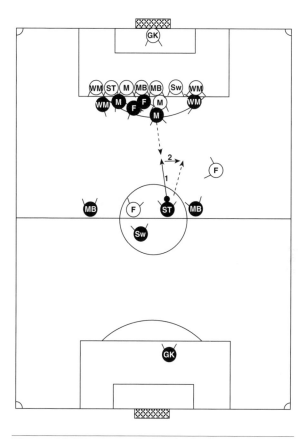

Figure 12.29 A simple free kick play.

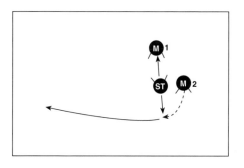

Figure 12.28 Setting up a left-footed shot at a free kick.

Summary

The hardest offensive component to coach is improvisation. Players must be willing to play with flair and dare to take risks. You must create an atmosphere and environment in which players aren't afraid to do that. In the meantime the points below will help you in making your team more effective and efficient in offense.

- Be aware that when your team is attacking it must find ways to play through, around, or over the opposing defense.
- Design realistic soccer practices against groups of defenders to practice the three options above.
- Teach the forwards to push up on the line of the opposing sweeper. They will be more successful in receiving the ball.
- Stress that forwards should time their runs to coincide with what is happening on the ball.

- Coach two (or more) forwards to work harmoniously. If one goes to the ball then the second should hold on the line of the opposing sweeper.
- Make the second forward understand that if the first forward is able to turn with the ball, the second forward must provide one of three options—a diagonal run behind the defense, a move away to create space for the first forward to dribble, or a target for the pass.
- Instruct forwards always to be alert to one-two and one-three opportunities.
- Show attacking players how to create space for others by taking defenders out of covering positions.
- Compliment forwards who are willing to create space for the other forward(s).
- Remember that if you're playing with three forwards, it may be best to play with one advanced (primary) striker and two withdrawn (secondary) strikers.
- Instruct the primary striker to push up on the line of the opposing sweeper while the withdrawn strikers look for the ball in the space in front of the defense.
- Demonstrate that if the ball sticks with one player for longer than a couple of seconds, then it is likely that the opposing defense will have sufficient time to reorganize. Use wide-angle videos to bring the point home.
- Remember the key offensive principles: support, penetration, width, mobility, and improvisation.
- Practice set-play organization diligently.
- Calculate the degree of risk or possession when taking throw-ins.
- Know that when you are awarded a free kick near the goal, the simpler the plan and the fewer players involved, the more likely it is that the free kick will succeed.
- Realize that, in general, the quicker a free kick, corner kick, or throw-in is taken, the less likely it will be that the opposing team will have time to organize.

Part V

Coaching Matches

Chapter 13

Preparing for Matches

During the regular season you will often have opportunities to watch your next opponent play and have one or two practice sessions to prepare your team for that particular game. On the other hand, in a tournament or play-off situation, you will not be able to watch your opponent play or to have a practice session specially designed to combat the opponent.

Your true worth as a coach is established when you can watch your next opponent and have one or two practice sessions to prepare for the match. Have you identified the key strengths and weaknesses of the opposing team and players? How do they relate to your team's strengths and weaknesses? Have you designed practice sessions that will clearly show your players how they can combat the strengths and weaknesses of the opponent?

Scouting the Opposition

There are two extremes of thought about preparing teams for matches. The first school will tend to ignore all information about the upcoming opposition and concentrate all energies on perfecting the team's own game. The second will make detailed reports of the upcoming opposition, relay this information to the players, and make whatever adjustments are needed to counter any major strengths in the opposing team.

Both approaches hold dangers. The first might ignore some major tactical strategy, the influence of a key player, or a match-deciding set play the opposition frequently uses. The second might create "paralysis by analysis," whereby the strengths of the

183

opposition are overexaggerated and the team makes too many changes in its tactical plan in an attempt to nullify those strengths.

Probably the most sensible approach is a compromise, whereby a report on the opposition might include information on the following areas:

- Team formation
- Defensive strategy
- Midfield shape
- Forwards
- Key players
- Set plays
- General conditions

Team Formation

The single biggest factor in looking at team formations is to discover how many forwards the opposition uses. Do they use one, two, three, or even four forwards? If so, who marks each opponent?

The number of forwards used in the opposing team's offense will also indicate the likely number of players they employ in the midfield. If they use four midfield players it will usu-

ally be in the formation of two wide midfield players and a pair of central midfield players. This pair will play either as one attacking midfield player and one defensive midfield player, or as right-central and left-central midfield players who pivot on each other. If they use five midfield players, it will usually be in the formation of two wide midfield players and a triangle of three central midfield players. This triangle can take different forms; it can be with two stoppers and one attacking midfielder, or with one stopper and two attacking midfield players. If they use six midfield players it will almost invariably be with two wide midfield players and a box of four central midfield players made up of two stoppers and two attacking midfield players.

The second biggest factor is identifying how the opposing team initiates its attack. Does it aim to get around, over, or through the opposing defense? This will determine the method of defense that your team must use.

Defensive Strategy

When preparing a scouting report, the scout should determine where the opposition decides to defend. Do they play a high-pressure game in the opponent's half of the field, or do they retreat nearer to their own goal? Usually one player organizes a team's defense. It is advantageous to know which player has this task as it is possible to preoccupy that player with a marking situation.

Midfield Shape

As previously stated the team that controls the setup area usually ends up winning the game. The scouting report should look closely at the opposition players who are deployed in the setup area. Do they use a single or twin stopper? Are there one or two playmakers? What are the qualities of the wide midfield players?

Forwards

The scouting report should include information on the physical, technical, and tactical attributes of the opposing forwards. Are they big, fast, and powerful or small, quick, and skillful? Do they come to the ball, or do they seek to run onto passes in the area behind the defense?

JIMMY THE SCOUT

In the early days of the North American Soccer League (NASL) my good friend Dave Jones was the coach of the Toronto Toros. Dave was a meticulous planner and organizer, and would scout all league opposition and prepare comprehensive reports that he passed on to his players. Imagine his dismay when he found out that an exhibition game had been arranged between the Toros and Moscow Dynamo and that he would be unable to scout the Russians because the Toros had league matches on the days the Russians played their other exhibition matches.

It was decided to send the assistant coach to watch the Russians in their exhibition games in Miami and Tampa Bay, but to Dave's consternation the assistant coach took ill the day before he was due to begin his long journey to Florida. Dave now had a problem. He wanted desperately to have a scouting report on the Soviets, but he had no coach available to travel. Seemingly, the only person available was Jimmy, an old-timer who had long ago played professional soccer in his native Scotland and now did odd jobs for the Toros. Dave decided that Jimmy should go since he needed certain knowledge and information about the Moscow Dynamo team.

Dave read in the newspapers that Moscow Dynamo had recorded impressive victories over both their Florida opponents, and he eagerly awaited Jimmy's return from his long and expensive trip. On Jimmy's arrival at the stadium, Dave assembled all the players and coaching staff to receive the scouting report. "Well, Jimmy," said Dave, "tell us about this Moscow Dynamo team." "Ehh!" said Jimmy, "They're a fine team." There was a long silence before Dave repeated his request for information on the Russians.

"Ehh!" said Jimmy again, "They're a fine team—a *real* fine team."

The players began to chuckle and snigger as it was obvious that this brief summary was the extent of Jimmy's report.

Key Players

The scouting report should identify the key players in the opposing team. Who leads their defense? Who orchestrates their midfield? Who threatens to score?

Most teams will have a leader in their defense. The goalkeeper or sweeper is usually in the best position to give defensive organizational instructions. Your report should indicate if either, both, or neither organizes the defense. If it is the sweeper then your offensive plan should include some measure to fully occupy him or her in marking and covering one of your attackers. Do not allow the sweeper a free role with time to organize the defense.

Again, there will usually be a leader in the midfield. The opposing stopper will usually assume this role and will be well positioned to accomplish it if allowed to play unopposed behind the midfield. On the other hand, this player will have less time to think and organize the midfield if your team has a player in direct opposition. Make the opposing stopper work defensively to deny him or her time to orchestrate the midfield offense.

The opposing goal threat must, of course, be stifled. You must heavily mark the striker(s) on the opposing team. Be careful that you do not have a mismatch where your smallest or slowest defender is marking their biggest or fastest attacker.

Set Plays

You should probably direct as much attention to the opposing team's set plays as to any other issue. It takes much practice to develop a successful set play, and it is unlikely that a team will change its set plays while they continue to be successful. The scouting report should, therefore, include

details of how your opposition handles the following set plays.

Corner Kicks For

Who takes them?

To which area do they serve the ball?

Where do the attacking players line up?

Where are the players not immediately involved in the corner-kick situation? What do they do?

Corner Kicks Against

How do they guard against a near-post corner?

How do they guard against a far-post corner?

How do they defend against a short corner kick?

Do they mark on a player-to-player basis or in a zone defense?

How does the goalkeeper perform against near-post and far-post crosses?

Free Kicks For

Do they take free kicks quickly?

Do they have prearranged set plays at direct and indirect free kicks near the opponent's goal?

If so, what are they? Who are the players involved?

Free Kicks Against

Who decides if a wall is required and how many players are in the wall?

Who lines up the wall?

Who is the "keystone" player in the wall?

Who are the other players in the wall?

What do the other players do?

What position does the goalkeeper take?

 RAY CLEMENCE

Even amid Liverpool FC's rich tradition of goalkeeping excellence, the name and achievements of Ray Clemence stand out above those of all others. Ray always believed that the best saves are not the spectacular ones but those that influence a result.

Liverpool FC was drawn to play the East German powerhouse, Dynamo Dresden, in the first leg of the UEFA Cup quarterfinal in March 1976. Tom Saunders, then the youth development officer at Liverpool FC, had scouted Dynamo Dresden in a game in which they had been awarded a penalty kick. Tom had briefed Ray that their penalty-kick taker would put the ball to Ray's right. When Dynamo was awarded a penalty kick that is what happened, and Ray made the save.

General Conditions

The scouting report should include information such as the nature of the field, its dimensions and surface, prevailing wind conditions, the sun, proximity of fans, and so on. The laws of the game in soccer require that the field be rectangular with a minimum and maximum length and width and stipulate that the length must exceed the width. The shape and dimensions of a field will, of course, affect the type of game that will be played. It is much easier to defend on a small field with a bumpy surface, while it is easier to build up good attacking play on a larger field with a good surface. On a narrow field, goals are more likely to be scored from corner kicks and throw-ins than from wing play.

The prevailing wind and sun conditions should also help you determine which direction to play in the first half if you win the coin toss. Do you want to play with the wind at your backs and the sun in the opposing goalkeeper's eyes or wait until the second half of the game for such advantages?

The proximity of fans to the field can affect the game by reducing the space for the run-up to a corner kick or the approach run to a throw-in. The closeness of these fans can also adversely affect your players unless they are prepared for it.

Preparing Your Team

In the prematch practices the coach should focus on negating the strength of the opposition while making minimal changes in the team's style and method of play.

Playing Against Three Forwards

For example, it may be necessary to adjust the regular 3-5-2 formation if the opposition plays with three forwards. Consequently, one of the stoppers will have to take on the role of a marking back.

Playing Against an Attacking Wing Back

The opposition might have a wing back who likes to attack by overlapping the wide midfield player. You can instruct one of the forwards to take a wide defensive position thus forcing the play to the other side of the field.

It will be useful for you to run through such situations on the field in a practice situation with your players. It is remarkable how many players fail to understand a chalkboard session but grasp the problem when the coach shows it on the field.

Playing Against a Star Player

If the opposition has a star player, such as a playmaker or a striker, you should assign one of your players to mark this player tightly. Whenever possible the marking player should get assistance from a teammate to double-team. If this star player favors one foot or a particular move, then instruct the marking player to force the star player to go to his or her weak side (usually the left foot).

Your Team's Set Plays

Devote some of the time in prematch practices to refining your set plays based on knowledge of any opposition weakness. For example, do they only send one player out to defend against a corner kick? If so, then the team should practice short corners to develop goal-scoring opportunities from the initial two-versus-one situation. You should probably also spend some time perfecting the defense against the opposition's favorite set plays, particularly corner kicks or free kicks near the goal.

 STOP THE SUPPLY

Albert Finely was a giant of a man, 6-foot-3-inches tall, weighing nearly 220 pounds, with wide shoulders, narrow waist, and rippling muscles. He was a striker of immense power, and he terrorized the league, particularly with his heading ability.

After scouting Albert's team I decided that the best means of defense was not to try to combat or stop Albert, but to cut off the supply of the ball to him. At the time I had a marking player, Stan Allen, with amazing quickness, tenacity, and concentration. Stan's task was to stop the supply of crosses delivered to Albert by their right winger. It worked to perfection. We won the game and Albert had a frustrating afternoon with hardly a touch of the ball.

The team will need to know the following information to defend well on set plays.

Corner Kicks

Who marks players and who covers space?

How to stop a short corner kick.

The goalkeeper's position.

Where to clear the ball—high, far, and wide.

How to come out of defensive positions when the ball is cleared.

Who takes the leadership role?

What is the role of the team's forwards when defending a corner kick?

How to mount a counterattack.

Free Kicks

Is a wall necessary? Who decides?

If so, how many players?

Which players go into the wall?

Who lines them up?

Where do the other players position themselves?

What does the goalkeeper do?

A team that you are scouting will often receive a penalty kick. It is useful to give the goalkeeper full information on the following:

Penalty Kicks

Who took the kick?

The distance of the kicker's approach run.

The angle of the kicker's approach run.

The plant of the nonkicking foot.

The strike of the ball—inside of foot or instep, or outside of foot, or even the toe.

Did the kicker concentrate on power or accuracy? Where did the ball go?

Watching the opponent play before your match, or a detailed scouting report, is of immense value. Not having either, your team needs to be able to make adjustments when the match starts and as it progresses. You should have prepared them to make adjustments, on their own, to any system employed by the opponent. Identify dangerous players early. Defend against the opponent's set plays with extreme caution. You can often identify shooting strengths and goalkeeper weaknesses in the opponent's warm-up. By observing closely in the early going of the match, you can help your team make adjustments.

Summary

Consider the following points as you prepare your team for matches:

- Compromise between the two schools of thought regarding prematch preparation. That is, spend time both perfecting your team's game and preparing to counter any major strengths in the opposing team.
- Pay attention to the opposing team's set plays. The scouting report should include details of corner kicks for, corner kicks against, free kicks for, free kicks against, throw-ins, and penalty kicks.
- Also consider the general conditions for play—the field (its dimensions and surface), prevailing wind, the sun, proximity of fans, and so forth.
- In prematch practices, focus on negating the strength of the opposition while making minimal changes in your team's style and method of play.
- Run through any adjustments you make to the team's formation or style of play in an on-the-field practice.
- Devote some prematch practice time to refining your team's set plays based on knowledge of any opposition weakness.

Chapter 14

Handling Match Situations

There are many types of coaches. Some excel at organizing fun-filled, physically demanding, and informative practice sessions. Others excel at recognizing talent and can put teams together that will constantly overachieve. And still others can immediately identify the strengths and weaknesses of any team, including their own, and design situations and strategies to exploit such strengths and weaknesses. But no matter how good you might be as an organizer of superior practice sessions or as a talent spotter, you will always struggle unless you can handle match situations. That includes prematch and postmatch situations.

Prematch situations include determining the starting lineup. During the match your keen observation should tell you if your team is playing according to plan and if the plan is working. At the same time it is your job to see what weaknesses the opponent may have. From your observations you may have to adjust the match plan and make substitutions.

Explicit instructions at halftime are essential to a better second half. And, no matter what the outcome of the completed match, well-chosen comments after the match can leave the team mentally ready for its next practice or match.

Setting the Starting Lineup

A critical consideration in deciding the starting lineup is the substitution rule for the particular match. Is unlimited substitution permitted or is the match to be played according to FIFA rules with a designated number of substitutes and no reentry after substitution?

Obviously, if the match is to be played with limited substitution and no reentry, then you should put the best starting lineup on the field. You should have referred to your scouting report and prepared for the match in the prematch practices.

In matches where unlimited substitution is permitted you should reward the players who have performed the best in previous matches or shown the greatest dedication and determination in training. You run a risky course if you try to give all your players equal playing time. You should have a policy of equal opportunity rather than a policy of equality.

In matches against weaker opponents you can reward increased playing time to some of your weaker players who have displayed commitment, dedication, and determination in practice time.

Matchups

One of the greatest mistakes made by beginning coaches is that they allow mismatches to develop on the field. Very often you will see a team's biggest and fastest player marked by the other team's smallest and slowest player. In most instances, teams are punished for such mismatches.

You shouldn't allow mismatches to develop. You should prepare for such events before the match and be ready to make adjustments during match play.

Of course, you should not only avoid mismatches that work against you but also attempt to create mismatches that work in your favor. For instance, you may be able to create mismatches in the following situations:

- *The opponent leaves a big space between the goalkeeper and the last defender.* You may have an opportunity to play over the defense, especially if you have a fast forward.
- *The opponent plays the offside trap.* Can a deep player, like a defensive midfielder or stopper, dribble through the defense? Or, can you play the ball wide behind the defense to a wide midfielder who starts the run late?
- *The opponent has a slow defender.* Obviously, you can attack this player with a quick player.
- *The opponent marks player-to-player at corner kicks, direct free kicks, and so forth.* Can you ghost in an open player? Can you pull the opponent into poor positions?

It is an easy task to prepare your team for or against such situations.

During the Match

During a match, your immediate and primary objective is to ascertain what your team is doing well and what weaknesses your opponent has. You should be prepared to help your team solve any critical problem that arises. For example, does the opposing team play with three forwards, and have your players readjusted by using three marking backs? If so, has your central midfielder adjusted to the loss of one of the stoppers? Does the opposing team play with a deep-lying sweeper, and if so does your primary forward push up to make the opposing defense play flat across the field?

Coach Conduct

Your conduct and demeanor on the touchline can have an impact on your team. In my experience, I have found that a coach who either sits on the bench or stands still (leans on something) has the most calming effect on the team. It is as if your body language oozes confidence to your players, who will then perform in a calm, confident, calculated manner.

On the other hand, if you move up and down the touchline shouting instructions at your players, you're likely to have a nervous, underachieving team prone to moments of violent behavior. It is as if your anxiety is transmitted to the players, who will then perform in a tense, insecure manner.

It is all right, on occasion, to convey instructions to your players, but you should do this in a calm, quiet manner when the ball is at the other end of the field. It is of little use to shout instructions to a player who is in possession of the ball. The player's attention should be on making a decision regarding the next move and on sending messages from the brain to the muscle groups to achieve the best technical performance. Instead, focus your attention on players far from the ball, who have the opportunity and the time to absorb your instructions. Figure 14.1 offers a simple example.

Here, the coach has observed that some of the defenders are ball watching (or cheerleading) and are vulnerable to a counterattack. He instructs the goalkeeper and the sweeper to reorganize the other defenders into a solid defensive shape.

 COACHING TO DEFEAT

I made a causal analysis of coaches who had been ejected from matches in the English Foot-

ball League during the period between 1970 and 1982. These ejections were for a variety of reasons, but by far the most common was dissent by the coach and the use of foul language. I also made a causal analysis of players who had been ejected in the same matches in the same league. Player ejections were caused by a wide variety of violations, but what was interesting was that when a coach was ejected a player from his team was usually ejected too. Invariably, that team lost the match. It was as if the coach's demeanor—anxiety, stress, or tension—had been transmitted to the players, who then underachieved.

Player Conduct

Player conduct is often a product of coach's conduct. It is remarkable how often teams with coaches who scream and shout at their players and who rant and rave at referees have the worst discipline record. On the other hand, teams who have a calm, level-headed coach who accepts referee mistakes have few discipline problems.

There are, of course, some players who will have discipline problems no matter which coach they play for. These players are usually prone to macho behavior and carry around giant chips on their shoulders. I have found that I can help such players by giving them guidance and advice on the practice field. I try to explain the following ideas:

- Players who are repeatedly fouled are special because this is the only way that opponents can stop them. It is a mark of respect for their ability.
- A brave person will walk away from a confrontation, while the coward will enter into a war of words, ultimately falling afoul of the referee.
- The best answer to a provocative opponent is to score against him or her.
- Players should be yellow carded and red carded in practice matches, just as they would be in regular matches.

Substitutions

The United States is one of the few places in the world where we find unlimited substitution in soccer. Elsewhere, only limited substitutions are allowed, which means that the main considerations for substitution are injury or tactical adjustment.

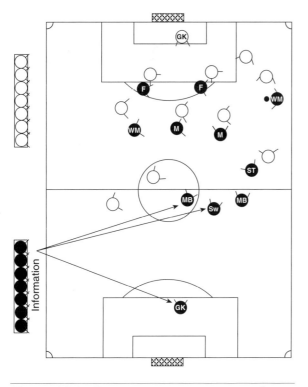

Figure 14.1 Focus your instruction on players who are far from the ball.

These are not often the primary considerations when unlimited substitution is in force. Rather, playing time becomes the major issue. Teams usually have between 15 and 18 players on the roster, and it is normal to find that all these players will demand some playing time during each match. Sometimes, you may have planned your substitutions to give each player a certain number of minutes of playing time, but you may have to change these decisions depending on the score. If your team is comfortably in the lead early in the match then it is possible to put in the weaker players earlier than planned. However, if a match is even and you put in your weaker players to give them their playing time, and consequently end up losing the match, you can be certain of some criticism. In my opinion unlimited substitution is a "lose, lose" situation for both coaches and players. No one likes to be substituted and no one likes to be a substitute. Nearly everyone ends up being disgruntled.

Match Plan Adjustments

Sometimes the best-laid match plans can go awry. Despite total dominance in most aspects of play a team can still be trailing in scoring. There may be many reasons for that to happen:

- Superb goalkeeping
- Missed goal chances
- Field conditions
- Weather conditions

On such occasions it might be necessary for a team to change its match plan. It might be necessary to push up an additional forward and risk being outnumbered in midfield; or it might be necessary, if the team is holding on to a narrow lead, to add an additional defender. There may be a strong wind blowing straight down the field or wet conditions at one end of the field. In such situations it may be necessary to adjust the match plan depending on which end a team is defending.

Halftime

Most coaches make adjustments to a match plan at halftime. It is during this short interval that you can demand the total attention of all your players. Your instructions should be clear, concise, and to the point. All players must understand how any adjustment affects them and their roles on the team.

You may miss the opportunity of making telling changes during the halftime talk by being too general. Remarks such as "We must pick up in the midfield," "We must improve our marking," "We've got to talk more," or "We've got to move off the ball" are meaningless clichés. Rather, it should be "John, you must pick up your man in midfield," "Kristen, you must tell Gina which way to force the play," "Nicole, mark your player tighter and don't let her turn with the ball," or "Adam, take up a better support position that will allow Matt to pass the ball to you."

After the Match

If the team and the players have performed very well in a match, you should compliment them immediately afterward. Reinforce the pleasant memory of a successful play. On the other hand, refrain from immediately criticizing a particular player if he or she has failed or if the team has had a disappointing match. You don't need to add to the players' feelings of frustration.

Postmatch Conduct

Emotions are usually high immediately after the match, but no matter how frustrated or disappointed you might feel, refrain from making any negative comments to your players. You should understand that, nearly always, players try their best. When they fail, or the team loses, they will be extremely insecure and disappointed. It serves no purpose to blame or castigate players in the immediate postmatch period. Rather, if disappointment and frustration prevail, you should make it a habit to simply inform the players of the immediate administrative messages and then leave.

Conduct the match postmortem the next day when emotions have cooled and everyone can discuss the match in a calm, sensible fashion. But even 24 to 48 hours after the match you will achieve little if you set out to blame any player or players for failure. Instead, you should point out the good points in the performance and praise the players involved.

If the loss of a match could be directly attributed to poor performance by a player, then reassure the individual that he or she is still the same player who was on the team when they won some previous matches. Try to work with the player to identify the cause of the poor performance so that the athlete has the opportunity to correct the problem.

Postmatch Lessons

If you and your team allow yourselves to learn from a match—win, lose, or draw—then you have gained. Ultimately, *the game* is the greatest teacher. You and your players should understand this statement and commit it to memory.

The focal point of the next practice session should be the lessons learned in the previous match. If, for instance, the goalkeeper dropped some crosses in the match, then spend at least some of the next practice session on having the goalkeeper deal with crosses in realistic situations.

I am always amazed to see coaches who sincerely believe that they are addressing the problem that cropped up in the match by setting up drills without opposing players. That's not realistic. You will address the match problem only by providing the player a similar opportunity to solve the problem in practice under match conditions.

There are literally thousands of problems that can occur in a match. These can be the problems of an individual player, group of players, or even the whole team. They can be physical, technical, tactical, even psychological or social in nature.

Some examples are the following:

GOALKEEPER

Positioning

Distance—took up a position too far off the line

Angles—left too much space at the near post

Crosses

Had problems dealing with left-wing crosses

Shot stopping—sat down in crucial one-versus-one situation

MARKING BACKS

Positioning was too loose, allowing opponents to turn with the ball

Did not mark on inside line

Marked too closely when the ball was a long distance away

SWEEPER

Did not recognize double-team opportunities

Did not communicate and failed to provide organizational leadership

CENTRAL MIDFIELDERS

Gave the ball away too easily

Did not track down opposing players

WIDE MIDFIELDERS

Marked immediate opponent even when team in possession

Failed to provide penetration down the flanks

FORWARDS

Did not get in behind defense

Lost possession too easily, too quickly

Failed to bring the midfield into the attacking play

Shot poorly

THE TEAM ON ATTACK

Played too many risky long passes and repeatedly gave away possession

Gave no real threat of going around opposing defense

Had no mobility in central midfield—passing lanes were clogged up

Had very little support from defenders

THE TEAM ON DEFENSE

Too slow to organize against counterattack

Failed to pass on players in midfield

Very little forcing of play by forwards and midfielders

Did not communicate

Summary

Here are some basic guidelines to follow during a match:

- Consider the substitution rule for the particular match as you decide your starting lineup.
- Avoid mismatches that give an advantage to the opponent.
- Attempt to create mismatches that work in your team's favor.
- Be in control on the touchline. Your conduct is transmitted to your players.
- Communicate only with players well away from the ball, when they have the opportunity and time to absorb your instructions.
- On the practice field provide guidance and advice to your players about their match conduct.
- Be prepared to change your match plan *during* the match if things have gone awry.
- Make sure that every player understands the adjustments discussed at halftime.
- Refrain from making any negative comments to your players immediately after the match
- Don't blame any player or players during the postmatch meeting. Instead, point out the good points in the performance and praise the players involved.
- Design your team's practice program on how the team performed in the previous match.
- Help your players improve on match problems by giving them an opportunity to solve the problem in practice under match conditions.

Part VI

Coaching Evaluation

Chapter 15

Evaluating Your Players

I believe that observation and evaluation are important parts of coaching. When we are evaluating, we have to do more than just determine the individual skill level of a player. We must also evaluate how the player will fit into our program and contribute to the team's competitiveness and culture.

Player evaluation should start early. You should try to learn as much as possible about a player long before the first practice. The more you know about a player, the better you can prepare to coach him or her. In preseason evaluations try to observe a potential player under the pressure of match conditions. Go to competitive matches and observe. I find it just as valuable to observe

a potential player during training sessions. There I can learn much about the player's attitude, concentration, motivation, work ethic, willingness to learn, and social skills.

To help me with my early evaluations I have developed some tools. They include a player evaluation form, a player profile form, and a player self-evaluation form.

Regardless of all preseason evaluations, your most critical period of evaluating occurs during the first days of practice before making cuts. The most traumatic part of coaching is making cuts. It is hard on you but can be devastating for the player. So make sure that each player cut has had a fair opportunity to prove himself or herself.

Once you have made the cuts, evaluations should focus on technical ability and tactical awareness of the remaining players. From those evaluations put the players into positions best suited for them at the time. After a few practices with players in assigned positions you can begin to put the starting team together.

Evaluating doesn't stop there. You should evaluate players before, during, and after every practice and every match. Through attentive observation and thorough evaluation you can increase your effectiveness immensely and thereby your chances for success.

Preseason Evaluations

Players do play soccer before trying out for high school or college teams. You have numerous opportunities to watch potential players in action. There are competitions for club teams, tournaments, and indoor centers. Go watch matches, especially those of the players that may try out for your program. By beginning to familiarize yourself with potential players you are laying a foundation for a thorough evaluation.

Watching Matches Before Tryouts

Coaches in high school programs do not recruit. Many coach club teams. If that is legal in your conference, by all means do it. It is a great way to see numerous players under match conditions. Many conferences and school districts, however, have ruled it illegal for a high school or college coach to coach other teams of the same age. In that case watch matches and observe players who may be trying out for your team. In these early observations you may want to evaluate only technical abilities, like how well the player controls the ball, passes, shoots, heads, tackles, and dribbles. After awhile you may want to figure out how to bring the player along and where the player might fit on your team. When watching, don't be position conscious. Although the player is playing defense in the match you are watching, that may not be his or her strongest position.

 THE RELUCTANT FORWARD

Two years ago I looked at Kevin Mosher, a high school junior. His coach had told me that Kevin could probably make a contribution to our team. He looked impressive, but I felt that he didn't function all that well in his outside midfield position. His lack of speed over distance often caused him to be caught either too far up or too far back. When he had the ball, however, he was magic. He could screen the ball well, was hard to get off the ball, had excellent fakes, was deceptively quick over a short distance, and could shoot well with either foot. I recruited him and told him that I was going to play him at forward. He was somewhat reluctant, but cooperative. During Kevin's first season with us he tied for the honors as the conference's leading scorer, he was selected to the conference all-star team, and he shattered a 15-year-old conference record for most goals scored by one player in a match.

The time to evaluate a player fairly is when the player is performing under match pressure, especially if the teams are of similar quality. The trick is not only to observe the player as a part of a team but also to evaluate the player's individual strengths and potential.

I have another reason for wanting to see as many players as possible before our actual tryout, especially those I am actively recruiting and those who have signed a letter of intent. I also want to see those who have interviewed and have said that they will be turning out. After one week of practice we make our first cuts. We make the final cuts one week later. I have never liked tryouts; I feel they don't really give the coach a true picture of a player's ability. Over the years I have learned that a number of players just don't show well in a tryout. And although our tryouts are long, I still believe that some players hold back or overdo it in a tryout atmosphere. Too many players equate self-worth with succeeding or failing in a tryout. The stress defeats them. I have known players who could not eat or sleep during tryouts. I don't want to lose a good player before I have a chance to work on his confidence and hardiness.

When one of my assistants or I view a player in a match, we prepare a written evaluation. Our form is simple, but it gives me the information I need (see figure 15.1).

Player Evaluation Form

Name:_____

Age:_____Date:_____

School or team:_____

Match versus:_____

Team coach:_____

Team coach phone:_____

Rating Scale:

5 - College caliber—starting

4 - College caliber

3 - Needs work; has possibilities

2 - Needs work

1 - Take a look next year

1. Overall technical ability in training (ball control, passing, dribbling, shooting, heading, tackling): **Rating_____**

Specific comments:_____

_____

2. Overall technical ability in a match: **Rating_____**

Specific comments:_____

_____

3. Tactical ability in training (awareness, transition, position, decisions, communication, use of space, support, vision):   **Rating_____**

Specific comments:_____

_____

4. Tactical ability in a match: **Rating_____**

Specific comments:_____

_____

5. Overall physical fitness (agility, flexibility, speed, endurance, strength): Height____Weight____**Rating_____**

Specific comments:_____

_____

6. Overall psychological wellness (attitude, concentration, motivation, confidence, courage, hardiness): **Rating____**

Evaluator:_____Overall rating:_____Date:_____

Figure 15.1 Sample player evaluation form.

Player Profiles

After the first contact with a new player, the college sends him a packet of information. That packet includes our player profile form (see figure 15.2). Again, it is a simple form that gives me some basic information, which is particularly useful if I'm not familiar with the player. For instance, if the player indicates on the profile that he has played select or premier soccer and that he was selected to an Olympic Development team, I know that I'm dealing with an experienced player who is used to competitive soccer.

The profile also gives me information about his speed, scholastic success, and financial needs.

Player's Self-Evaluation

Most of the evaluating of a player is done by me, an assistant, or one of the many club and

Soccer Player Profile

Full name:_____

Home address:_____

City and state:_____Zip:_____

Home phone: (_____)_____Social security number_____-_____-_____

Mother's name:_____Occupation:_____

Father's name:_____ Occupation:_____

High school:_____ Coach's name:_____

Age:_____Date of birth:_____Height:_____Weight:_____

Grade point average last 3 years:_____

Position played:_____ School uniform number:_____

Time 100 yards:_____ Time 1 mile:_____

Other sports played:_____ Positions:_____

Youth soccer experience (mark all applicable): Club_____Select_____Premier_____ODP_____

Coach's name(s):_____Phone(s):_____

Athletic honors received (captain, all-star, all-conference, etc.):_____

_____

_____

_____

What course of study are you interested in:_____

Have you applied for financial aid:_____

Uniform sizes: Shirt_____Shorts_____Warm-up_____

Figure 15.2   Soccer player profile.

school coaches who help our program by bringing my attention to talented players. I also find it useful to know what a player thinks of his ability. After the first cut I schedule a self-evaluation session. I first talk to the players and tell them that this is a simple exercise, but that I want them to be candid with their answers to the questions on the form (see figure 15.3). I also tell them that this is not a goal-setting session, that we do that later.

The form asks players to address their strengths and weaknesses. If the player's view of his strengths and weaknesses is the same as mine, we can go to work, because we both know what strengths he can enhance and what he needs to improve. If we differ, I'll have to alter my approach. I may do that by having a private meeting with the player and asking him to tell me more about the reasons he gave for feeling strong or weak in the areas we viewed differently. During those conversations I let the player do most of the talking. Usually he comes around, and eventually we agree. If not, it doesn't really matter. The self-evaluation form has told me to approach this player differently from the one who saw himself the same way I did.

Constant evaluation is necessary. Some athletes look, talk, and walk like soccer

Self-Evaluation Form

Name:_____Date:_____

In soccer, I feel that my three strong qualities are:	I feel that my three weaknesses are:
1.	1.
2.	2.
3.	3.

Figure 15.3 Sample self-evaluation form.

players. Don't be fooled. Looks don't count, performance does. Like any coach, I have no difficulty at tryouts picking out of 70 to 80 players the 20 who most look, talk, and walk like soccer players. What is difficult is to pick the 20 who are skilled, coachable, academically motivated, competitive, proud, honest, forgiving, team oriented, willing to work, and who have a sense of humor and complement each other's capabilities.

Evaluating Before Cutting

During the early practices most of our time is spent on conditioning. However, we do play a number of five-versus-five games and have some full-field, coached scrimmages. Throughout these activities my assistants and I are evaluating each player's technical and tactical development, fitness, and psychological characteristics. We are also looking at the players who seem to work well together. I'm not saying players who like to work together, although that could be a bonus; I'm saying players that work well together regardless of their likes and dislikes. Some players read each other well and anticipate a teammate's actions, while others constantly misread or miscue. The misreading and miscuing can be overcome. It is helpful, however, to have at least some players who are tuned in to each other at the start of practices.

While we evaluate all the above during the early practices, the characteristic we look for more than any other is work ethic. As stated earlier, in soccer all the hard work is done in practice. Therefore, a player who gives only 80 percent in practice will give a like effort in a match. That's not acceptable. I can encourage players to give their all in practice, but in the end only the player can make the decision to be ready and go 100 percent. The player who makes that decision has the edge in my selection process. Frequently I have picked a player less skillful than another because of superior effort.

Making Cuts

Coaching is the most exciting, challenging, and rewarding job I can think of. Every day is filled with positive anticipation except for the two days when I have to make cuts. I find it difficult to sleep the night before the first cut and even more difficult the night before the last cut. I haven't been able to find the ideal way to do it—a way in which everybody understands and accepts the cuts, a way in which no one gets hurt. There is no easy way to do it. All I can really do is be as sure as possible about the cuts and then, somehow, attempt to ease the disappointment players feel when told they didn't make the team.

I don't believe in posted lists. They are cruel, uncaring, and impersonal. No player should find out that he or she didn't make the team when surrounded by peers. Some coaches will finish the tryout by informing the team that the players who made it will be called over the weekend. The phone call method is just as cruel, if not more so, because of the waiting involved.

There is no easy way, but I treat my players the way I would like to be treated in such a situation. First, I want to make sure, or be as sure as possible, that I am making the right decision. For that I thoroughly study all the evaluations we made. After that I solicit the help of my assistants. Even though the final decision is always mine, their counsel is extremely important, especially when we discuss players who are on the borderline. My assistants may have seen or heard something that I missed. Many players find it easier to confide in an assistant coach than in the head coach. Before making a decision,

I may even go as far as getting comments from the two team captains.

The Hardest Part of Coaching

After I finally make the decisions, I schedule a meeting with each player who is being cut. Several already have a good idea that they will not make the team, especially during the first cut, when I cut down to 30. However, don't kid yourself, none has given up hope and all are disappointed. They have dreams. They have worked hard. They came up through youth teams; they played for their high schools. Now they are being told that they are not good enough. It hurts. It hurts badly, especially for the last 10 who made it through the first cut. Some accept the decision stoically, others become angry, and still others cry bitter tears.

 A TALE OF TWO REACTIONS

One year four goalkeepers tried out, two freshmen and two sophomores. All had similar skills. I decided to cut one freshman and one sophomore, although the sophomore was a bit better than the freshman I was keeping. By keeping a freshman I have a year to work with him. The sophomore I cut was Randy Crum. Randy is mature and is blessed with a great attitude. It hurt to cut him. The freshman took it very hard; apparently this was his first major setback. Three days after the cut, Ken Warren, the freshman I had kept, broke his jaw and was out for the season. I needed another goalkeeper. Since the freshman had taken it so hard, I called him first. He declined; he just was not willing to try again. I didn't like it, but I understood, although with a heavy heart. I next called Randy. He was delighted and joined us the next morning. Both Randy and the team had a great season.

When I meet with a player about to be cut there are just the two of us. No assistant sits in. I don't want the player to feel ganged up on. I arrange the office so that we can sit down to talk without anything, like a table or desk, between us. I want the conversation to be as open as possible. I know there will be disappointment, but I want to give myself every opportunity to help the player salvage his sense of self-worth. I don't want him to equate his setback with feelings of inadequacy. I hope that when he leaves my office he feels good about himself, although still disappointed.

To achieve that, I try to point out as many positive things about him as I can. I may say, "First of all I want to compliment you on your work ethic in practices. You have a lot going for you. You are personable, a good leader, people like you, and I also noticed from your transcripts that you are a very good student. With all those qualities I know you will go far in your chosen major. I'm not saying that you won't encounter some setbacks in life; they'll be there. But I feel that when they come, you'll handle them. I hope that you will view what I'm about to tell you as just that, a temporary setback."

I then take time to point out areas that he should be working on to improve and better prepare himself for next year's tryout. I also tell him about some of our players who didn't make it the first year, but worked hard and came back a year later and won a starting position. If possible I try to have a contact for him. Usually that is the phone number of a coach in the adult league who is looking for players. At the time of our meeting he may not be all that interested in the phone number, but I ask him to take it and hang on to it for a few days.

I may end the conversation by saying, "I know you are disappointed and may be a little angry. I understand. No one likes setbacks, and an unmotivated athlete will view it as the end of the world. But a motivated athlete, like yourself, will see this setback as a challenge to work harder and be better prepared the next time around."

Obviously, this is an emotional time for me, but it is far more emotional for the player. I don't want him to leave the office feeling totally without recourse. Since we make the cuts on Friday, I ask him to take the weekend and think about everything that has happened and all that has been said. If on Monday he feels that I have made a mistake or if he feels that he wants to talk some more, I will be available. I actually give him a time to meet me should he be inclined to do that.

 THE JEFF COLYAR STORY

During our last season, Jeff Colyar, a defender, came back to keep his Monday appointment with me after being cut in the second cut. Jeff explained that he had been nervous throughout the tryout and felt that he really was better than what he had shown. He asked if he could keep coming to practices even though he would not be competing with the team. I gave my permission.

During the next few weeks Jeff was far more relaxed and indeed looked better. His work rate was intense. Three matches into the season, Bryan Ruby, our right wing defender, broke his hand. We decided to activate Jeff, since the player who would have taken Bryan's place was not working out too well. Jeff did an excellent job and was in the starting lineup when we played for the regional championship.

Again, I don't like tryouts and I detest making cuts. I would hate them even more if in my heart I knew that I hadn't done everything in my power to be fair and to protect the player's self-esteem.

Evaluating Practice

Once you have made all the cuts, it is time to start molding the players and the team. The task now facing you is to view each player and determine how he or she fits into the team structure. As said earlier, Charles Hughes, the famous British coach, felt there were only two kinds of players on the field—attackers and defenders. All players are attackers when the team is in possession of the ball and all are defenders when the ball is lost. Simplistic? True, but not without merit. Every player on the field has attacking and defending duties. Certainly, when the ball is lost the forward closest to the ball becomes the first line of defense, and the defender in possession with space in front should attack. In other words, every field player should be able to play every position on the field. That a player will play certain positions better than others is a given. I like to compare the players to physicians. All know everything there is to know about medicine in general, but most of them specialize in a certain aspect. Our players have to know all principles of play, but most specialize in certain positions. The players with stronger defensive awareness will probably feel most comfortable in defensive positions. The risk takers will prefer attacking positions. Regardless, a player can't be strictly a defender

or strictly an attacker. There is no black and white; there are only shades of gray. In today's soccer all players on the field should be well rounded. For a good example, watch the Brazilian team in action.

Putting Players in Positions

After you have evaluated the players' overall abilities, you can begin to assess players for certain roles. You will need to evaluate defensive strengths, midfield characteristics, and forward capabilities. It's time to bring out the specialists.

Once you determine who the specialists are and what capabilities they have, it is time to start thinking about the style of play most suitable for the talent you have available.

After you have completed that task, you can begin to look for the strongest players in each of the three groups. Position assignment comes next. My friend Bobby Howe, former under-20 U.S. national team coach, likes to start by first selecting the strongest goalkeeper, then the strongest central defender, then the strongest center midfielder, and finally the most effective striker. He calls that the backbone of the team. After that he fills the other positions based on evaluated strengths. This creates the starting 11—for the moment. Remember, be flexible. The team you start in your first match never consists of the 11 players first selected. At least mine never has. There are too many questions still unanswered, such as the following:

- Are the selected players capable of playing the chosen style?
- How are the players responding to each other?
- How are they handling specific assignments?
- If we change the system, do all players adjust equally well?
- Does one system work better than another?
- How are individual players handling various degrees of pressure?
- Is this really the best position for this player?
- Is this really the best player for this position?
- Is there a good team culture?
- Who is communicating and who is not communicating?

Only hard practices, keen observation, and evaluation can answer these questions or questions like them. Asking questions will force you to be flexible and willing to make adjustments or changes. And flexibility is one of the keys to coaching soccer successfully.

Determining Your Starters

When you have decided who is going to play where and who will probably start, you will have to let the individual players know about your decisions. The starters should know why they are starting. What is more important is that you give the players who do not start specific reasons for your decision. You can be honest and candid; the players will appreciate that. You should also work hard with them to bring them to starting caliber. Earlier in this book I talked about the important role the nonstarting players play on the team. You need them, the team needs them. Make sure they understand that.

In most cases I have a nonstarting player understudy one or two starting players. So, in case of injury, nonperformance, or any other tactical reason for substituting, the player goes in well prepared.

Meeting With Assistants

During practice water breaks my assistants and I briefly meet to discuss each segment of the practice. Since we frequently work in small groups, each with his own group, we comment on the success rate, or lack thereof, that we have achieved. Directly after practice we meet again to discuss the practice. After consulting the practice plan for the next day, we may make some adjustments. However, we seldom veer far from the plan. If pertinent information comes out of the after-practice meeting, we enter it into our files. It always astounds me how much my assistants contribute to the success of our program and the welfare of our players.

Evaluation Tools

Sometimes words and demonstrations alone are not enough to help players evaluate their strengths and weaknesses. I have found that video, especially when shown in slow or stop motion, can help the player understand what it is that you saw or want him to do.

Another tool I find essential to help me keep track of everything we do is a personal computer. I have one in my office and a compatible one at home. It helps me with mailing lists, keeps track of practice plans and practice suggestions, lays out match schedules, provides accurate statistics, and writes form letters. The only thing it doesn't do is brew my coffee, but I'm working on that.

Video

All our matches are videotaped. We also use video for specific purposes. For instance, players develop faults over a number of years. I try to correct the faults in practice, but I am not always successful. Sometimes the player thinks he has corrected it, but he hasn't. Before everybody gets frustrated we shoot a video of the error. It's much easier for the player to make corrections if he can see himself committing the error.

Video is also very useful when you want to see an action in slow motion. For that reason we often use it at goalkeeper practices, particularly when we are working on foot movement. Before a jump or dive many goalkeepers have a tendency to move their weight to the wrong foot for a split second. That wastes time. The movement is so quick, however, that he's unaware of it. Video, in slow motion, convinces him quickly.

We also use it during shooting practices. Again the action of the shot is so fast that faults are difficult to detect and therefore almost impossible to correct. Using slow motion, I can clearly show a player who has been shooting high that he hits the ball too much below center. Seeing this, the player will start to make corrections.

Computers

We collect a tremendous amount of information before, during, and after a season. It is difficult to keep track of it all and to file it so that we can find it when needed.

I have a friend who can fix almost any car with a pair of pliers and a screwdriver. I have another friend who could fix every car because he has every tool. The problem is he can't find the key to his toolbox. It goes that way with information. It's useless unless you have a key.

My key is a computer. All the information and notes I gather are stored in easy-to-find files on a well-organized hard disk. I don't own stock in IBM or Microsoft; however, I do recommend the use of a computer in your coaching endeavors.

Evaluating Matches

Evaluating a match is hard work. It consists of constant observation and evaluation of the match and the players, and then making necessary adjustments. I have never understood coaches who seem to have time to yell and scream, argue with referees, or give a constant barrage of emotional advice to their players.

Staff Responsibilities

The stress that comes with match day can be significantly reduced if everyone involved knows exactly what to do.

Rick Harrison, our administrative assistant, watches the opposing team warm up and reports anything noteworthy, such as strengths and weaknesses of the goalkeeper, the identity of the good shooters, and anything else that can benefit us.

Another assistant visits with the officials to answer any questions regarding league rules, such as substitution rules, and rules about overtimes, if any. He also asks the officials to stay after the match long enough to sign the match report.

The scorekeeper doubles as statistician and keeps track of who starts, who enters later, who scores, who assists, who shoots, who saves, who fouls, who gets cautioned, who gets ejected, who gets a corner, and who takes it. A spotter helps the scorekeeper.

Even though we probably have a scouting report and have practiced accordingly, once the match starts it is still my job to evaluate weaknesses in the opponent's defense and their strengths on attack. I also look for obvious mismatches on the field of play. I carry a very small voice-activated micro tape recorder on which I can catch my comments and the comments of my assistants.

One assistant totally concentrates on the opponent to determine its style and tactics. He also looks for opposing players who are losing their concentration or becoming tired later in the match. Another assistant concentrates on our team to determine the effectiveness of our tactics and game plan, and views our players for fatigue and loss of temper. All report to me orally when they feel I should know about something. If at times I feel that I should have had an oral report, but didn't, I may ask for it. Sometimes one of the observers sees something that has no immediate bearing on the match. He jots it down on a notepad so that we can discuss it afterward or during the next prepractice meeting.

During the first half Rick Harrison draws the movement of the ball on a small sketch pad for me. This little drawing also shows who brought the ball up, who lost it, who shot, and who scored. He hands me the drawing every 15 minutes. It is a tremendous tool because it quickly gives me a two-dimensional overview of what occurred in the preceding 15 minutes. It shows who had possession and where on the field the opponent likes to have possession. Among other things, it shows where the opponent likes to attack and if we are using the field according to our game plan.

Figure 15.4 is a good example of one of these match drawings. It is Rick's sketch from a match we played against Shoreline Community College on October 11, 1995. It shows the action from the 15th to the 30th minute. We play from left to right. In the opponent's half, the sketch shows the action and numbers of our players only. The lines show the path of the ball. If the number of a player appears more than once on a line, it means that the player dribbled the ball to the point where his number appears last.

If a number is at the end of a line, the player lost the ball one-on-one. If a line proceeds to no particular receiver, then the shot was missed or a pass was intercepted. When a line has no number or starts without a number, it simply means that Rick missed that particular detail on that play.

We show the action of the opponent in our half but not the players' numbers; there just isn't time. Besides, I already know who their dangerous players are, and I'm only interested in how they move the ball. Do they come through the middle? Do they attack wide? If so, which side do they favor? Do they play long or short? Where do they shoot from?

Obviously, during those 15 minutes illustrated in figure 15.4, we dominated—especially on our right side. That was pretty much according to game plan. The opponent's defender on our left side was strong, and you can see that when we tried a few attacks on that side our player was promptly fouled (F). We wasted the resulting free kicks. You can also see that we took seven shots at their goal during the period. Two were stopped by the goalkeeper. We were awarded one corner kick (C) and two throw-ins. The opponent had one good opportunity. It came from a throw-in to the top of the box from where it was crossed to the far post. A Shoreline player took a hard shot from there; however, our goalkeeper deflected it and gave up a corner.

Rick's drawings are a tool that usually confirms our observations. As such it serves as an additional opinion to help us make decisions. I also find the drawings very useful at halftime. My instructions are more effective if I have a picture to back me up. For example, I can say, "You're not using Adam enough. Adam can beat the right outside

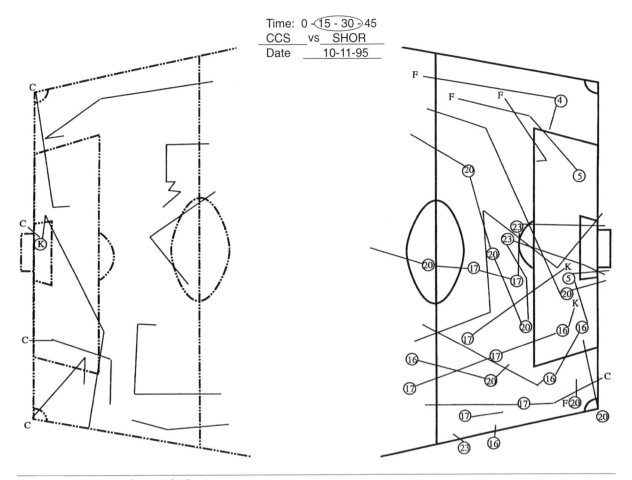

Time: 0 ⟨15 - 30⟩ 45
CCS   vs   SHOR
Date   10-11-95

Figure 15.4   Sample match drawing.

defender. The goal Clayton scored came after we played the ball wide to Adam. He beat his man and short-crossed to Clayton. Goal. But since then, you have hardly used him. Here, let me show you on the drawing."

When I tell the stopper to shift a bit to the right since most of their attacking play is on that side, it helps when I can show him a picture of heavy traffic on the right and very little on the left. He will understand better.

We instruct the trainers to watch for injuries and to know how they occurred. We ask them to have water ready for any player who needs it and has time during a stoppage to get it.

One of our managers watches the referee to see what he calls, how much he lets go, his cooperation with his linesmen, and the precision of the linesmen's offside calls.

Starting with the opening whistle, we gather information and make tactical adjustments accordingly. For instance, we may have given one of our players instructions to tightly mark an opposing player. After a while we find that the opposing player isn't all that dangerous. During the next stoppage in play we may get a message to our player to ease up. Or, we may find that the opposing wing forward is just too fast for our outside defender. We substitute a quicker defender.

At halftime we make final changes, and some of the players may get one or two new assignments. During the second half all of us evaluate the effectiveness of our adjustments. If things are working out I leave it alone. If not, I may have to make other changes. If we are behind late in the match I may bring in an attacking midfielder for a defensive midfielder. If we are ahead I may do the reverse.

I still maintain that soccer is not a coached sport. I call what we do during the matches observation, evaluation, and modification.

We don't teach during a match. Instead, we take what we learn from the match to the next practice session.

Postmatch Evaluations

After a match is completed I have a lot of information. There are the recorded notes, a videotape, the scoresheet with the stats, Rick's drawings, plus all the information that is still in our heads. To not lose the latter, the assistants and I meet directly after the match to discuss our observations. That discussion, combined with the hard information, determines the plan for the next few practices. Invariably during the next practice we will walk the players through the problem situations we saw. We can show why it became a problem and what could have prevented it. We also walk through the areas where we had success and again show why it was successful. No matter what happens in a match we gain from the experience. Since we always gain, we never lose.

Summary

To thoroughly, fairly, and expertly evaluate players is a crucial coaching task. I believe that the following suggestions help coaches become better evaluators.

- See players early. Observe them in competitive matches and at practice.
- Keep written records or computer files of your evaluations.
- Use tools like the player evaluation form, the player profile form, and the player self-evaluation form.
- Prepare yourself mentally before making cuts and know in your heart that the player has had fair and meticulous evaluation.
- When making cuts protect the player's self-esteem as much as possible.
- When putting players in positions ask yourself constantly, "Is this the right player for that position and is that the right position for this player?"
- Let players know why they are starting or why they are not starting.
- If you have a staff, use their talent.
- Make use of tools that can help you evaluate players, practices, and matches. Video and computers are essential to coaching and record keeping.
- During matches observe, evaluate, and modify.
- Don't neglect to have an in-depth postmatch evaluation. Record information while it is still fresh in your mind.

Chapter 16

Evaluating Your Program

No matter what happened during the season it is essential that you promptly evaluate all aspects of your program. Sometimes, if it has been a bad season, you may want to step away for a few days and recover from your disappointment. On the other hand, if the season was great you may be tempted to take some time off to come down from cloud nine. Neither is a good idea. You must evaluate while everything is still fresh in your mind and in the minds of others who will give evaluations—the players, assistant coaches, and administrators. In other words, the next season starts the day after the current season ends.

Postseason Evaluations

Only if you thoroughly evaluate the past season can you plan the success of the next season. What happened during the past season? Did it progress the way you had anticipated? Was the progress satisfactory—considering schedules, quality of players, strength of competition, and performance of staff? Were there discipline problems? Would any area benefit by making changes? Your evaluations are important, but they reflect only the impressions of one person and may be biased or limited in scope. To truly evaluate your program solicit comments on the season from as many sources as you can.

My college, in particular my athletic director, Dr. Maury Ray, also feels that immediate evaluations are crucial to the continued success of a program. But then Maury was a successful basketball coach. He personally conducts several evaluation sessions—one with the head coach, one with the players, and one with the coaching staff. All sessions are scheduled and completed within five days of the end of a season.

The agenda for Maury's initial meeting with me is short. He solicits some general comments, and together we schedule a session with the players and a session with the staff. I usually make general remarks about my satisfaction with the team's performances during the past season, my satisfaction with my staff coaches, the support staff, budgets, recruiting plans, and suggested changes to the conference's code.

Evaluation by the Players

When I was first told about being evaluated by players, I had some misgivings. My anxiety increased when I found out that the evaluations were anonymous. I knew that it was difficult to please all players and feared their judgment, whether it was biased or not. But over the years player evaluations have become one of my greatest learning sources. The few negative comments that have come out of the evaluations have helped me improve. Some of the negative comments were about areas where I needed to pay more attention.

Maury leads the session, explains the importance of evaluation, and asks the players to be honest and fair in their appraisals. All evaluations are in writing. To ensure that they are candid, names or signatures are not required. The players are asked to complete a player evaluation form like the one in figure 16.1.

After everyone finishes, Maury collects the evaluations, makes a few comments, and leaves. Before the meeting with the staff coaches, he studies the evaluations.

Even if your athletic director does not require an evaluation by the players, I suggest you execute it on your own. Be prepared

for some harsh criticism. Some of it will be unfounded, but some will have merit. Learn from it. You can only get better.

Evaluation by the Assistant Coaches

A few days after the meeting with the players at the end of the season, my assistants and I will meet with the athletic director. Maury's questions will deal mainly with team management. I need the assistants to evaluate the quality and effectiveness of our practices and our on-the-field performance. I require each assistant coach to write a detailed report that evaluates the overall season. The reports may include comments and suggestions on our physical condition, technical skill level, tactical understanding, practice and game management, coaching decisions, and efficiency of our trainers. I also ask them to analyze whether we were successful when we made style adjustments, changed the system of play, or reassigned players. Those reports become part of our permanent file and are a terrific tool for planning the next season.

The meeting with Maury is casual, and everyone has an opportunity to candidly discuss the good and bad points of the season just finished. Since he has studied the evaluations done by the players, he takes time to discuss concerns players may have expressed. Maury also requires all assistants to complete a written evaluation. He solicits comments like those in figure 16.2 on pages 213-215.

This evaluation is effective because it not only addresses the program but also includes self-evaluation and a reality check of how the assistant coaches feel about the program compared with the players.

Evaluating the Assistants

Maury's process includes some self-evaluation by the assistants. However, it is somewhat limited. I need to let my assistants know how I feel about them and their performance. Before we meet I ask the assistants to list both their coaching strong points and where they feel they need to improve. I, too, have made a list. Usually our observations

Postseason Player Evaluation Form

1. Was your coach (or coaches) well organized and prepared for each practice?
   Comments: _____
   _____

2. Were the practice sessions too long, too short, or about right?
   Comments: _____
   _____

3. Were there open lines of communication between you and your coach (coaches) so that you could solve problems together?
   Comments: _____
   _____

4. Did you feel your coach (coaches) had favorites or did your coach (coaches) treat everyone fairly?
   Comments: _____
   _____

5. Did you feel there was enough discipline, too much, or not enough?
   Comments: _____
   _____

6. Would you like more matches at home or away, if possible?
   Comments: _____
   _____

7. Was your coach (coaches) well organized and prepared for each match?
   Comments: _____
   _____

8. Did you enjoy the trips themselves, see new places, meet new people, and enjoy the company of your teammates and others?
   Comments: _____
   _____

   What can be done to improve the trips?
   Comments: _____
   _____

9. Were your home matches well organized by the staff so that they ran smoothly from your point of view?
   Comments: _____
   _____

(continued)

Figure 16.1 Sample postseason player evaluation.

What can be done to improve match management?

Comments: _____
_____

10. Were you and your teammates and the opposing team treated well by match managers so that the home matches were first-class events?

Comments: _____
_____

11. Were the uniforms, equipment, and supplies furnished by the college adequate, more than adequate, or inadequate?

Comments: _____
_____

12. List the major strengths you see and like in the program. _____
_____
_____

13. List the major weaknesses you see and would like to change in the program. _____
_____
_____

14. Do you have a positive or negative feeling about your participation in the soccer program?

Comments: _____
_____

15. Do you have additional comments on strengths, weaknesses, and feelings about your coach and the soccer program?

Comments: _____
_____

Figure 16.1   *(continued)*

are the same. Be sure to bring out all the positive points. The assistant also has a right to know where you feel improvement can be made.

Choose your method and your words carefully when making suggestions for improvement. Don't trample on their self-esteem. Usually the sandwich approach works best. Begin the conversation by pointing out the qualities you admire in the assistant. Next, discuss the area where you feel the coach could make improvements. Make suggestions and offer your help. Finish the discussion by again pointing out the coach's positive qualities and your satisfaction with his or her performance.

 MANAGING STRESS

Kammie Jacobs, my assistant for women, is an excellent coach. She was, and still is, an exceptionally good player. She is also very competitive, and the team's performance is extremely important to her. There was one area where I felt she should try to make an improvement. I'd like to give you the gist of our conversation.

"Kammie, thanks for taking the time to meet with me. Before we discuss anything else, I want to say again how happy I am with your performance as a coach. You are an essential part of our success. Your knowledge, reliability, and consistency have a very positive influence on the team. But most of all, I believe that your enthusiasm motivates not only the team but

Assistant Coaches Evaluation Form

ADMINISTRATION

    1. Rate (on a scale from 1 to 10, with 1 being poor and 10 excellent) your overall relationship and communication with the athletic director.   **Rating** _____

    2. What needs to be done to improve in this area?

EQUIPMENT

    3. Rate overall handling of uniforms, equipment, and supplies.   **Rating** _____

    4. Rate your relationship and communication with the equipment staff.   **Rating** _____

    5. What needs to be done to improve your communication and relationship in the equipment area?

PUBLIC RELATIONS

    6. Rate your overall relationship and image with the general community.   **Rating** _____

    7. Rate your relationship and image with the student body.   **Rating** _____

    8. Rate your relationship and image with the press.   **Rating** _____

    9. What needs to be done to improve in this area?

ORGANIZATION

    10. Rate your overall organizational skills (paperwork, travel advances, eligibility, forms, etc.) in the total program.   **Rating** _____

    11. What needs to be done to improve in this area?

DISCIPLINE

    12. Rate the amount of discipline you demand in your team.   **Rating** _____

    13. What needs to be done to improve in this area?

(continued)

Figure 16.2 Sample assistant coaches evaluation form.

TEACHING-COACHING TECHNIQUES
  14. Rate your overall effectiveness in teaching and coaching techniques.   **Rating** _____
  15. What areas need improvement?

MATCHES
  16. Rate your overall coaching ability in competitive matches.   **Rating** _____
  17. What needs to be done to improve?

RECRUITING
  18. Rate your overall effectiveness in recruiting.   **Rating** _____
  19. What needs to be done to improve it?

PRACTICE
  20. Were the practice sessions too long, too short, or about right?
      Comments:

  21. Were you well organized and prepared for each practice?
      Comments:

TRIPS
  22. Would your team like more home matches or trips?
      Comments:

  23. Did you give your athletes opportunities to see new places, meet new people, and time to enjoy themselves and their teammates?
      Comments:

Figure 16.2 (continued)

COMMUNICATION

24. Were there open lines of communication between you and your team so that you could solve problems together?

Comments:

25. Were there open lines of communication between you and the head coach?

Comments:

26. Did you feel you played favorites or did you treat everyone the same?

Comments:

OVERALL

27. List the major strengths you see and like in your program.

28. List the major weaknesses you see and would like to change in your program.

29. Do your athletes have a positive or negative feeling about their participation in the soccer program?

Comments:

Figure 16.2 *(continued)*

also the people you work with. I know that you are striving to improve constantly. I would like to make a suggestion that, if you apply it, will make you even better.

"I feel for you during the moments right before a match and during the time it takes to play the match. Your mouth gets a tight set, your eyes glare, and you are breathing rapidly. During the match you pace a lot. I can feel your stress. I can identify with your emotions because I used to do the same things."

Kammie said, "That's hard to believe. You seem so calm."

"I'm not. But, some time ago, a friend pointed out to me that if he could feel my stress, so could the team. I was probably transferring some of my stress to the team, or at least showing them that I wasn't quite as confident as I said I was. That might cause them to doubt their preparedness. I have learned to manage my stress and purposely force myself to relax. I do that by doing deep-breathing exercises whenever I feel the stress coming on. If you'd like I'll teach you how to do the exercises."

Kammie said that she would like to learn and did. She is now more relaxed and so is the team. I finished the conversation by again pointing out my satisfaction with her work, and I also mentioned how great it was that we could sit down and help each other get better.

Constructive criticism, if you deliver it properly, is appreciated by coaches eager to learn and improve.

I have been very fortunate with my assistant coaches. They did an excellent job while working with me. They learned. Those who left did so because they accepted head coaching positions elsewhere.

We encourage all our staff coaches to attend at least one clinic per year at the college's expense. After evaluating the assistants I also suggest which clinics they should attend. First, I like them to get their United States Soccer Federation licenses. But since the USSF teaches very little about coaching effectiveness, I suggest to our coaches that they study selected courses in that subject area. I also make them aware of other courses, such as sport psychology, sport management, sport marketing, physiology, and so forth.

Evaluating the Players

In a two-year system the team is forever changing. Each year I lose about half the players. Building a team is an ongoing challenge, but the building will be strong if it stands on a firm foundation. The returning players are that foundation.

After coaching a competitive season, my assistants and I know our players well. We are then in the unique position of being able to fully evaluate each of them. I ask my assistants, before the Christmas break, to write an evaluation for every returning player. I do the same. Once we have done the evaluations, we prepare an off-season training program for each player.

We may recommend certain classes like strength training and other fitness activities.

We make them aware of playing opportunities. I also conduct a technique development class in spring. At this meeting we discuss eligibility rules again.

We also have a few get-togethers like picnics. A number of players work and play at our five-a-side tournament; others work in our summer camps.

Kammie Jacobs, my assistant coach for women, is a runner. Once a week she brings the team together for a run. Jim Martinson, who assists me with the men, likes to do circuit training with them during the off-season.

All I'm really concerned with in the off-season is that the players succeed academically, stay fit, and take advantage of every opportunity to improve on their playing skills.

In a short meeting with each player I go over the evaluations and the newly written training program. I explain each item on the program and show how it will benefit him or her. I also schedule times for the player to report back to me to check his or her progress. This time is well spent. After all, these players are the foundation on which we build our dreams for the next season.

Evaluating Yourself

The allure of coaching is that it is forever a learning process. Each year, each season, there are new and different challenges. The challenge may be playing a formidable opponent, trying a new method or system, managing a difficult player, building a team culture, handling fatigue, or another problem. Numerous challenges present themselves during a season of play. We should evaluate all of them. Since I have probably evaluated practice and match performance challenges with the staff during season and postseason sessions, I don't need to evaluate them again. There is one significant area, however, that I still need to look at—the effectiveness of my own performance.

Within one week of completing a season, I evaluate my performance in areas other than practices and matches. I use a checklist with questions like the following:

- Was I always physically and mentally prepared to perform my tasks?

- Did I separate my personal life from my life as a coach?
- If I became fatigued, did I maintain a positive attitude?
- Did I stay positive even after a defeat?
- Did I manage or lead?
- How well did I communicate, in groups and one-on-one, with players, staff, administrators, media, and community? Did I listen?
- When problems occurred did I procrastinate or handle them immediately?
- How well did I handle confrontations? Did I listen?
- How patient was I when players or staff wanted to discuss personal problems with me? Did I listen?
- Did I stay performance oriented throughout the season?
- Was I fair to everyone I met this season?
- Did I, at all times, consider the athlete's welfare first?
- What am I willing to do to improve?
- If I need to improve in any area, where can I go to learn?

I believe that giving honest answers to my questions will make me a better coach from season to season.

Building for the Future

My grandfather was a sea captain. As a child I listened to his stories in fascination. One day he took me to the harbor and we went aboard his ship.

"She's a good ship," he said.

I asked, "Why, grandpa?"

He said, "Because she's well built, she has an excellent crew, and she has a destination to go to."

Build your program well, surround yourself with ambitious, hardworking people, and set realistic goals. You'll have a good ship. Once you are sailing, stay on course.

It's not all that difficult to get to the top. Staying there is. No matter how successful you become keep evaluating each situation, each new plan, each change in course. Keep listening to your players, your assistants, your boss. Evaluate what they say; it may be important.

Talk to and study other coaches, not just soccer coaches, but any successful coach. Learn from them, but in the end be yourself. Only you can be the best you.

Coaches earn respect. It doesn't automatically come with the job. To earn it, maintain your integrity and always stick to your philosophy. It is your plan, your map to the future.

A man once said, "Winning isn't everything, it's the only thing." I agree. If by winning he means taking a program from scratch and building it into a successful entity, if by winning he means giving young aspiring coaches an opportunity to develop, if by winning he means taking a group of athletes and helping them play as close to potential as possible, then I agree. Winning is everything. As long as you care for your athletes and staff, and stay focused on performance improvement, you'll never lose. By the way, eventually your efforts will be reflected in your win and loss record.

The most important part of your program is your athletes. They are your messengers. They look to you for guidance, leadership, values, integrity, and consistency. Be the role model they can emulate. Instead of knowing many athletes, you will have hundreds of friends who fondly call you Coach.

Summary

A stronger future can be built by evaluating the past. Next year's program will be better if you take the time to evaluate the strengths and weaknesses of the season just completed. Here are some suggestions for making the task easier.

- Do all evaluations within days of the season's completion.
- Allow administrators, players, and your assistants to evaluate your program.
- Don't let candid criticism bother you. Learn from it.
- Evaluate your players and assistants fairly and candidly. Be tactful.
- Do a thorough self-evaluation.
- Build the future of your program on the facts presented by your evaluations.

Index

A

Academics, importance of, 21
AC Milan, 85, 114
Administration, school, 39-40
Administrative assistant, 57, 205-206
Affirmations, for motivation of players, 27-28
Al-Dhain, Adeeb, 8
Allen, Stan, 187
Almost Free activity, 97-98
American Youth Soccer Association, 3
Angles, between challenging and covering players,
    95
Assistant coaches
    communication with, 19-20
    evaluation of, 210-215
    in evaluation of players, 199, 201, 202, 205
    evaluation of program by, 210
    hiring of, 57
    licensing of, 215
    responsibilities during matches, 206-207
    training and continuing education for, 215
Athletic trainers, 19-20, 55-56, 207
Attacking midfielder (playmaker)
    defensive skills for, 85-86
    offensive skills for, 140-141
Attacking wing back, tactics for playing against,
    187
Attack in Numbers activity, 168
Audiovisual production manager, 57
Away matches. *See also* Travel, planning for
    selecting players for, 18
    staff at, 57

B

Baba brothers, 109
Baggio (player), 85, 137
Balance, in defense, 119-121
Balls, 53
Big Ben activity, 160
Big Sky Tournament, 8
Bishop, Wilbur, 45
Blake, John, 14
Body composition, 61-62
Books, on soccer and coaching, 4-5
Brown, Terry, 39
Budgeting, 39, 52, 63

C

Campos, Jorge, 111
Cardiovascular endurance training, 58-59
Caring, about players, 30
Carle, Tory, 55-56
Cascade League, 22
Central midfielder, postmatch lessons for, 194
Chadwell, Joe, 8
Charlton (player), 85
Clemence, Ray, 186
Climate, and playing style, 36
Clinics, coaching, 5, 215
Coaches
    conduct during matches, 10, 17, 190-191
    mission summarized, 9-10
    responsibilities with injuries, 56
    role in practices, 90-91
    self-evaluation by, 216
    weekly meetings for, 5
College, player planning for, 65
Colyar, Jeff, 203
Communication, 13-23
    with assistants and staff, 19-20
    basic techniques for, 14-16
    with community, 22
    with faculty, 21-22
    during matches, 17, 190-191, 192-193
    with media, 22-23
    nonverbal, 15-16, 17
    with officials, 20-21, 206
    off the field, 17-18
    with parents, 21
    with players, 16-18, 69, 190-191, 192-193,
        202-203
    at practices, 17
    with student body, 22
Community Colleges of Spokane (CCS), 35-36,
        38, 39, 42-44, 55-56, 62-63, 205-208, 209-
        216
Community support, 22, 41-42
Compactness, in defense, 114-116
Computers, for evaluating players, 205
Conditioned games. *See* Small-sided, conditioned
    games
Conditioning, for players, 57-62
    basic guidelines, 57-58

Conditioning, for players, *(continued)*
    for body composition, 61-62
    cardiovascular endurance training, 58-59
    communication with trainers about, 19
    flexibility training, 60-61
    strength training, 59-60
Conduct
    after matches, 193
    during matches, 10, 17, 190-191
Confined to Base activity, 93, 164-165
Continuous One-Versus-One activity, 100-101
Continuous Two-Versus-Two activity, 101
Contracts, team-player, 32
Corner kicks
    defensive tactics, 123-124, 187
    offensive tactics, 174-175
    scouting reports of, 186
Cover, in defense, 116-118
    skill development activity, 101-102
Creativity, in offense, 170-172
Cross and Finish activity, 150
Crosses, dealing with, 79-80, 108
Crum, Randy, 202
Cruyff, Johan, 36, 85, 137, 171
Curfew, 43
Cutting, 197, 201-203

D
Daily practice plans, 68, 70
Dalglish (player), 85, 137
Daws, Cindy, 123
Defender. *See also* Fullback, tactics for; Marking
        back; Sweeper; Wing back
    defensive tactics for, 111, 113, 114, 116-117,
        119, 121, 125
    skill-building activities for, 98-99, 101, 118
Defensive skills. *See also* Defensive skills and
        techniques activities; Defensive tactics
    for specific positions, 75-87
        attacking midfielder (playmaker), 85-86
        forward, 86-87, 93, 94
        goalkeeper, 75-81, 93-94, 104-108
        marking back, 82-84, 92, 93, 94
        stopper, 84-85
        sweeper, 81-82, 93-95
        wide midfielder, 85
    teaching of, 89-108
        basic positioning, 92-93
        defensive responsibilities, 93-100
        goalkeeper skills, 104-108
        small-sided, conditioned games for, 90-91, 114
        tackling, 103-104
Defensive skills and techniques activities
    for covering, 101-102
    for defensive responsibility, 95-99
    for defensive skills in general, 100-103
    for midfielders, 95-96, 98-99
    for positioning, 93
    for tactical skills, 115-121
    for specific positions

        for defenders, 98-99, 101
        for goalkeeper, 104-108
        for marking players, 100-101, 102-103
        for sweepers, 95-96, 102-103
Defensive tactics, 109-128
    against attacking wing back, 187
    formations, 113-114
    goalkeeper in, 111-114, 123, 124, 125, 126-127
    key principles, 114-121
    line of confrontation, 112-114
    phases of play in, 122-123
    postmatch lessons on, 194
    scouting reports of, 184
    set plays, 123-128, 187
    for specific positions
        forward, 114, 125
        fullback, 114
        goalkeeper, 111-114, 123, 124, 125, 126-127
        marking back, 113, 121, 122-123, 128
        midfielder, 111, 113, 114, 122, 124, 125, 127-128
        stoppers, 128
        sweeper, 113, 116, 119, 122, 126-127
        wide midfielder, 124, 127-128
        wing back, 114
    against star player, 187
    teamwork in, 122-123
Delay, in defense, 118-119
Depth (cover), in defense, 116-118
Depth (support), in offense, 164-165
DeSailly (AC Milan player), 85
DeStefano (player), 137
Diagrams, legend for, 91
Direct free kicks, defensive tactics with, 124-126
Discipline and rules, 22, 31-34, 43-45
Distances, between challenging and covering play-
        ers, 95
Distributing the ball, by goalkeeper, 80-81
Dorrance, Anson, 7
Dress code, 44
Dribbling, 91, 110-111, 158-159
Drills, 90. *See also* Defensive skills and tech-
        niques activities; Offensive skills and tech-
        niques activities
Drug abuse, 43-44
Duke, Phoebe, 55
Dunga (Brazilian player), 85
Dynamo Dresden soccer team, 186

E
Eating disorders, 61-62
Eaton, Kristen, 123
Education, importance for athletes, 21
Ejection, 33, 191
Endurance training, 58-60
English Football League, 191
Equipment, 52-53
Equipment manager, 57
Europe Cup match, 1988, 6
Evaluation, of players, 197-208
    by assistant coaches, 199, 201, 202, 205

before cutting, 197, 201-203
during matches, 205-208
postmatch, 193, 208
postseason, 215-216
during practices, 201-202, 203-205
preseason, 197, 198-201
tools for, 197, 198-201, 205
Evaluation, of program, 51, 209-217
by assistant coaches, 210
of assistant coaches, 210-215
by players, 44-45, 210, 211-212
of practices, 71-72
of yourself (coach), 216

F
Facilities
planning of, 53-54
scouting reports of, 186
Faculty
communication with, 21-22
support for soccer program from, 39-40
Fahey, Erin, 123
Faking, 158, 159
Family. *See* Parents, communication with
Feeder system, 42-43
Field diagrams, legend for, 91
Field manager, 57
Fields. *See* Playing fields
Finely, Albert, 187
Fitness. *See* Conditioning, for players
Five-Second Delay activity, 119
Five-Versus-Two activity, 160
Flexibility, in coaches, 8, 204
Flexibility training, 60-61
Flick-Ons activity, 152-153
Fluid intake, 61
Footwear, 52-53
Formations, defensive, 113-114
Forward
defensive skills for, 86-87, 93, 94
defensive tactics for, 114, 125
offensive skills for, 132-137
offensive tactics for, 164-165, 166-168, 169, 170-171
postmatch lessons for, 194
scouting reports of, 184
Four-Back Defense activity, 117-118
Free at Last activity, 98-100
Free kicks
defensive tactics, 124-127, 187
direct, 124-126, 177
indirect, 126-127, 177-179
offensive tactics, 177-179
scouting reports of, 186
Fullback, tactics for, 114, 168
Fun, 10-11, 31, 72
Furman University, 124

G
Game officials. *See* Referees

Games. *See* Small-sided, conditioned games
Goalkeeper
in defensive tactics, 111-114, 123, 124, 125, 126-127
postmatch lessons for, 193
scouting reports for, 187-188
scouting reports of, 185, 205
skill-building activities for, 104-108
skills described, 75-81, 93-94
Goals (equipment), 53
Goal setting, 28-29
Graduation, plans for after, 65
Greaves, Jimmy, 150-151
Greeter, 57
Gullit, Ruud, 6, 152

H
Halftime procedures, 25, 189, 192-193, 207
Harrison, Rick, 17, 205-206
Havens, Jerry, 28
Head coaches. *See* Coaches
Heading, 151-153
Heading in the Right Direction activity, 152
Hearing impaired players, 15-16
High Pressure activity, 116
High pressure defense, 116, 147
High shots, stopping by goalkeeper, 76-77, 78, 106
Higuita, Rene, 111, 112
Howe, Bobby, 7, 83, 204
Hughes, Charles, 37, 174, 203
Humiliation, avoiding, 16-17
Hydration, 61
Hyndman, Tony, 176

I
Imagery, 26-27
"I'm OK, You're OK" game, 31
Improvisation, in offense, 170-172
Indirect free kicks, 126-127
Injuries
communication about, 19, 69
handling during play and practice, 55-56, 207
preventing during practice, 68
Insurance coverage, 55
Inswinger kick, 175

J
Jacobs, Kammie, 212, 215, 216
Jasso, James, 30
Johnson, Adam, 17
Jones, Dave, 185

K
Keegan (player), 137
Keep It Safe activity, 154
Keep to Shoot activity, 154-155
Kinder, Matt, 21
Koemans, Ronald, 6
Kubistant, Tom, 27-28

L

Legend, for field diagrams, 91
Letter of agreement, 32
Licensing, of assistant coaches, 215
Limited Freedom activity, 95-97
Line goalkeeper, 111, 112-113
Line of confrontation, 112-114
Lineup, starting, 45-46, 190, 204
Listening techniques, 14
Liverpool FC soccer team, 186
Liverpool University soccer team, 76, 91
Long Shots, High Shots activity, 106
Losing, postmatch reaction to, 193
Low Pressure, High Pressure activity, 116
Low shots, stopping by goalkeeper, 76, 78, 105-106
Low Shots Straight at Goalkeeper activity, 105-106

M

Managers, 20, 57, 207
Maradona, Diego, 137, 171
Marking back
    defensive skill-building activities for, 100-101, 102-103
    defensive skills for, 82-84, 92, 93, 94
    defensive tactics for, 113, 121, 122-123, 128
    postmatch lessons for, 194
Martens, Rainer, 9
Martinson, Jim, 19, 216
Master plan, for practices, 62, 67, 68, 69
Matches
    communication during, 17, 190-191, 192-193
    conduct during, 10, 17, 190-191
    discipline during, 33
    evaluation of players during, 205-208
    facilities for, 53, 186
    halftime procedures, 25, 189, 192-193, 207
    imagery as preparation for, 26-27
    plan adjustments during, 192
    player matchups for, 190
    postmatch procedures, 193-194, 208
    prematch procedures, 186-188, 189, 190
    during preseason, 62-63
    scheduling of, 62-63
    staff responsibilities during, 205-208
    starting lineup for, 45-46, 190, 204
    substitutions during, 191-192
Matchups, 190
Matlock, Irene, 40
Matthew, Cris, 43-44
McCarthy, Michelle, 123
McCrath, C. Clifford, 25
McGuire, David, 109
Media support, 22-23, 40-41
Medical care, planning for, 55-56
Medical examinations, 55
Medical screening, of players, 54-55
Michels, Rinus, 36, 148
Midfield, scouting reports of, 184, 185

Midfielder. *See also* Attacking midfielder; Wide midfielder
    defensive skills for, 85-86
    defensive tactics for, 111, 113, 114, 122, 124, 125, 127-128
    offensive skills for, 138-142
    offensive tactics for, 167-168, 176-177, 178-179
    postmatch lessons for, 194
    skill-building activities for, 95-96, 98-99, 167-168
Mobility, in offense, 168-170
Montgomery, Amy, 21
Montgomery, Jeff, 21
Moscow Dynamo soccer team, 185
Mosher, Kevin, 198
Motivation of players, 25-34
    coach's role in, 30-31
    discipline in, 31-34
    fun in, 10-11, 31, 72
    tools for, 26-30
Mullins, Rick, 18
Muscular strength and endurance training, 59-60

N

NASL (North American Soccer League), 20, 185
Noah's Arc activity, 155
Nonverbal communication, 15-16, 17
North American Soccer League (NASL), 20, 185
Northwest Athletic Association of Community Colleges (NWAACC), 35, 52
Notre Dame University, 123
Nutrition, 43, 61
NWAACC (Northwest Athletic Association of Community Colleges), 35, 52

O

ODP (Olympic Development Program), 8, 42
Offensive skills. *See also* Offensive skills and techniques activities; Offensive tactics
    for specific positions, 131-143
        attacking midfielder (playmaker), 140-141
        forward, 132-137
        midfielder, 138-142
        stopper, 139-140
        wide midfielder, 141-142
        withdrawn striker, 137-138
    specific skills
        dribbling, 91, 110-111, 158-159
        heading, 151-153
        passing, 80, 91, 110-111, 146-147
        receiving and turning, 155-158
        runs, 159-160
        screening, 153-155
        shooting, 91, 147-151
Offensive skills and techniques activities
    for dribbling, 158-159
    for forward, 164-165, 166-167
    for heading, 152-153
    for midfielder, 167-168

for passing, 146-147, 151
for receiving and turning, 155-158
for runs, 160
for screening (ball protection), 154-155
for shooting, 149-151
for tactical skills, 164-174
Offensive tactics, 110-111, 163-180
    key principles, 164-172
    postmatch lessons on, 194
    scouting reports of, 184
    set plays, 174-179
    teamwork in, 172-174
    for specific positions
        forward, 164-165, 166-168, 169, 170-171
        fullback, 168
        midfielder, 167-168, 176-177, 178-179
        stopper, 177, 178-179
        wide midfielder, 168-169
        wing back, 168
Officials. *See* Referees
Off-season, 17-18, 216. *See also* Postseason
        evaluation; Preseason preparations
Off the Wall activity, 146-147
Olympic Development Program (ODP), 8, 42
One-Versus-One in Breakaway Situations activity,
        106-108
One-Versus-One Plus One activity, 101-102
On Guard activity, 101
Open-door policy, 15
Opposition
    evaluation during matches, 206
    scouting of, 63, 64, 183-186, 205-206
    selection of tournaments and, 63
Ostander, Lothar, 7
Outswinger kick, 174, 175
Overarm throw, 80-81
Overcoaching, 90

P
Parents, communication with, 21
Pass, Turn, Shoot activity, 157-158
Passing, 80, 91, 110-111, 146-147
Patience, in defense, 121
Pele, 83, 137, 171
Penalty kicks, scouting reports on, 187-188
Penetrating With Three Against Five activity, 167
Penetration, in offense, 165-167
Personnel. *See* Staff
Phases of play, in defense, 122-123
Philosophy of coaching, 3-11
    basic principles of, 6-9
    on fun, 10-11, 31, 72
    questions to be answered by, 4
    sources of information for developing, 4-6
    on winning, 8-9, 10-11, 217
Physician's approval to participate, 55
Pibluvich, Dang, 8
Pin Ball activity, 146
Planning. *See also* Playing season, planning for
    for after graduation, 65

for practices, 62, 67-72
for program future, 216-217
for travel, 14, 52, 63, 65
Platform for Success activity, 151
Platini (player), 85, 137, 171
Players. *See also* Evaluation, of players
    comments on performance of other players, 30-
        31
    communication with, 16-18, 69, 190-191, 192-
        193, 202-203
    conduct during matches, 191
    cutting of, 197, 201-203
    evaluation of program by, 44-45, 210, 211-212
    personal conflicts with soccer responsibilities, 8
    prematch preparation for, 186-188
    profiles of, 199, 200
    self-evaluation by, 199-201
Playing fields, 53-54
    scouting reports of, 186
Playing season, planning for, 51-65
    budgeting, 39, 52, 63
    conditioning players, 57-62
    equipment, 52-53
    facilities, 53-54
    insurance coverage, 55
    medical care, 55-56
    medical screening, 54-55
    preseason preparations, 62-63, 197, 198-201
    scouting the opposition, 63, 64, 183-186, 205-
        206
    staff, 56-57
    travel, 14, 52, 63, 65
Playmaker. *See* Attacking midfielder
Plyometric training, 60
PMR (progressive muscle relaxation), 26, 27
Porter, Ryan, 19
Portland Timbers soccer team, 159
Positions, evaluation of players for, 204. *See also*
        Defensive skills, for specific positions; De-
        fensive tactics, for specific positions; Offen-
        sive skills, for specific positions; Offensive
        tactics, for specific positions; *specific posi-
        tions*
Postmatch procedures, 193-194, 208
Postseason evaluation, 51, 209-216
Practices. *See also* Defensive skills and tech-
        niques activities; Offensive skills and tech-
        niques activities; Small-sided, conditioned
        games
    communication at, 17
    evaluation of, 71-72
    evaluation of players during, 201-202, 203-205
    facilities for, 53-54
    master plan for, 62, 67, 68, 69
    planning for, 62, 67-72
    preparing for, 68-69
    principles for, 69-72
Praise, 29-30, 193
Prematch procedures, 186-188, 189, 190
Preparation area, 110-111

Preseason preparations, 62-63, 197, 198-201
Pride, team, 34, 45
Prim, Micah, 45
Program development. *See* Soccer program development
Program evaluation. *See* Evaluation, of program
Progressive muscle relaxation (PMR), 26, 27
Protect Your Territory activity, 105
Punching the ball, 78-79
Punctuality, 44-45
Push pass, 80
Puskas, Ferenc, 137

Q
Quick Cover Game activity, 118

R
Rapid Fire activity, 105
Ray, Maury, 18, 34, 39, 210
Receiving and turning, 155-158
Red cards, 33, 191
Reep, Nicolas, 8
Rees, Roy, 7
Referees
    communication with, 20-21, 206
    observation of, 207
    skills of, 20-21
    weekly meeting for, 5
Reinforcement, 29-30, 193
Relaxation, for motivation of players, 26
Relay Turns activity, 155, 157
Rewards, for motivation of players, 29
Reyes, Adrian, 149
Reyna, Claudio, 109
Road trips. *See* Away matches; Travel, planning for
Ruby, Bryan, 203
Rules and discipline, 22, 31-34, 43-45
Run and Shoot activity, 149-150
Runs, 159-160
Run the Gauntlet activity, 159

S
St. John, Ian, 150-151
Saunders, Tom, 186
Scheduling
    of matches, 62-63
    of practices, 62, 68
Schilperoort, Todd, 17
Schmeichel, Peter, 81
School administration, support for program from, 39-40
Scorekeeper, 206
Scouting the opposition, 63, 64, 183-186, 205-206
Screening (offensive skill), 153-155
Screening, medical, 54-55
Scuderi, Kevin, 33

Seale, Elson, 159
Season. *See* Off-season; Playing season, planning for; Preseason preparations
Security, and motivation of players, 30
Self-evaluation
    by coach, 216
    by players, 199-201
Self-talk, for motivation of players, 27-28
Set plays
    defensive, 123-128, 187
    offensive, 174-179
    pregame practices for, 187
    scouting reports of, 185-186
Setup area, command of, 110-111
Shoes, 52-53
Shooting, 91, 147-151
Skelmersdale United soccer team, 136
Skills. *See* Defensive skills; Defensive skills and techniques activities; Offensive skills; Offensive skills and techniques activities
Small-sided, conditioned games. *See also specific games*
    basic principles, 70-71
    for teaching defensive skills, 90-91, 114
    for teaching offensive skills, 160-161, 164, 172
Smoking, 44
Snickers USYSA National Under-16, 133
Soccer Association for Youth, 3
Soccer program development, 35-47
    implementation of plan, 42-46
    playing system development, 37-38
    starter selection, 45-46, 204
    style development, 36-37
    support for program, 38-42
    team leader selection, 46
    team pride in, 34, 45
Sociograms, 45-46
Spin to Win activity, 150
Sportsmanship, 33
Spotter, 57, 206
Square Off activity, 173
Staff
    assessment for style development, 36-37
    communication with, 19-20
    planning and hiring, 56-57
    postseason evaluation of, 210-215
    responsibilities during matches, 205-208
Star player, tactics for playing against, 187
Starting lineup, 45-46, 190, 204
Statistician, 57, 206
Stiles, Nobby, 139-140
Stopper
    defensive skills for, 84-85
    defensive tactics for, 128
    offensive skills for, 139-140
    offensive tactics for, 177, 178-179
    scouting reports of, 184, 185
Strategic Withdrawal activity, 115

Strategy. *See* Defensive tactics; Offensive tactics
Strength training, 59-60
Students body, support for program from, 22, 40
Style of play, development of, 36-37
Suarez, Temoc, 127
Substitutions, during matches, 191-192
Success, measures of, 8-9, 11, 46. *See also* Winning
Support, for program, 38-42
Support, in offense, 164-165
Sweeper
  defensive skills for, 81-82, 93-95
  defensive tactics for, 113, 116, 119, 122, 126-127
  postmatch lessons for, 194
  scouting reports of, 185
  skill-building activities for, 95-96, 102-103
Sweeper-keeper, 111, 112-113
Systems of play, development of, 37-38

T
Tackling, 103-104
Tactics. *See* Defensive tactics; Offensive tactics; Systems of play, development of
Teachers. *See* Faculty
Team culture, 30-31
Team leader, selection and role of, 46
Team pride, 34, 45
Team Vancouver, USA, 53
Teamwork
  in defensive tactics, 122-123
  in offensive tactics, 172-174
Terriers soccer team, 15-16
Texans Soccer Club, 133
Three and One activity, 167-168
Three-Back Defense activity, 117-118
Three-Cone Game activity, 171-172
Three-Pronged Attack activity, 166-167
Three Zones activity, 120-121
Through the Minefield activity, 147, 148
Throw-ins
  defensive tactics, 127-128
  offensive tactics, 175-177
To and Fro activity, 158-159
Toronto Toros soccer team, 185
Tournaments, selection of, 63
Trainers, 19-20, 55-56, 207
Training facilities, 53-54
Training grids, 53-54
Travel, planning for, 14, 52, 63, 65. *See also* Away matches
Travel manager, 57
Triangle activity, The, 169-170
Triangle defensive shape, 93-95
Troppmann, John, 43-44
Trowbridge, Brandon, 55-56
Tryouts, 198, 201, 203
Turning, receiving and, 155-158
Two-Goal Game activity, 173

Two Goals, Two Balls activity, 173-174
Two-Versus-Two Plus One activity, 102-103

U
Umbro Soccer Education Division, 124
Underarm roll pass, 80
Under-17 World Cup, 109, 123, 127, 160
Uniforms, 52
United States Soccer Federation, 215
United States Youth Soccer Association, 3
U.S. Soccer, 3
Use Your Head activity, 152

V
van Basten, Marco, 6
van der Meer, Gerard, 4
van der Meer, Reinier, 4
Vargas, Nelson, 127
Videos
  on coaching, 5-6
  for evaluating players, 205
Visualization (imagery), 26-27

W
Waiters, Tony, 7
Warren, Ken, 202
Washington School for the Deaf, 15
Washington State Youth Soccer Association, 7-8
Weather conditions
  playing style and, 36
  scouting reports of, 186
Wide midfielder
  defensive skills for, 85
  defensive tactics for, 124, 127-128
  offensive skills for, 141-142
  offensive tactics for, 168-169
  postmatch lessons for, 194
Widener, Scott, 32-33
Width, in offense, 167-168
Wing back
  defending against attack from, 187
  tactics for, 114, 168
Winning, 8-9, 10-11, 217
Withdrawn striker, offensive skills for, 137-138
W/M system, 35-36
Wood, A.J., 109
World Cup, 20-21, 36, 40, 110, 112, 139-140, 174. *See also* Under-17 World Cup
Wouters, Jan, 636

Y
Yakima Reds soccer team, 17
Yellow cards, 33, 191

Z
Zico (player), 85
Zoff, Dino, 111, 112

About the Authors

Roy Rees

Cor van der Meer

Roy Rees, director of coaching for the Texans Soccer Club, had a long career as a professional soccer player in the English Football League before becoming a full-time soccer coach. He has coached soccer at the youth, college, professional, and World Cup levels. From 1961 to 1982 Roy worked as an English Football Association staff coach at various national coaching schools in England. He also served as coach of the British Universities All-Star team, which played annually against Holland, Belgium, Germany, France, and Ireland.

While coaching in England, Roy led the Skelmersdale United team to F.A. Amateur championships in 1967 and 1971. During his years as head coach in Altrincham (1971 to 1977), the team won the Vauxhall Conference championship twice and the F.A. Trophy once. Roy also coached the national teams in Iraq, Iceland, Sudan, and Algeria, and was coach of the British team in the 1978 World University Games. From 1985 to 1993 he coached the U.S. national team (under-17 group).

Roy is the author of the best-selling book, *Manual of Soccer Coaching.* He holds both a Master of Education degree and a Master of Arts degree from Liverpool University.

Cor van der Meer's involvement in soccer spans nearly fifty years and includes experience as a player, coach, referee, and administrator. He began playing soccer as a child in the Netherlands, where he was on the Dutch National Youth team for two years. In 1960 Cor emigrated to the United States and began coaching and working with soccer organizations in Vancouver, Washington. He not only helped organize the Columbia Youth Soccer Federation, which grew from 36 players to more than 6,000 under his leadership, but also coached Team Vancouver, USA, a semi-professional team in the Pacific

Northwest Soccer League. He also served the Washington State Youth Soccer Association (WSYSA) as district commissioner, vice president of organization, vice president of competition, and vice president of development.

In 1982 Cor moved to Spokane, Washington, where he coached the Spokane Youth Sports Association's elite Skyhawks Club. As head soccer coach for the Community Colleges of Spokane since 1985, he has led both the men's and women's clubs there to several successful seasons.

Cor is the author of *Soccer Guide for Coaches* and *Keeper of the Goal*. He also writes two newspaper columns, *Nutrition for Athletes* and *Playing to Win*. Cor was named Coach of the Year by the Northwest Athletic Association of Community Colleges (NWAACC) in 1989 and 1992. The Northwest Collegiate Soccer Conference also named him Coach of the Year in 1992.

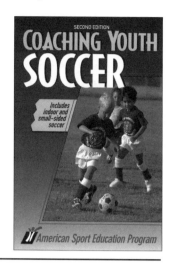

Joe Luxbacher

1995 • Paper • 152 pp • Item PLUX0554
ISBN 0-87322-554-6 • $13.95 ($19.95 Canadian)

Here are 120 practice games that provide players with conditioning exercises, drills, simulated game experiences . . . and *fun*. Excellent for coaches who want to teach specific soccer skills or who need drill ideas for their practices, as well as for players who want to work on skills on their own.

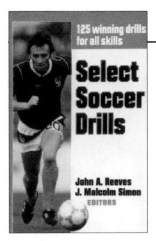

**John A. Reeves and
J. Malcolm Simon, Editors**

1991 • Paper • 152 pp • Item PREE0408
ISBN 0-88011-408-8 • $13.95 ($19.95 Canadian)

Provides 125 drills from top coaches. Each drill is presented in an easy-to-read manner that shows you at a glance what skills or movements are emphasized, the recommended playing area, how many players are needed, and what equipment is necessary.

(Second Edition)
Joseph A. Luxbacher and Gene Klein

Foreword by Tony Meola
1993 • Paper • 176 pp • Item PLUX0397
ISBN 0-87322-397-7 • $14.95 ($21.95 Canadian)

Includes new and improved drills and game-simulated competitions, modern training regimens such as plyometrics, chapters on footwork and defending against restart situations, more information on positioning, and updates on the attacking role of the goalkeeper.

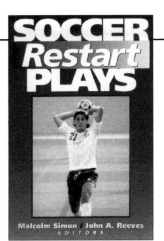

J. Malcolm Simon and John A. Reeves, Editors

Foreword by Cliff McCrath
1994 • Paper • 152 pp • Item PSIM0521
ISBN 0-87322-521-X • $12.95 ($17.95 Canadian)

Inside you'll find 68 effective restart plays and 48 variations. The book contains plays from three categories: free kicks, corner kicks, and throw-ins and kick-offs. Each play provides a detailed diagram, the formation for beginning the play, and a complete description of the procedure.

Prices are subject to change.

Human Kinetics
The Premier Publisher for Sports & Fitness
http://www.humankinetics.com/

2335

Place your order using the appropriate telephone number/address found in the front of this book, or call TOLL-FREE in the U.S. 1-800-747-4457.